Landmark Visitors Guide

Italian Lakes

Richard Sale

D1045368

A research scientist before concentrating on writing and photography, Richard Sale began visiting the Italian Lakes area in the 1970's. At first he climbed in the 'undiscovered' Dolomites above Lake Como, but soon he became fascinated by the mix of history, art, scenic beauty and the enviable climate offered by the Lakes. He now has many friends there and returns each year.

Richard is also the author of a walking guide to the Italian Lakes and a general guide to Milan. His other titles published by Landmark include Landmark Visitors Guides to the Cotswolds & Shakespeare Country, Dorset, Dartmoor, Somerset, Provence & the Côte d'Azur and Madeira.

Published by
Landmark Publishing
Ashbourne Hall, Cokayne Ave, Ashbourne,
Derbyshire DE6 1EJ England

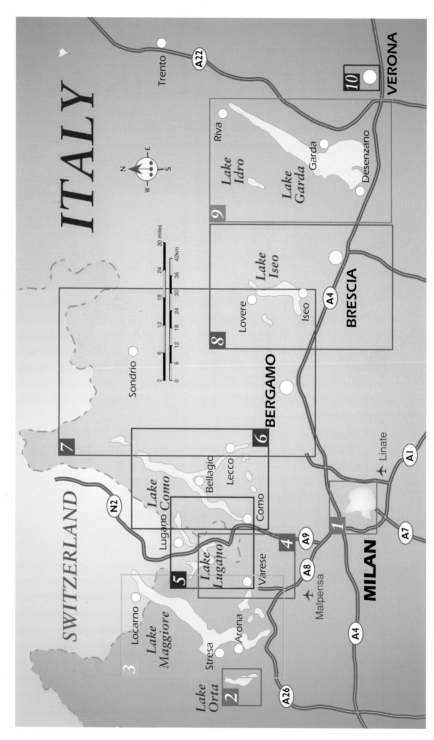

Opposite: The lakeside village of Menaggio, ablaze with colour

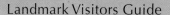

Landmark Visitors Guide

Italian Lakes

Richard Sale

Contents

I n the north of Italy, away from the sea resorts of the Adriatic and Mediterranean coasts, is an area whose climate is every bit as enticing, an area with a fascinating history, and one from which day trips can be made into the high mountains of the Italian Alps. This is the Italian lakeland.

The lakes are huge, long, ribbon-like bodies of water stretching down towards the Lombardy Plain, Europe's most important trade route in medieval times.

They have long been popular with rich folk seeking tranquillity. The Romans Pliny and Catullus had villas here, as did others down the years. Today the sumptuous villas of the last three centuries can be visited or, in some cases, lived in as they have been converted into luxurious hotels. The villa builders also laid out fine gardens. With an enviable climate and the abundant lake water, these are now recognised as among the finest in Europe.

The lakes themselves can be enjoyed by sailors, indeed by anyone who finds their excitement on water, but for those looking for a quieter holiday there are historic buildings and churches, old towns and villages to explore and savour, and cable cars to some of the most spectacular views in Italy.

To extend the sightseeing, the city of Milan is close by with its cathedral, La Scala opera house and streets of expensive shops, as is Verona with its evocative buildings linked with Romeo and Juliet. Venice, too, is just a couple of hours away.

For those seeking more dramatic scenery or excitement, the Alps are within easy reach, particularly the mountains around Monte Rosa and the Brenta Dolomite to the north of Lake Garda, while southwards the Monza race track, Europe's most famous venue, lies just an hour's drive away from Como.

When describing the area, Stendhal wrote *"What can one say about Lake Maggiore, about the Borromean Islands, about Lake Como, unless it be that one pities those who are not madly in love with them"*. Arriving at Lake Maggiore after crossing the Simplon Pass, Dumas noted that *"the sky is pure, the air mild, and one recognises the land beloved of the gods, the happy land that neither barbarous invasions, nor civil discords could deprive of its heaven-sent blessings"*.

This guide sets out to prove the truth of these quotes, exploring the area of the northern Italian lakes from west to east – from Orta to Garda. The upland country between the lakes, including the large area between Lake Como and Lake Iseo, is covered, together with the cities that border the area, Varese, Bergamo, Brescia and Sondrio. For completeness, Milan, Italy's richest city, and Verona are also included, though they are dealt with only briefly.

GEOGRAPHY

On very rare days it is just possible to view, from the southern edge of the Alps, the Apennines, the ridge of mountains that form the bones of Italy's leg-shaped country. Similarly, it is a lucky visitor who sees the white alpine wall from the Apennines. Yet each of these mountain chains has helped to create the land that separates them, the Po plain, a wide valley covered with the deposits brought down by the rivers that drain the high peaks.

Back in the Pleistocene era, during the time of the Quaternary Ice Age, it was not rivers but glaciers that flowed south from the Alps towards what is now the Po plain. These glaciers were confined by the ridges of hard rock that still define the northern valleys, gouging out the bottoms of those valleys and depositing, as terminal and lateral moraine, the material they removed.

The over-deepening of the valleys, and the thickness of the morainic deposits, produced deep basins that filled as the glaciers retreated, leaving huge lakes of fresh water bounded by rich bands of soil that separated them both from their confining ridges and the Po plain. The depth of both the lakes and the moraine deposits are impressive. Lake Garda, for example, is 1,135ft (346m) deep, the moraine deposits contributing 484ft (149m) to that depth. The lake's deepest point lies 922ft (281m) below sea level.

Lake Garda, though not unique in this thickness of morainic deposit, is slightly unusual, because the deposit's thickness allows it to extend far out of its valley into the plain. Alone of all the lakes, Garda has almost a third of its length beyond the end of its confining ridges. In common with the others, however, its more northerly end is confined by high ridges, the lakes pushing northward into the Alps so far that they have an almost fjord-like appearance at their extreme northern tips. The best example of this is Como, whose northern end is not only fjord-like, but shows quite spectacularly the V-formed cross-section of ridges that is such a characteristic of glacial valleys.

Travelling from Lake Garda in the east, westward towards Lake Maggiore, it is noticeable that the confining mountains of the lakes change. Initially the rock is calcareous – dolomitic limestone – that gives the peaks their name, the Dolomites. Ironically for a mountain area that is so famously characteristic of Italy, the name derives from that of a French geologist, Dolomieu, who first identified this magnesium-rich rock.

Continuing westward there are occasional intrusions of crystalline rocks which become more frequent towards Lake Maggiore, by which time the mountains (strictly the pre-Alps, rather than the Alps themselves) are wholly crystalline, a mixture of schists and gneisses. This change of rock type changes the vegetation and its profusion. The most obvious change is in the woods, where the abundant and apparently ubiquitous chestnut trees grow only where the crystalline rocks intrude.

In general the western area has a more varied and luxuriant growth, but this really only applies to the upland areas. Near the lakes the growth is governed by the deposition of the lateral and terminal moraine, with Garda's considerable deposits giving its shorelines a richness that the other lakes can barely match.

To the south of the lakes, before and after the Ice Age, the moraines and the

Lake Statistics

Lake Maggiore

Despite the name Maggiore is not the biggest of the lakes, but it is the longest. From Magadino, in Switzerland, to Sesto Calende is 41 miles (65km). The lake covers 215 sq km (84 sq miles). At its deepest point Maggiore is 1220ft (372m) deep. About 15 per cent of the lake lies in Switzerland.

Lake Lugano

The lake is 22 miles (36km) long, but very narrow, rarely being more than 1.25 miles (2km) wide. The maximum depth is 945ft (288m). About 60 per cent of the lake lies in Switzerland.

Lake Como

At 1345ft (410m), Lake Como is the deepest of the lakes. The deepest point, which lies off-shore of Argegno, is 984ft (300m) below sea level. The lake has an area of 58 sq miles (148 sq km). Because of its shape, the lake's shore line measures 106 miles (170km), the same as that of Lake Maggiore. Although the lake has two arms, only one of them (the Lecco arm) has an outflowing river.

Lake Garda

Lake Garda is the largest lake, covering 145 sq miles (370 sq km), but despite its size, the lake's shore line measures only 78 miles (125km). Garda has a maximum depth of 1135ft (346m). It is the only lake without a significant island, though it does have a handful of tiny islets.

The Po river, into which all the outflowing rivers from the lakes empty, is Italy's longest river at 263 miles (420km).

---

river-borne silts formed the immensely fertile Lombardy plain that constitutes the northern part of the Po plain. This was, and is still, the most productive area in Italy and, as a consequence, has always been one of the most important areas in the country.

HISTORY

The area's fertility was noted in the wake of the glaciers that had carved the lake basins, retreating as the Ice Age ended, and was immediately exploited. The very early Bronze Age Remedello culture is named after the earliest known site, near Brescia, and there are also other very early sites, chiefly pile dwellings, at the edges of several of the smaller lakes. Later, Iron Age peoples also moved into the area, though the most famous of these, the Etruscans, are commemorated by the regional name Tuscany to the south.

While the Etruscan civilisation was flowering, Romulus founded Rome – in 753BC according to legend – so that its first governors were Etruscans rather than Romans. These early Romans were defeated in northern Italy around 400BC by Gauls who swept across the Alps to found Cisalpine Gaul, Cisalpine meaning 'this side of the Alps'. It was to be more than a century before true

Romans reconquered northern Italy as the Roman Empire expanded.

THE ROMANS

Surprisingly, the area covered by this book has very sparse Roman remains. Those at Brescia, dating from the first century AD, are about the best, though there are some isolated pieces at other places. The reason for this is partly the conversion of the Roman Empire to Christianity and the replacement of pagan temples with Christian churches on the same sites.

The Emperor Nero presided over the first persecution of Christians in AD64. The persecution lasted for 250 years, and was at its most severe under Diocletian in AD303. He failed to reverse the tide of religious history,

The Roman Lakes

The lakes have alternative names, derived from those given them by the Romans, which the visitor will occasionally still see. Maggiore is Verbano, Lugano is Ceresio, Como is Lario and Garda Benaco. The Roman names for the two smaller lakes, Orta and Iseo, were Lacus Cusius and Lacus Sebinus respectively.

however, which flowed ever faster following the Edict of Milan in AD313 when Constantine the Great granted religious freedom to the empire's Christians. In AD391 Theodosius made

Looking out over Lake Garda from the viewpoint at Tignale

Looking across Lake Iseo towards Monte Isola from Sulzano

Christianity the religion of the state. This reason for the apparent lack of Roman remains also partly explains the lack of very early Christian remains, later churches having been built on the sites of earlier ones. Some of the best preserved treasures from the early Christian era can also be seen at Brescia, in the Christian Museum.

Ironically, the two emperors Constantine and Theodosius assisted the fragmentation of the empire, but at the same time laid the foundation for later Italian greatness. In AD330 Constantine moved the capital of the empire to Byzantium, renaming it Constantinople, and in AD395 Theodosius divided it into eastern and western halves.

The link with the east that followed this transfer of power had profound implications for the Italian city states in the early Middle Ages, while the division of the empire made the plundering of the western half by the northern barbarians easier, though it would almost certainly have happened at some stage even if there had been no division. The names of the 'barbarians at the gates' are now household words for the atrocious – Huns and Vandals – but they also included the Longobards or Lombards, who named the province which is mainly covered by this book.

THE LOMBARDS

The origin of these people is not absolutely clear, though their route to Italy, across the Alps from the Danube basin, suggests somewhere around Hungary. They were pagan, but not really the barbarians of legend, having some impressively modern ideas. It is no coincidence that Lombard Street is the home of London's bankers.

11

The 'True Nail' Crown

The Lombards were converted to Christianity by Theodolinda, the daughter of a Bavarian duke, who married the Lombard king, and for this act of conversion Pope Gregory III sent her a 'True Nail'. This was incorporated into an iron crown which was thereafter used to crown the kings of Lombardy and, later, Italy. Both Charlemagne in the eighth century and Napoleon in the nineteenth century were crowned with the Iron Crown, as were more than forty kings in the thousand years between those two. Today it can be seen at Monza Cathedral a little way northeast of Milan.

Charlemagne had defeated the Lombards in 794 taking the area into his Frankish kingdom, but the Lombards had retaken the crown by the ninth century following the invasion of the Magyars of Hungary who plundered the whole of northern Italy. The widow of King Lothar, who had been defeated and killed by King Berengar of Ivrea, appealed for help to the German emperor Otto. This plea was answered by invasion. Berengar was defeated, Otto married Adelheid and was crowned emperor in Rome.

THE RISE OF THE CITY STATES

Thus began three centuries of German rule of the majority of Italy. This time was important for the rise of the Italian city states, and also for the conflict between the papacy and the emperors for overall control of the country.

This conflict was given voice by struggles between noblemen supporting either the pro-pope 'Guelfs' or the pro-emperor 'Ghibellines'. These two 'party' names are often encountered on museum visits, though neither had any direct bearing on Italian cultural or political history. However, the same is not true of the rise of the city states. The towns of northern Italy were at the crossroads of the civilisations of west and east, on the pilgrimage routes to Rome and, most importantly, on the routes of the Crusades that kept the kings and noblemen of Europe active for many years around the twelfth century.

Venice, Pisa and Genoa arose as ports, growing rich on trade from the east and on the transportation of soldiers. Milan, and later Florence, grew rich on their geographical position. Milan, in the fertile Po valley, was on trade routes inland from Genoa and Venice, Florence was on the trade route to Rome.

From earliest times the cities were controlled not by feudal lords but by elected councils of rich merchants: Venice's Doge was an elected official, more mayor than duke. These councils encouraged innovations in agriculture and expanded markets in every possible direction. Feudalism required few innovations, power being maintained by keeping the peasants down.

By contrast the merchants of the city states wanted increased efficiency and trade because that brought wealth. Marco Polo was a Venetian, and Leonardo Fibonacci, who brought Arabic numerals to Europe to replace the cumbersome Roman system, was Pisan.

Renaissance Masters

When the city states were at the height of their power, their wealth encouraged art: Dante was born in Florence in 1265 and a century later the same city saw the work of Donatello.

By the fifteenth century the Renaissance had created perhaps the finest artistic climate that has ever existed at any time, anywhere, with Michelangelo, Leonardo, Raphael and Titian all alive and working at the same time, and Palladio designing buildings that still inspire awe. The work of these masters make any visit to northern Italy worthwhile because, although only a limited amount of their work is visible, the effect of their presence on contemporaries and pupils is frequently seen.

The rise and domination of the city states was far from painless. There were frequent inter-city rivalries: Florence fought Pisa, Genoa fought Venice, Milan fought Como in the Ten Years' War (1118-27), destroying that city. Aided by Emperor Frederick I, known as Barbarossa – red beard – Como rose again, destroying the Island of Comacina in revenge and assisting the emperor against Milan. At first the emperor was successful, but the city states combined to form the Lombard League, defeating Barbarossa at Legnano in 1176 and winning significant concessions in the Treaty of Constance in 1183.

Later, some of the cities succumbed to lordships, though these remained chiefly benign. The Viscontis ruled Milan at first, later being replaced by the Sforzas, while the castles of Verona's Scaligeri family will be seen in almost every town on Lake Garda's shore.

INVASION BY FOREIGN POWERS

Elsewhere in Italy the influence of the eastern states was declining. The Normans invaded Sicily and southern Italy around the same time as they were invading England. French influence was destroyed following the 'Sicilian Vespers' in 1282 when all Frenchmen were murdered or expelled. The House of Aragon which succeeded them supplied emperors for the Holy Roman Empire and ensured Spanish domination of much of Italy: Charles V's son, Phillip II, was given Milan in 1540 and it remained a Spanish colony for 150 years.

Eventually, a divided Italy with its small city states left the country open to attack by foreign powers. Not all of the business acumen of the cities failed however. In 1768 Genoa sold Corsica to France! By then, indeed 50 years before then as far as Lombardy was concerned, much of northern Italy had fallen under the rule of the Austrian Hapsburgs. Napoleon briefly freed the area, but declared himself King of Italy and replaced Hapsburg rule with small republics – the Cisalpine covering much of Lombardy, the Ligurian around Genoa – under the umbrella of France.

When Austrian rule was re-established, Italians began to awaken to the fact that they had a national identity and that they could throw off foreign rule. A real voice was given to this awakening by the appearance of a newspaper *Il Risorgimento* in Turin in

(cont'd on page 16)

13

Sirmione with Scaligeri Castle, which includes a embattled quay

1842. Its title was taken up by the disparate groups fighting for unity and freedom: Carlo Alberto, the Piemontian king of Sardinia, Count Camillo Cavour from Piemonte, an ardent monarchist, Guiseppe Mazzine, an anti-monarchist from Genoa, and Guiseppe Garibaldi, an enigmatic but effective guerrilla leader.

With help from France, particularly at the battles of Magenta and Solferino, much of northern Italy was freed from Austrian rule and voted, with the remainder of mainland Italy, for unity with Sardinia and for monarchy. In 1861 Vittorio Emanuele II, son of Carlo Alberto, was crowned King of Italy. Under his kingship war with Austria incorporated Venice into Italy, and World War I added South Tirol and Istria, apart from the city of Fiume.

MUSSOLINI

Sadly, following World War I, the expansionist policy that had unified the country and brought the return of *Italia Irredenta* – 'Unrecovered Italy', continued. Mussolini's fascists took over the government, Annunzio took Fiume, Abyssinia and Albania were invaded and the 'Pact of Steel' with Hitler came into being. Despite Mussolini's attempts at mediation, the latter brought Italy into the war with France and Britain in June 1940. In 1943 Italy changed sides, the fascists were routed and later Mussolini was shot, but in the Treaty of Paris Italy lost Istria to Yugoslavia.

ITALY TODAY

In 1946 King Vittorio Emanuele III abdicated and a national referendum abolished the monarchy. Today Italy is a respected member of the European Union and of NATO.

ECONOMY

Economically, Italy is a country of staggering contrasts. In the north the standard of living is as high as in any country in western Europe while in the south it is almost the equal of any economic low spot. This is in part due to the groundwork of the medieval free city states; the climate, which is more amenable to agriculture in the north than in the very hot south; and the existence in the north of hydro-electricity and natural gas in a country that is chronically short of indigenous power sources.

Milan, with a population of almost two million, is Italy's second biggest city behind Rome, but is the country's undoubted economic capital. Its shops, fashion houses and restaurants are the equal of any other European city, and its artistic and architectural interests are considerable. Lombardy as a whole – Italy's fourth biggest region, of which Milan is the regional capital – is equally rich.

However, the region does not rely on its wealth alone to attract the visitor. It is of considerable artistic interest, has virtually unsurpassable scenic beauty – particularly the area of the lakes – and a climate that is enviable. All in all there can be few more attractive areas to spend a holiday.

FOOD

Although a recently published poll suggested that only about one per cent of foreign tourists listed food as a contributing reason for visiting, few tourists pass up the opportunity to sample a local specialty.

It will come as no surprise to discover that the local specialties are fish dishes. The lakes and rivers hold a variety of coarse fish which are served in many different ways. The most popular fish are trout and perch, which are usually served with herbs or soused. For something very different try the *missoltini* – sun-dried fish.

Away from the lakes, the mountain areas specialise in the serving of salted meats (try the spit-roasted salted mutton, perhaps with a few slices from a big, round, dark brown rye loaf) sausages and dairy products. The sausages are chiefly *polenta*, a maize-based pudding, often served flavoured with rabbit or the mountain fungi for which the areas are also famous, or with the Italian delicacy currently under fire from conservationists – song birds.

The Ossola valley near Lake Maggiore is noted for its *viulin*, leg of goat salted and stuffed with herbs and spices. Nearby, in Val Vegezzo, Santa Maria Maggiore is famous for its smoked ham. The Valtellina, near Sondrio, is well known for its dried salted beef while the Valganna, near Varese, has its own *risotto*. Try too, the

Special Cheese & Honey

Many of the valleys have their own cheese specialties, the best known being Taleggio from the valley of the same name that links the Val Brembana and the Valsassina to the north of Bergamo, but try also the goat's cheese of the Brianza, south of Lake Como. Many also have honey in numerous flavours, assisted by the profusion of alpine flowers, azaleas and rhododendrons.

gnocchi, a pasta of white and chestnut flour, mashed potato and pumpkin, with breadcrumbs and egg yolk, seasoned with nutmeg and the local area's secret spice recipe.

DRINK

Italy has a huge number of wines, usually drunk locally since they do not travel well. Since there is no strictly local specific naming system, some caution must be exercised because occasionally quite disparate wines have the same names. It is usually best to look for labels that refer to the government's grading system.

The lowest grade – DS (*Denominazione Semplice*) – has no quality standard. DOC (*Denominazione di Origine Controllata*) wines meet defined quality standards and come from officially recognised production areas. DCG (*Denominazione Controllata & Garanzia*) wines are of the highest standards.

Well known wines from Novara, the region that includes the western shore of Lake Maggiore, are Barolo and Barbaresco – dry, full-bodied red wines, and Asti Spumante, the sparkling white. Lombardian wines tend to be white from the plains – Moscato and Reisling dell' Oltepro Pavese, and red from the mountains – the famous Valtellina wines, Sassella, Grumello and Inferno. Lake Garda is famous for three wines, the full-bodied red Valpolicella, the lighter red, dry Bardolino and the dry white Soave.

In addition, there are many distilled spirit drinks. The most famous are those sold at Como's Piona Abbey, but there are also those from other mountain areas, which are distilled from alpine herbs and wild fruits such as strawberries and bilberries.

This will necessarily be a short introduction to the city of Milan. Italy's second city, with two million inhabitants, is its undoubted economic capital and has enough points of interest to fill a sizeable book of its own. Here the emphasis is on the heart of the city with its real treasures that no day-tripper should miss, and details of where the determined traveller can find the museums and galleries which deserve more time.

HISTORY

Milan derives its name from *mediolanum*, the middle land, after the area's capital founded by the Gauls in the fifth century BC in the centre of the Lombardy plain, which was strategically positioned near the rivers Po, Ticino and Adda. The Romans captured the city from the Gauls in 222BC and it grew rapidly in importance. In AD286 Diocletian made the city capital of the western empire, a position it held until the barbarian invasions of AD402. Between these two dates, in the Edict of Milan in AD313, the Emperor Constantine gave Christians freedom of religion.

In AD539 the city was completely destroyed in the war between the Goths and the Byzantines, recovering only when it was taken by the Lombards. For defying Barbarossa the city was partially destroyed in 1157, but rose to organise the Lombard League, the army of which defeated Barbarossa at Legnano in 1176. Then followed the rise of the city as one of Italy's city states under the chiefly benevolent control of firstly the Viscontis, and latterly the Sforzas. This period lasted until 1499 when the French took control of the city. Thereafter it was held by the Spanish for almost 200 years before being taken by the Austrians.

Napoleon made the city capital of the Cisalpine Republic in 1797, and then capital of his kingdom of Italy when he was crowned in 1805. Following Napoleon's fall, Milan returned to the Austrians, becoming part of the new Italy after the wars of the Risorgimento. In these the city fought bravely, most notably during the Five Days of Milan (18-23 March 1848) when the citizens threw the Austrians out of the city and barricaded its street. However, the rebellion was short-lived and the Austrians regained total control by early August.

TOUR OF THE CITY

The tour of Milan, which can use the city's trams and metro to cut down on walking, starts at the city's heart, in Piazza Duomo.

PIAZZA DUOMO

At the centre of the square is a bronze statue of Vittorio Emanuele II, but the *piazza* is dominated by the **Duomo**

MILAN

KEY

1. Duomo
2. Palazzo Reale
3. Church of San Gottardo
4. Palazzo della Ragione
5. Palazzo dei Giureconsulti
6. Church of San Maurizio
7. Archaelogical Museum
8. Church of Santa Maria delle Grazie Leonardo's 'Last Supper'
9. Science and Technology Museum
10. Naval Education Museum

11. Siloteca Cormio
12. Basilica of San Ambrogio
13. Basilica of San Lorenzo
14. Basilica of San Eustorgio
15. Church of San Satiro
16. Ambrosiana Art Gallery
17. Church of Santa Maria della Passione
18. La Scala
19. Poldi Pezzoli Art Gallery
20. Brera Gallery
21. Risorgimento Museum
22. Public Gardens and Zoo

23. Museum of Natural History
24. Planetarium
25. Palazzo Dugnani and Museum of the Cinema
26. Museum of Modern Art
27. Museum of Contemporary History
28. Church of San Marco
29. Sforza Castle
30. City Aquarium
31. Arch of Peace
32. Monumentale Cemetery

The Building of Milan's Duomo

History records that work began on the new cathedral on 17 September 1387, despite the plaque in the south-west corner of the building claiming it was actually in 1386.

On 17 September a group of the city's armourers gathered, in what is now the Piazza Duomo, and were blessed before a makeshift altar and turned the first shovelfuls of earth on the foundations of the new building. Before the end of the month the armourers had been replaced by the city's drapers, followed by the butchers, bakers and millers as the various craft guilds offered the services of their members to help with construction.

The marble for the building came from Candoglia in Val d'Ossola (near the western shore of Lake Maggiore). It was floated down the lake, then by river and canal to a quay close to the cathedral site. Each stone was marked AUF, *ad usum fabricae* – for building use – so that it avoided the tax usually employed by the city on building stone. The long drawn-out proccess of building the duomo, with its frequent stops when money or material ran out and the use of free labour from the city folk, meant that eventually *auf* became a local term for a long wait and for working for nothing.

(cathedral) which was started in 1386 but took centuries to complete, such is its complexity. It is the third largest church in the world (only St Peter's in the Vatican and Seville Cathedral are bigger) covering almost 125,000sq ft (12,000sq m).

It is 515ft (157m) long, 302ft (92m) wide at its widest, and 356ft (108m) to the top of the gold Madonna on its highest spire. To add to this array of amazing statistics, the cathedral has 2,245 external statues and a further 914 inside. Those who climb to the terrace near the top of the façade will walk among a forest of spires, 135 in all. It all coalesces into a fairy-tale church, romantic, almost bewilderingly ornate, but having some quite beautiful component parts.

The exquisite central bronze door is by Ludovico Pogliaghi, and there is a monument to Il Medeghino (*see* Como chapter). Inside, the cathedral is huge, and beautifully lit by the large windows. A treasury of artwork is illuminated, some pieces of which are priceless. One of the more interesting, if somewhat macabre exhibits, is the tomb/body of San Carlo Borromeo (*see* Arona, Lake Maggiore).

Palazzo Reale

On the southern side of the Piazza Duomo is Palazzo Reale, the Royal Palace, parts of which date from the twelfth century, though it has been re-modelled by the Viscontis, the Sforzas, the Spanish, the Austrians and, sadly, following bombing in World War II. Today it houses the **Duomo Museum**, a must for all who found the cathedral itself of interest, as it explains the history of its building and decorating. Beside the *palazzo* is the **church of San Gottardo**, a fine fourteenth-century building with an elegant campanile.

On the opposite side from the Royal Palace is the **Galleria Vittorio**

Shopping and Eating

As Italy's richest city, Milan can readily satisfy the needs of the most discerning shopper or gourmet. In every respect, it offers services more usually associated with capital cities. The shopper should visit the area bounded by **Via Manzoni** and **Corso Vittorio Emanuele** that lies north of the Piazza Duomo. Here, especially in Via Montenapoleone, Via Sant'Andrea and Via della Spiga, shoppers will find outlets of all the major fashion houses, as well as world's leading jewellery and leather goods manufacturers.

With Italy's justifiable reputation as the world's leader in fashion, lingerie and particularly in leather, visitors can spend happy hours window shopping or a lot of money doing the real thing. As might be expected the city also has many art dealers, antique shops and outlets showing the latest in home design, furnishings, etc. With Italian flair for style the latter are certainly worth some time.

The gourmet is well catered for in Milan too, with several restaurants which are claimed to be as good as any in the rest of Italy. **Savini** in Galleria Vittorio Emanuele is the most famous restaurant in the city, especially for the evening of the opening night of the La Scala opera season when the rich and famous not only of Milan and Italy, but of Europe gather after the curtain has gone down. By common consent **Biffi Scala** in Piazza della Scala is the other great eating house in the centre, with the highest quality cooking from a menu that combines local and international dishes together with some surprises. For something a little cheaper, but no loss of quality, try **Al Mercante** in Piazza Mercanti, the beautiful Renaissance market square just a short step from Piazza Duomo. The food is great and the setting must surely be the most romantic in town.

Finally, vegetarians should try **Joya** at Via Castaldi, 18, which is claimed by many to be the best vegetarian restaurant in Italy.

As befits an international city, Milan's restaurants serve varied menus, but it is still possible to find typical local dishes. These specialties include *risotto allo zafferano*, rice broth with saffron, and *costolletta allo Milanese*, breaded veal cutlets. Try also *panettone*, a light cake with sultanas, now popular throughout Italy but having long been a Milanese speciality.

Emanuele II, the Victor Emmanuel Arcade, begun only in 1865 and housing an array of elegant shops and coffee houses. Note too the mosaics, high up near the wrought-iron and glass roofs. Close by is the city's most exclusive shopping area and two interesting museums. The **Bagatti Valsecchi** collection of Lombard Renaissance art is housed in a fine Renaissance-style mansion, while the **Museum of Milan** explores the history of the city with maps and paintings.

North-west from the Piazza Duomo, Via dei Mercanti leads to Piazza Cordusio. In this street, the **Palazzo** della Ragione, to the left, dates from 1233, the last remaining building, and a beautiful Romanesque one, from the era of the city-state. The **Palazzo dei Giureconsulti**, opposite, is three centuries older.

CORSA MAGENTA

From Piazza Cordusio, go west along Via Meravigli to Corso Magenta. To the left, is the **church of San Maurizio**, also known as Monastero Maggiore. It is the largest monastic house in the city built in the early sixteenth century for Benedictine nuns. The church is famous for its frescoes by Bernardino Luini and its mid-sixteenth-century organ.

Beside the church is the city's **Archaeological Museum** with items from the city's Roman and pre-Roman eras, and from Greece and Egypt.

At the other end of Corso Magenta is the **church of Santa Maria delle Grazie**. A magnificent church in Lombard Gothic style, built by Donato Bramante in the last half of the fifteenth century, and well worth exploring.

Many who visit the church unfortunately fail to go inside, being drawn instead to the small building beside it, the refectory of a Dominican convent, where between the years 1495 and 1498 Leonardo painted *The Last Supper*. The painting, though almost miraculously surviving the bombings of 1943, has not withstood the ravages of time and has deteriorated despite extensive restoration. It remains a masterpiece of subtle colouration and dynamic realism suffused with formidable emotions. It is not to be missed, though time should also be given to the Donato di Montorfano *Crucifixion*, a fresco from 1499, which stands opposite the Leonardo and is too often casually bypassed.

Piazza Duomo

23

Via San Vittore

South from Piazza delle Grazie, in Via San Vittore, lies an interesting series of museums. The largest is the **Science and Technology Museum** which has a section dedicated to Leonardo and holding a large collection of records on the great man's work in science. In addition, there are galleries for railways, planes and physics. The **Naval Education Museum** covers ships and shipping.

East from the museum complex is the **basilica of San Ambrogio**, perhaps the most notable building in Lombardy. It was begun in AD379 and consecrated by San Ambrogio himself in AD386. In AD739 a Benedictine monastery was added and, in the ninth and twelfth centuries, the campaniles. The porticoed building is magnificent, and the interior artwork equally so. The work of the goldsmith Volvinio is breathtaking.

South-east from the basilica of San Ambrogio, in Corso di Porta Ticinese, is another, dedicated to **San Lorenzo**, which has a row of columns from a third-century Roman temple, as well as work from a fourth-century Christian church.

North again is a museum showing the work of the sculptor Francesco Messina, who died in 1995, set up in his studio.

South again, it is worth visiting the **basilica of San Eustorgio**, built in the fourth century, which was a place of pilgrimage for its relics of the Magi until these were removed by Barbarossa, who all but destroyed the church. Today it is more famous for the Portinari chapel, a marvel of Renaissance architecture, and the frescoes by Vincenzo Foppa.

Return towards the Piazza Duomo to find the **church of San Satiro**, another masterpiece by Donato Bramante, and the **Ambrosiana Art Gallery**. This gallery, set up by a member of the Borromeo family in the early seventeenth century, includes work by Raphael, Titian, Botticelli and Caravaggio.

East from Piazza Duomo is the **church of Santa Maria della Passione**, an impressive church with a museum of seventeenth-century Lombardian artwork attached.

Piazza della Scala

An alternative walk from Piazzo Duomo is through the Victor Emmanuel Arcade to reach Piazza della Scala, and **La Scala** (closed for refurbishment from September 2002), the most famous opera house in the world.

The opera house was built in 1776 on the site of a church dedicated to Santa Maria della Scala, which had been named after Beatrice della Scala, wife of a fourteenth-century Visconti, but it had to be rebuilt exactly following its devastation in 1943.

Today it is revered as *the* opera house, but it was not always so. It was once considered a den of vice for having gambling tables – and that on once consecrated ground. Its reputation was born with the coming of Verdi, whose arrival coincided with the Risorgimento and whose initials spelled out Vittorio Emanuele Re d'Italia. Everywhere 'Viva Verdi' appeared on walls, an association that did no harm to composer or theatre. The visitor who cannot see a performance in the house, which holds 2,800, can visit the museum with its collection of operatic memorabilia.

In front of La Scala stands a monument to Leonardo, while another famous Italian, writer Alessandro Manzoni, has a monument in front of the nearby church of San Fedele. Near here, in **Via Morone**, is a museum dedicated to the writer, in the house he occupied for almost sixty years until his death in 1873. It contains numerous personal items and his library.

Via Manzoni

North-west from the Poldi Pezzoli gallery is the **Brera Gallery**. Here is a series of frescoes by Bernardino Luini and the *Christ Dead* of Andreas Mantegna that cannot fail to move the visitor.

There are also works by Rubens, Rembrandt, El Greco and Raphael, as well as a huge collection of Italian Renaissance work. The building also houses an ancient telescope, once the treasure of the city's observatory.

Near the Brera is the **Risorgimento Museum**, with a fascinating collection on the history of Italian nationalism from Napoleon's campaign (1796) to final success in Rome (1870).

South of the Public Gardens, in Via Palestro, is the **Museum of Modern Art,**

Public Gardens

At the top of Via Manzoni is the Porta Nuova, which was part of the city's fortifications when Barbarossa attacked in 1156, and beyond which are the **Public Gardens,** in English style. Here, in addition to the flowers, trees and shrubs, there is a lake, plenty of amusements for children, a zoo, and the city's **Museum of Natural History** with 2 million in-sects, 100,000 fossils, 30,000 birds, and 25,000 mineral specimens. The collection also includes a lifesize dino-saur. Next to the museum is the city planetarium, reputedly the best in the world. Also, backing onto the gardens, is **Palazzo Dugnani**, a seventeenth-century build-ing with good frescoes, which houses the **Museum of the Cinema**, with a fine collection from magic lanterns to modern equipment.

Poldi Pezzoli

In nearby Via Manzoni, named after the writer, is one of Milan's most famous art galleries, the **Poldi Pezzoli**, named after its nineteenth-century aristocratic collector and one of the most interesting private collections ever established. Here can be seen Mantegna's *Madonna and Child*, and a Botticelli of the same title, an agonising *Pietà* by Bellini and the famous *Portrait of a Young Woman* by Antonio Pollaiolo.

housed in the eighteenth-century Villa Comunale. Here is a fine collection of Italian work, together with work by many leading modern artists including Renoir, Gauguin, Corot, Monet, and Cézanne. A little way out of town – and visible from the Duano's roof – the San Siro Football Stadium is one of the wonders of modern Milan. Football enthusiasts will find the museum, to the two sides, which share it, fascinating.

Going westward along Via Fatebenefratelli, observe on the right the **church of San Marco**, in fine Lombardian style, and containing excellent frescoes and canvases. Further on again, to the right in Via San Semplicano, is a basilica of the same name built in the fourth century, though much restored and altered since then.

Ahead now are the **Sforza Castle** and the parkland that surrounds it (*see* below).

The parkland behind the castle offers excellent walking. At its eastern corner is the **City Aquarium** with reptiles as well as fish, while beyond its north-western edge is the **Arch of Peace**. This was started in 1807 to celebrate Napoleon's victories, but was only about half finished when the battle of Waterloo rendered the monument inappropriate. It was finally completed in 1838 and dedicated to peace. The spectacular bronze chariot and horses on the arch was sculptured by Sangiorgio.

North from here is the **Monumentale Cemetery**, with a most impressive façade. Manzoni and Toscanini are buried here, as well as other famous Milanese citizens.

Finally, to the north-west of the centre, in the district of Lambrate, the Palazzo dei Martinitt houses the **Museum of Toys and Childhood**, a collection of some 1,500 toys dating from the eighteenth to nineteenth centuries.

Sforza Castle

The original castle was built by Galeazzo Visconti in the late fourteenth century, but this was partially destroyed in the mid-fifteenth century. What can be seen today is largely from the late fifteenth century, built under the direction of Francesco Sforza.

The central tower, the Filarete Tower, was destroyed in 1521 when lightning struck it and detonated a considerable quantity of gunpowder stored inside. Its rebuilding was part of several restorations carried out as Milan's rulers changed, but eventually warfare outstripped the need for castles and it fell into disrepair. Thankfully, when it was threatened with demolition in 1880, a good sense of history prevailed and it was restored. Today it is seen as one of the great Renaissance castles, and rightly so: the Filarete Tower is an expanded, Russian-doll-like delight of architectural styles; the round towers are beautifully constructed; the entrance gateway is massively functional.

In addition, the castle houses an excellent art museum in the fine rooms of the Ducal Court and the Roccheta wing. In the museum, pride of place must go to the *Pietà Rondonni* by Michelangelo and a frescoed room by Leonardo. The *pietà* is an unfinished sculpture, almost the more brilliant for being so, the work seeming to climb out of the stone like a half-emerged butterfly from a chrysalis.

Ambrosiana Art Gallery (Pinacoteca Ambrosiana)
Piazza Pio XI
Open: all year, Tuesday-Sunday 10am-5.30pm. Closed certain days in August.
☎ 02 806921

Aquarium (Civico Acquario)
2 Via Gadio
Closed for restoration at time of writing.
☎ 02 86462051

Archaeological Museum (Civico Museo Archeologico)
15 Corso Magenta
Open: All year Tuesday-Sunday 9am-5.30pm.
☎ 02 86450011

(cont'd overleaf)

Right: The Leonardo Gallery at the Science & Technology Museum

Leonardo looks across to the La Scala Theatre in Piazza della Scala

(cont'd from previous page)

**Bagatti Valsecchi Museum
(Museo Bagatti Valsecchi)**
10 Via Santo Spirito
Open: All year Tuesday-Sunday
1-5.45pm
☎ 02 76006132

Basilica of San Ambrogio
15 Piazza San Ambrogio
Open: all year, Monday-Saturday
7.15am-12noon, 2.30-7pm;
Sunday 7.15am-1pm, 3-8pm.
☎ 02 86450895

Basilica of San Eustorgio
Piazza San Eustorgio
Open: Monday-Saturday 7.30am-
12.30pm, 3.30-6.30pm, Sunday
7.30am-1.15pm, 3.30-6.30pm.
☎ 02 58101583

**Brera Gallery
(Pinacoteca di Brera)**
28 Via Brera
Open: All year Tuesday-Sunday
8.30am-7.15pm.
☎ 02 722631

**Brera Observatory (Osservatorio
Astronomico Brera)**
28 Via Brera
Open: all year, Monday-Friday
9am-4.30pm.
☎ 02 50314680

Church of San Maurizio
15 Corso Magenta
Closed temporarily.
☎ 02 86450011 for more details

**Church of Santa
Maria della Passione**
2 Via Vincenzo Bellini
Open: all year, Monday-Saturday
7am-12noon, 3.30-6pm, Sunday
7am-12noon, 3.30-6.15pm.

**Cinema Museum
(Museo Cinema)**
Palazzo Dugnani, 2b Via Manin
Open: all year, Friday-Sun 3-6pm.
☎ 02 6554977

Duomo
Open: daily, 7am-7pm.

San Carlo's Tomb
Open: 9am-12noon, 2.30-5.45pm.
Roof open: 9am-5.45pm (4.15pm
Nov-Feb). ☎ 02 86463456

**Duomo Museum
(Musepo del Duomo)**
Palazzo Reale, 14 Piazza Duomo
Open: all year, daily 9.30am-
12.30pm, 3-6pm.
☎ 02 860358

**Francesco Messina Museum
(Civico Museo Studio Messina)**
10 Via San Sisto
Open: all year, Tuesday-Sunday
9am-12.30pm, 1.30-5.30pm.
☎ 02 86453005

**Leonardo's Last Supper
(Cenacolo Vinciano)**
Piazza Santa Maria delle Grazie
Open: all year, Tuesday-Sunday
8.15am-7pm.
☎ 02 4987588
Booking is now compulsory and
usually only available on the
following day (☎ 02 89421146).

**Manzoni Museum
(Museo Manzoniano)**
1 Via Morone
Open: all year, Tuesday-Friday
9am-12noon, 2-4pm.
☎ 02 86460403

**Museum of AC Milan and
Inter Milan**
Stadio Meazza, San Siro
Open: all year, daily 10am-5pm
closed on match day.
☎ 02 4042432

**Museum of Milan
(Civico Museo di Milano)**
6 Via Sant'Andrea
Open: all year, Tuesday-
Sunday 2-5.30pm.
☎ 02 76006245

**Museum of Modern Art
(Civica Galleria d'Arte
Moderna)**
Villa Reale, 16 Via Palestro
Open: All year daily 9am-5.30pm.
☎ 02 76002819

**Museum of Naval Education
(Civico Museo Navale
Didattico)**
21 Via San Vittore
Open: All year, Tuesday-Friday
9.30am-5pm; Saturday &
Sunday 9.30am-6.30pm.
☎ 02 4817270

**Museum of Science
and Technology
(Museo Nazionale della
Scienza e Technica)**
21 Via San Vittore
Open: all year, Tuesday-Friday
9.30am-4.50pm; Saturday &
Sunday 9.30am-5.30pm.
☎ 02 485551

**Museum of Toys and Childhood
(Museo del Giocattolo
e del Bambino)**
*Palazzo dei Martinitt, 56 Via
Riccardo Pitteri*
Open: all year, Tuesday-Sunday
9.30am-12.30pm, 3-6pm.
☎ 02 26411585

**Natural History Museum
(Civico Museo di Storia Naturale)**
55 Corso Venezia
Open: all year, daily 9am-6pm.
☎ 02 88463280/88463337

**Planetarium
(Planetario Ulrico Hoepli)**
57 Corso Venezia
Lectures (in Italian): all year,
Tuesday & Thursday 9am;
Saturday & Sunday 3pm & 4pm.
☎ 02 88463340

**Poldi Pezzoli Gallery
(Museo Poldi Pezzoli)**
12 Via Manzoni
Open: all year, Tuesday-
Sunday 10am-6pm.
☎ 02 794889

**Risorgimento Museum
(Civico Museo del
Risorgimento)**
23 Via Borgonuovo
Open: all year, Tuesday-
Sunday 9am-1pm, 2-5.30pm.
☎ 02 88464170

**La Scala Museum
(Museo Teatrale alla Scala)**
Piazza della Scala
Open: All year daily 9am-
12.30pm, 1.30-5.30pm.
☎ 02 88792473

**Sforza Castle
(Civici Musei d'Arte e
Pinacoteca Castello Sforzesco)**
Open: All year Tuesday-Sunday
9am-5.30pm.
☎ 02 88463703

Zoo, Public Gardens
Open: November-February,
Monday-Saturday 8.30am-
4.30pm, Sunday and holidays
8.30am-5.30pm; March-
October, Monday-Saturday
8.30am-7pm, Sunday and
holidays 8.30am-7.30pm.
☎ 02 6554365

2. Lake Orta

Boats are available for hire at Orta San Giulio

The first lake visited is, by comparison with the main lakes to the east, a mere splash of water in a mountain cauldron, but despite that description Lake Orta is, in fact, 8.5 miles (13.5km) long, and 1.5 miles (2.5km) wide at it widest point. It sits at 950ft (290m) high, nearly 328ft (100m) above Lake Maggiore and is, at its deepest, 469ft (143m) deep.

The Romans called the lake *Cusius*, which later became *Cusio*, this also being the name given to the part of the Novara province that surrounds the lake. To add to the confusion, the lake was at one time – between being *Cusius* and being Orta – known as Lago San Giulio, after its most famous saint.

The lake can be reached from Gravellona in the north, from Gozzano in the south or, by the very intrepid, over the Mottarone massif on a lane that links Gignese (visited in Chapter 3) and Armeno which stands on the hill above Pettenasco. This tour will take the easiest way, a straightforward drive beside the river Strona from Gravellona to Omegna at the northern end of the lake.

Foot of the Mountain

The whole of Lake Orta lies in the Novara province of Piemonte, a region which takes its name from its position – foot on the mountain. Nowhere is the name more appropriate than at Lake Orta. It is filled by numerous streams draining down from the mountains that make the bowl in which it sits. The lake itself is drained by the Strona river that flows into the Toce at Gravellona Toce, and from there into Lake Maggiore. It is the only lake that drains northward, since the Alps are to the north and the rivers generally must go south into the Po valley.

La Nigoglia – a Stream Flowing the Wrong Way

The inhabitants of Omegna are proud of La Nigoglia, the stream that links the lake and the Strona. It is claimed to be the only stream in Italy which flows towards the Alps rather than away from them and the townspeople say that *"La Nigoglia goes up, and we make the laws"*, a firm stance for independence beside this most independent of lakes.

OMEGNA

Omegna is a pleasant enough place, a small industrial town with part of its medieval walls still standing, and the ruins of an old bridge that once spanned the river still visible. Some experts think the bridge is also medieval, but others think the ruins are much older, perhaps even Roman. The old part of the town, particularly part of the lake front, is excellent, having beautiful old houses, some with balconies and outside staircases, and with a fine array of shutters and wrought ironwork. The iron is a link with the town's industrial past. One old steelworks is now the **Forum Museum**, an applied arts centre.

The view lakewards is beautiful, the gentle curve taking the lake out of sight to the left as the mountains tumble in from the right. Equally good are the views to the valleys of the inflowing and outflowing Strona, with mountain peaks like the posts of some giant gateway.

ALONG THE WESTERN SHORE

From Omegna the lake can be circled in either direction, but it is a good idea to go first along the western shore, to keep the best until last. A road up and away from the lake leads to **Quarna Sotto** and **Quarna Sopra**, good villages set among chestnut woods. The first has a very interesting museum of musical instruments, the manufacture of wind instruments having been the local trade in the 19th century.

Stay close to the lake, pass **Cesara**, again set among woodland, and reach **Pella**. Here there is a medieval tower and an equally old bridge, picturesquely set over the Torrente Pellino pouring into the lake. There is also a fine collection of houses from the eighteenth and nineteenth centuries, with open galleries and porches.

Above Pella is **Madonna del Sasso**, the name given to a small collection of villages and hamlets. A visit to the area is very worthwhile and offers fine views of the lake, but the chief reason for a visit is to see the church of that name, set on a rock above the village of **Boleto**. It is beautiful, both in construction and setting, and contains some very interesting frescoes of the eighteenth century and some fine earlier artwork: a sixteenth-century painting and seventeenth-century wooden crucifix.

The road from the church has to be retraced to the lakeside road, which continues southward with exciting views across the water to Isola San Giulio and the promontory of Orta behind it.

San Maurizio d'Opaglio is a good holiday resort and is one of Europe's leading centres for the manufacture of bathroom fittings. This sort of information always raises a smile and an eyebrow but there is, after all, no reason why Italian towns should not make taps. Perhaps it is a surprise that, amid so much scenic splendour, something as mundane as real life should intrude.

Next head for Gozzano, passing, at Luzzara, the **Villa Jucker** standing in an English-style park (not open to the public) and a fine Romanesque church, the **Nativita di Maria.**

GOZZANO

Gozzano is another light industrial town, but in a good position, with a building complex known as the 'castle', even though there are no castle remains.

The complex includes the **church of San Lorenzo**, rebuilt in baroque style with a Roman marble font and a sarcophagus, reputedly that of San Giuliano. Beside the church the **Palazzo Vescovile** is thirteenth-century, and there are other fine houses from the seventeenth century.

The **parish church of San Giuliano** has a Romanesque campanile, while the **church of Santa Maria** has a seventeenth-century wooden altar. The whole complex offers an extremely interesting visit.

Also within the town, but set at the lakeside on a wooded headland, is the **medieval tower of Buccione** built by the Lombards. From the tower it is only a short journey to Orta and the chief interests of the lake.

Giulio and the Dragons

When Guilio's brother Giuliano stopped to found his church at Gozzano Giulio pressed on and reached the anvil-shaped headland opposite the lake's little island. The island attracted him immediately. It was gently wooded, quiet and remote and he wanted to be taken there to live as a hermit and teacher. The locals would not take him, telling him that it was inhabited by dragons and serpents, and was in the possession of the powers of darkness. Undeterred, Giulio flung his cloak on the water and stepped onto it. Then, to the astonishment of the locals, a wind picked up, blowing the cloak across the water, Giulio steering by using his staff as a rudder. By the time he reached the island the monsters had fled, overawed by the sight of him and not daring to fight. Giulio landed and built his hermit's cell, where he lived for the rest of his life converting and teaching the lake-dwellers.

In the fourth century AD two brothers, Giulio and Giuliano, were sent from Rome to preach the gospel to the inhabitants of the wild area around the lake, then known as Cusius. Giuliano founded his church at Gozzano and died there – some say he was murdered – his body being laid to rest in the sarcophagus in a church on whose remains the present church stands.

ISOLA SAN GIULIO

Isola San Giulio is reached from Orta San Giulio, as the town is known. It still has an 'other worldliness', many

Basilica of San Giulio

On Isola San Giulio the basilica of San Giulio is now recognised as the most important Romanesque church in the Novara province.

It was built in the ninth century on the site of the hermit's cell, but was altered and restored in the eleventh and seventeenth centuries. Much of what remains dates from the first period of alterations, when the campanile was also built.

Within the basilica there is a treasure house of artwork and architecture, but pride of place is given to an *ambo* (pulpit) in black Oira marble which dates from the eleventh or twelfth century. The three carved lecterns and the pulpit stand, which are supported on four columns, are also masterpieces.

Note too, the interplay of Christian and pagan symbols. The walnut choir stalls are very good, as are some of the painted wooden sculptures. The church preserves a 'monster's bone' said to be from the time of San Giulio (but which is probably a more recent whale bone) and the crypt holds a silver urn which contains the remains of the saint.

Beside the church, the **Palazzo dei Vescovi** is fourteenth-century and today houses a Benedictine monastery.

Opposite page: Isola San Giulio
Above: View across Lake Orta
Below: Orta San Giulio

visitors talking of the dreamy atmosphere of its narrow lanes, churches and piazze.

Elsewhere the island is worth all the time that can be given to its exploration. Its elegant, arcaded houses, narrow alleys and sudden lake views are treasures beyond words. The island is jammed tight with buildings: there can be very few patches of soil that have not been or are not built on. This is due in part to the island's religious past, and to its having been, until earlier this century, capital of the lake district. But some of the building work was for fortification due to various ownership struggles and a heroic defence by Willa, the wife of Berengar, against the forces of Otto the Great.

On your return to the mainland, if the lake is flat calm, and especially if there is a light mist that obscures the western lake shore and softens the focus of the island, just stand and stare. The island seems to float in mid-air, magically suspended, unsure of its position between heaven and earth.

ORTA SAN GIULIO

The mainland town of Orta San Giulio is also an excellent place, not least for its view of the island. At night, when both island and the **church of Madonna del Sasso** high above it are lit, this is a magical spot. Here too, there are narrow lanes whose curves and breaks give sudden views of mountains, lakes and occasionally the island.

The town square, Piazza Motta, at the quay, is open and airy, coolly shaded by trees and with a side dominated by the town hall, a sixteenth-century building with frescoed walls, an outside stairway and a tiny campanile breaking through the grey roof like a chimney. Elsewhere, find more frescoes

Orta's Sacre Monte

The treasure of Orta San Giulio is the Sacre Monte, which dominates the headland. The hill is delightfully wooded and has excellent views of the lake. Through the beech and pine woods a single path threads its way, passing twenty-one chapels, chiefly from the early seventeenth century, but one that has only recently been completed. Inside these are a total of 376 life-size terracotta statues by a number of sculptors, illustrating incidents from the life of St Francis of Assisi to whom the Sacre Monte is dedicated.

At the top of the hill is a building comprising two small oratories and the remains of a monastery which contains a Gothic wooden Madonna. Expert opinion differs slightly about which of the chapels is the best, but all agree that numbers eleven and sixteen are excellent. Chapel number fifteen is on a terrace from which the view is expansive. Beside the Sacre Monte, the secular is represented in sumptuous style by the Villa Crespi – It was on Sacre Monte in 1882 that Friedrich Nietzsche, after hearing the romantic song of a nightingale, realized he was in love with his Russian traveling companion, the poet, Lou Salomé. The love was not returned and Nietzsche never risked his emotions again, dedicating his life to his work. When he published his greatest work, *Thus Spake Zarathustra*, he dated it 'after Orta'. Sadly not open to the public.

at **Casa Morgarani**, called the 'House of Dwarves', though the reason for the name has been lost in time. In searching for that house the visitor will also pass many others which are of interest.

CLOSE TO ORTA SAN GIULIO

On the hillsides above Orta San Giulio are some good villages: **Miasino** with fine seventeenth- and eighteenth-century buildings and a really good baroque church; **Armeno**, also with a good church, and **Ameno**, a village clustered around a Romanesque campanile.

In the nearby hamlet of **Vacciago** there is a collection of paintings and sculpture, chiefly by the artist Antonio Calderara who died here in 1978, but including European, American and oriental work. The collection is in a superb house with triple tiers of porticoed balconies.

On the lakeside the last village is **Pettenasco**, with a pretty lake front and a very impressive viaduct taking the lake-edge railway line over the Torrente Pescone. There is also a museum of characteristic wood carving. Beyond is the *Punta di Crabbia*, a small headland so positioned that virtually the whole of the lake can be seen from it, the gentle curves in both directions melting into the enclosing mountains. From this point, the lake road goes back again to Omegna.

PLACES TO VISIT

ISOLA SAN GIULIO
Boat Trips
During daylight hours.
For information ☎ 0333 6050288.

OMEGNA
Fondazione Museo Arti Industria "Forum"
Open: All year, Tuesday-Saturday 10.30am-12.30pm, 3-7pm, Sunday 3-7pm. ☎ 0322 866141.

ORTA SAN GIULIO
Sacre Monte di Orta
For information ☎ 0322 911960.

PETTENASCO
Museo dell' Arte della Tornitura del Legno
Open: July-September, daily except Monday 9.30am-5pm.
☎ 0322 89622.

QUARNA SOTTO
Museum of Musical Instruments
Open: August, daily 3-7pm.
At other times by request.
☎ 0323 826141/826368

VACCIAGO (NEAR AMENO)
Calderara Collection
Open: mid-May to mid-October, Tuesday-Sunday 10am-12noon, 3-6pm.
☎ 0322 998192

LAKE STEAMERS
There is a limited service on the smallest of the big lakes, linking Omegna, Pettenasco, Orta San Giulio and Pella, a full trip taking about 1 ½ hours.
For information on the steamers ☎ 0322 844862.

Maggiore is a squiggle of a lake, its northern region (about fifteen per cent) lying in the Swiss canton of Ticino, its western shore lying in Piemonte, its eastern shore in Lombardy. The lake covers 84sq miles (215sq km).

It is approached from the south by anyone entering Italy through Milan's airports or railway stations. Those entering from Switzerland, via the Simplon Pass, Domodossola and the Val d'Ossola reach the Borromean Bay, and although this is a wonderful entrance to the land of the lakes – the high gorges of the Simplon making it one of the finest alpine passes – it is an unsatisfactory place to join the lake. Those crossing the St Gotthard or the San Bernardino Passes arrive in Italian Swiss Bellinzona and can choose to go down either the west or east side of the lake.

This tour will go through Locarno. There, as a digression, it is worth mentioning that one of the finest short rail journeys in Europe links the town with Domodossola, via Val Vigezzo. Those who take the lake steamer from, say, Stresa to Locarno, the Vigezzo train to Domodossola and a return train to Stresa, have a really magnificent day.

THE SWISS SHORE

Locarno

Nestling in a sheltered bay, Locarno has one of the finest positions of any town on the lakes, and makes full use of its sunny position. In summer the public gardens on the southern side of Piazza Grande are glorious. The gardens are the first sight of the town for those who arrive by lake steamer.

A delightful walk past an imposing bronze bull takes the visitor to the **Kursaal** (to the left), a casino and elegant restaurant, and galleried shops (to the right). Continuing, the visitor will soon reach the **Castello Visconti.** The castle was built in the fifteenth century by the Dukes of Milan, but was almost destroyed in the early sixteenth century. Today it houses a small archaeological museum and a collection of modern art.

From Via della Stazione, which runs north towards the station from Piazza Grande, a *funivia* or cable car rises to the fifteenth-century **church of Madonna del Sasso**, a superb vantage point and interesting for its fine altarpiece of the *Flight into Egypt* by Bramantino. From the *funivia*'s top station it is only a short walk to the continuing chair lift, which climbs to Cimetta di Cardado at 5,482ft (1,672m) from where the views are tremendous.

South of Locarno

From Locarno the road that heads south along Lake Maggiore's eastern shore cuts off the delta of the Maggia river, which flows into the lake between the towns of Locarno and Ascona. A road leads up Valle Maggia, a good valley, but less scenic than the enchantingly named Val Centovalli – the Valley of a Hundred Valleys – that leads off westward at Tegna and is named after its numerous side valleys.

Ascona occupies the bay on the Maggia delta's southern side, another sheltered spot whose climate has helped turn an old fishing port into a thriving holiday centre. The town has a long artistic tradition: Isadora Duncan, Herman Hesse and Paul Klee all spent time here, as did both Lenin and Jung. Today the Museo Communade d' Arte Moderne and the Music Weeks in September continue the tradition.

South of Ascona is **Porto Ronco** from where the **Isole di Brissago** (occasionally also known as the Isole dei Conigli or 'Rabbit Isles') can be reached. On the larger of these there is a superb sub-tropical garden.

Southward again is **Brissago**, after which the islands are named. Once this was a cigar-making centre, famous for having given its name to a long, thin cigar.

THE PIEMONTIAN SHORE

Cannobio

After Locarno the visitor crosses into Italy at Piaggio di Valmara, though there is not enough of a village there for him to feel he has really arrived. Cannobio is the first town, a fine place, but not as popular as it should be, mainly because it is a long way up the western side of the lake.

Its old quarter, with its narrow winding streets (note especially Via Marconi and Via Umberto I) and towers (the campanile is twelfth-century) is typically Italian, speaking of ancient trades and allegiances. Cannobio was fortified by the Romans – there is evidence of pre-Roman occupation – and in 1859 the people of the town attacked an Austrian fleet over a period of two days. This is commemorated by a memorial stone.

The town quay, where there is a market each Sunday, is excellent, as is the walk along it which passes the **Santuario della Pietà**.

Santuario della Pietà

In 1522 a picture *(pietà)*, showing the dead Christ removed from the cross, with Christ between the Virgin Mary and St John – hung in a house near the lake shore and bled real blood from Christ's wounds. This was miraculous in itself, but soon Cannobio escaped unscathed from a plague that devastated the area around. To enshrine the painting the house was demolished and a small chapel was built. Other miracles followed, and about fifty years later San Carlo Borromeo ordered that a church should be built to do justice to the painting, which should itself be given a silver frame, as befitted its status. Almost immediately, in 1575, Cannobio was spared when plague again devastated the area. Today, the ornately framed picture is kept at the high altar, in a church interior that is almost equally ornate.

Elsewhere in the town there is another church, beside which is the

Excursions from Cannobio

From Cannobio a road leads up the **Val Cannobino**, and at about 1.5 miles (2.5km) from the town is the gorge (*orrido*) of Santa Anna, with a church dedicated to the same saint beside it. Here the Torrente Cannobino falls through a narrow gorge before emerging into a wide, calm pool. The gorge can be viewed from either of two bridges, one reputedly Roman, or from the pool in a hired boat.

Continue along the road to the **Val Vigezzo**, already mentioned in connection with the Domodossola to Locarno railway. Val Vigezzo has been a favourite with artists since its 'discovery' in the eighteenth century because of the variety of shades and tints of greens and browns, and the pure quality of the light. Today it is equally famous for winter sports, for walking, and for its art and crafts.

For a really unusual trip try the **Chimney Sweep's Museum** at **Santa Maria Maggiore** or the museum at **Gurro**, a small village with Scottish connections (Scots settled there after the Battle of Pavia in 1537) – these being two of several small but interesting museums. The lover of food and drink should try the smoked ham at Santa Maria Maggiore, the valley honey, and spirit drinks distilled from alpine herbs. The church at **Re** is magnificent, It owes its size to a miraculous painting, Santa Maria del Sangue, the Virgin of the Blood. In April 1494 the painted Virgin was struck by a stone thrown in temper by a man who had lost a game, and bled for 20 days. A phial of blood is still kept at the church and the painting has become a centre for pilgrimages.

fine thirteenth-century Palazzo della Ragione also known as the **Palazzo Paradiso**, with a fine, column-supported barrel roof at ground floor level.

Back at Lake Maggiore, take the lake hugging road to **Carmine**, a small village near an elbow in the lake. The village is divided into two, as are several on the sloped lakeside, **Inferiore**, the lower lake village, and **Superiore**, the higher cliff village. In this case the upper village really does cling to the cliff, and in that cliff is a *ricetto*, a medieval hermitage. Maintaining the religious theme, the **church of San Gottardo**, a fourteenth-century building with beautiful fifteenth-century frescoes and paintings, is well worth visiting.

Beyond Carmine the road rounds the elbow headland and the Cannero or **Malpaga castles** come into view.

The Pirates of Malpaga

There were two Cannero or Malpaga castles, one on each of two islands, which were originally connected by a drawbridge. The castles date from the twelfth century and were once occupied by five brothers who terrorised the local villages and pirated any ship unfortunate enough to come too close. Eventually the Viscontis – rulers of Milan – became exasperated by the lawlessness (and the occasional loss of their merchandise from pirated ships) and decided to capture the brothers, though it is said that it took six months to winkle them out of their strongholds. When they had, the Viscontis destroyed the castles.

The islands were later used by the Borromeo family as the site of a fortified villa. It is the ruins of that the visitor sees. The ruins are not open to the public, but boat trips around them are available from Cannero.

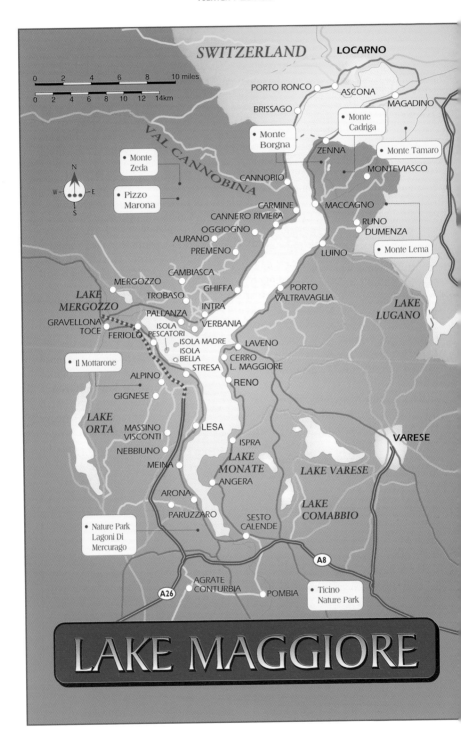

Cannero Riviera

Cannero was once described as a *"Genoese Riviera in miniature... a pearl in a necklace of vineyards and villas"*. The vineyards have largely gone now, but the villas remain and the town is now known as **Cannero Riviera**, claiming the title of the 'Nice of Maggiore' because of its very mild winter climate. At one of the villas, Villa Sabbioncella, Garibaldi stayed after the battle at Luino.

The town has fine old houses in narrow streets, a delightful tiny harbour, and the beautiful gorge of the Torrente Cannero which rushes under a picturesque old bridge. At **Oggiogno**, a village above the town, there is a fine view of the town, lake and castles which can be considerably improved by a climb of some 2,990ft (850m) to the top of the **Cima di Morissolo**.

The public gardens in Locarno

A quiet corner in old Cannero Riviera

Drive along the shore of the lake, round the lake elbow and the view is expansive. Stresa, ahead across Borromean Bay, nestles below the Mottarone, while to the right the Piemonte Alps are green cascades.

Next pass through a succession of tiny villages, each with its own special charm, and reach **Ghiffa**, perhaps the best of them, with its elegant array of villas and fine gardens grouped around castle ruins. An interesting church is found here, the **Santuario della Trinitá**, from which there are excellent views, and from a small headland at Ghiffa the view is the most expansive of any from the lakeside. The village was once famous for hat-making and a museum in the old hat factory (which provided work for exactly a century, from 1881-1981) explores the trade with the help of the old factory machinery and a collection of hats.

Intra, Verbania and Pallanza

Beyond Ghiffa, at a sharp angle in the lake as it cuts back into the Borromean Bay, is the largest stretch of habitation on the lake, the towns of **Intra**, **Verbania** and **Pallanza**. They are now so close that they virtually merge into one, and usually take the name of the smallest – **Verbania**. This choice of name can cause confusion as the lake's only car ferry links the village complex to Laveno and is called the Laveno-Intra ferry.

Intra is the most industrialised town on the lake, but the industry is powered by electricity not smoke-stained chimneys, and is light, keeping to the back of the town, to leave the lakeside area fresh and airy. The area between the two streams, the San Giovanni and the San Bernardino (the town's name derives from this position) was certainly settled by the Romans and may even be older, but what is seen today is all many centuries newer, and the town is still being developed as a tourist base.

The **basilica of San Vittore** is a good example of the comparative newness, for there, though the site is very ancient, the present church is of eighteenth-century origin. The town has older sections, however, and the more modern buildings were designed with an eye to architectural wholeness, and have been satisfactorily integrated into the town.

The lakeside villas make an elegant back-drop, viewed through the chestnuts and oleanders, to the walk along towards the ferry terminal, though the better ones, Villa Poss, Villa Adda and that of the Intra sculptor Paul Troubetzkoy, are closer to the mouth of the San Giovanni and are sadly not open to the public. The port itself is an elegant arc of masonry, its entrance guarded by a tall light with an external spiral staircase.

Beyond, cross over the San Bernardino to Verbania-Pallanza, and soon reach one of the highlights of a trip to Maggiore, the **Villa Taranto**, which has one of the world's finest botanical gardens.

Villa Taranto

The villa is named for the Duke of Taranto, one of Napoleon's generals who was an ancestor of Scotsman Neil McEacharn who created the garden early in the twentieth century. The garden covers 50 acres (16 hectares) and is criss-crossed by almost 5 miles (8km) of pathway, so that every aspect of its delights can be explored.

Those who visit the garden can see about 20,000 varieties of trees, shrubs and flowers, some very rare and some uniquely represented in Europe. The villa itself is used by the Italian government and is not open to visitors.

It is worth visiting Villa Taranto in spring during **Tulip Week** when over 80,000 tulips are in bloom, a sight that gathers crowds from all over the world. A little later, the blooming of the azaleas and rhododendrons is another of the garden's highlights.

Further along the lakeside, before the headland of the Verbanian spur, is the Romanesque **church of San Remigio**, an eleventh-century building with good fifteenth-century frescoes. Beside it stands the Villa San Remigio, with excellent gardens that sadly are no longer open to the public.

From the headland itself there are fine views of the lake, extending into most of the crevices it fills, and including the little island (the *isolino*) of *San Giovanni*, on which is a villa that was long the home of Toscanini. Beyond, the old town is dominated by the campanile of the **church of San Leonardo**, a much restored sixteenth-century building.

At the water's edge near the harbour is a memorial to Marshal Carlo Cadorna, commander-in-chief of Italian forces in World War I and a native of the town. It dominates the view of the lakeside from here onwards. Just offshore here is a line of fountains that are illuminated at night – a spectacular show.

Old Pallanza

Now go inland, first to Piazza Garibaldi at the heart of old Pallanza, with the maze of interesting narrow streets that lead from it. Strike northward for Piazza Cavour, where, in Palazzo Dugnani, is Pallanza's interesting **Museo del Paesaggio**, the Landscape Museum. Here there is a collection of paintings, including many landscapes, items from local Celtic and Roman history, and a collection of the work of Paul Troubetzkoy, the Intran sculptor.

From Piazza Cavour follow Via Azari and at the top (about 1 mile/1½ km) is the **church of Madonna di Campagna**, the town's finest piece of Renaissance architecture. The church was built in the early sixteenth century, on the site of another church whose mid-eleventh-century campanile has survived. Inside, the church has some fine frescoes, a baroque wooden choir and some good wrought ironwork.

Here in the old village it is possible to catch a glimpse of the world Hemingway described in *A Farewell to Arms*. In the book the characters planned "*to go to Pallanza. It is beautiful there when, in autumn, the leaves change their colour. ...There is a nice village at Pallanza and you can row out to the islands where the fishermen live...*".

CIRCULAR ROUTE INTO THE HILLS

From Pallanza, head not for Gravellone Toce and the head of the Borromean Bay, but upwards into the hills. The best route is to follow the eastern side of the Torrente San Giovanni up, and the western bank back, going from Intra to Campasca, then climbing steadily through a number of excellent hill villages, any or all worth allowing time to explore, to the delightfully named **Bee**, and on again to **Premeno**, the most famous of the villages in this area.

On a fine day Premeno is a spectacularly beautiful village, with its array of white and cream, mostly red-roofed houses. The village is high (about 2,600ft, 800m) and the air a little cooler, better for enjoying a mountain stroll with fine views of the surrounding scenery. The best views of the lake, and of Premeno, are obtained from **Pollino**, a short distance away, or from the **Albergo Belvedere** just beyond Pollino.

Beyond Premeno is the **Pian di Sole** where you can play golf in summer and ski in winter, and then the road winds round the Cresta della Cereso for Pian Cavallo and another spectacular view. From here the intrepid can follow a mountain track, drivable only to Colle, about 1 mile (2km), that leads after about 10 miles (16km) to Monte Vada at 5,900ft (1,800m). From there the even more intrepid can walk the high mountains of the **Reserva Naturale della Val Grande**, set aside for mid-alpine animals and birds. Such an expedition is for experienced walkers/climbers only and should not be undertaken lightly.

An adventurous alternative is to descend from Colle to Cannero, the journey getting easier the further you go, which offers the possibility of visiting either Trarego or Viggiona, each with good views over the northern end of Maggiore.

The return route leads down to **Aurano** which, with the nearby villages of Scareno and Intragna, is beautifully sited, and then descends to **Cambiasca** where there is a fine Romanesque church. From here a road goes up to Pala, offering a fine drive into the mountains and good views of them from the village. A drive can then be made to the memorial to the Alpini (the Italian Alpine Brigade), or it is possible to walk the 2 miles (3km) to Pian Cavallone, 2,000ft (600m) high, and from the refuge hut there to climb Pizzo Marona, a further 1 mile (2km) away and 1,650ft (500m) high. Such a trip will necessitate setting aside an entire half day at least.

From Trobaso, on the return to Verbania, a road leads off up the Val Grande, the valley of the Torrente San Bernardino, to **Cicogne**, a remote village high up under the peaks and a good walking centre. The less energetic can drive from Verbania to Monte Rosso's summit, 2,010ft (613m) with excellent views over Borromean Bay and islands.

CONTINUING AROUND THE LAKE

Back on the lakeside, continue to Fondotoce, beyond which a quick route to Stresa crosses the bridge over the Toce. Alternatively, leave the main road for one circling Lake Mergozzo for the village of **Mergozzo**. The lake is nicely positioned at the mouth of the Val d'Ossola, and the village is very picturesque with its medieval towers. From the village a road traverses the gap between Monte Órfano and the village of that name, with a church dedicated to San Giovanni which is one of the best examples of Lombard Romanesque architecture in the area. It is eleventh-century, made from granite blocks, with an octagonal dome.

The main road reaches **Gravellona Toce**, where it meets the road from Switzerland and from where a road goes to Lake Orta. Gravellona is a small industrial town, grown up because of its position at the mouth of the Val d'Ossola.

From Gravellona Toce the main road can be followed to **Domodossola**, and some of the most spectacular mid-alpine scenery in Italy. The Val d'Ossola is excellent itself, but from it lead: the Val Anzasca with **Macugnaga**, a famous winter sports centre; Val Antrona; Val di Vedro that leads

The Candoglia Marble Quarry

If you are driving up the Val d'Ossola, remember to look out for the village of Candoglia and for the marble quarries behind it. It was from these quarries that the marble for Milan's cathedral came, and the stone is still much prized for building where cost is less critical than quality and style.

The formal gardens on Isola Bella

through high-cliffed gorges to the Simplon Pass; the valleys of Antigorio and Formazza and Val Vigezzo.

Baveno

Baveno, the first holiday resort on this side of the bay, sits below a mountain of pink granite, the quarrying of which helped the town to prosper. It is an ancient site with Roman finds from the first century, and has a proud history in the fight for Italian freedom, first from the Austrians and later from the Fascists.

Today it is an elegant holiday resort, with a line of villas opposite the excellent flower-gardened lakeside testifying to a long and prosperous history in its newest industry. Villa Branca, the pink villa high up on the hillside on the way out of the town, is mid-nineteenth-century and very English looking.

Within the town there are some beautiful old houses, none more so than **Casa Morandi** which is an Italian national monument. Four floors high, each floor is reached by interwoven outside stairways. The house is Baveno's most photographed spot, and rightly so.

Also much photographed is the church square, the **church** at **Baveno** being set slightly apart from the rest of the village, though still in a central position. Dedicated to San Gervaso and San Protaso, it has a twelfth-century Romanesque façade and a Romanesque campanile, the rest having been almost completely rebuilt in the seventeenth and eighteenth centuries in baroque style.

Beside the church is a baptistery of great artistic importance. It is an octagonal building under a conical roof, with fifteenth-century frescoes on the domed ceiling which are of considerable historical interest. In the church

square, along the roadside, is an elegant arcade, completing the building in this dignified quiet spot.

Stresa

Next after Baveno is Stresa, without doubt the most elegant of all Maggiore's towns, and probably the most famous of all the Italian lake resorts. The lakeside speaks of prosperity, with its walks through fine gardens and trees.

On the other side of the lake-side road is an array of fine hotels, some of top international standard, especially the Grand Hotel des Iles Borromées, a truly sumptuous building both inside and out. Ernest Hemingway set part of *A Farewell to Arms* in the hotel. There is an old part to the town which is worth a visit.

Piazza Cadorna is a little square filled with café seats where you can sit and watch, and sniff in the scent from the flowers that seem to grow everywhere. But the lake soon draws the visitor back to its elegant walkways.

Il Mottarone

At the Baveno end of Stresa is a *funivia* that goes up to Il Mottarone. The lake terminus is easily reached, though at the top there is a short walk to the mountain summit, at 4,890ft (1,491m). From here the view extends to Monte Rosa, the valleys around Domodossola, the lakes near Varese, and the Lombardy plain, and on a very clear day as far as Milan and Switzerland's Jungfrau.

Borromean Islands

From **Carciano**, the tiny port near the lower terminus of the cable car, boats cross the lake for the three Borromean islands. Closest is **Isola Bella**, which is also the most famous.

Isola Bella

When, in about 1630, Count Carlo III Borromeo first laid plans for the transformation of the closest island to Stresa, the island was flat and rocky with a few fisherfolk's houses and a chapel or two that they used. Count Carlo wanted to change this island into his dream of a palatial ship anchored close to the shore.

He started by shipping boatloads of soil to the island which his landscape architects used to create a ten-terraced garden, 130ft (40m) high, sloping back from the island's southern tip to produce the effect of a snub-nosed boat. The result is an elaborate statement of the aims of Italian gardening, an architectural form in which man transforms nature into his own design. This is in sharp contrast to the English garden, where man aids nature in creating a naturalistic design.

To the gardens Count Carlo and his sons (for the work outlived the designer, indeed the island was not finally completed until 1958, three centuries after Borromeo died) added a baroque *palazzo*, positively subdued externally in comparison to the gardens, but inside echoing the extravagance.

The island was also transformed in name, Count Carlo calling it Isola Isabella after his wife. The now familiar, shorter form flows more gracefully from the tongue, and means 'beautiful island'.

The *palazzo* (palace) has a wealth of rooms, some of great beauty, some of great lavishness, almost invariably lit by chandeliers of Murano glass. The **arms room** displays the Borromeo coat of arms, while the **medals room** has carved wooden medallions depicting scenes from the life of San Carlo Borromeo, of the same family as the designer. The **music room** has antique instruments and some very fine paintings, while **Napoleon's room**, where he and Josephine slept in August 1797, is wonderfully elegant. Better still is the **great hall**, the last to be completed, with walls the colour of blue Wedgwood china, a geometrically patterned floor and a delightful balcony. The **library** contains rare volumes and some good paintings, while the **Luca Giordano room** contains fine works by the seventeenth-century Neapolitan master.

The **antechamber** has some good

The Borromean Family Puppet Theatre

Be sure not to miss the Borromean family puppet theatre. This flourished, chiefly for the amusement of the family, during the eighteenth and early nineteenth centuries, but was abandoned during the struggles of the Risorgimento, only coming to light again fairly recently. To a generation brought up on a television diet of instant action, the puppets seem a bit dull, even boring, but the faces are exquisitely carved, and the skill with which a mummy is brought out of its case (pre-dating the horror movie by more than a century!), a sedan chair turns into a woman, and elves appear from a giant, is very impressive.

paintings, and an excellent ceiling by Tiepolo, and from it the **family chapel** can be viewed, though permission for entry must be requested. It contains memorials to the Borromeo family. The **tapestry room** has a series of sixteenth-century Flemish tapestries in silk and gold depicting fantastic animals. They are really very good, as are some of the paintings in the room.

Finally, visit the **grottoes**, six cool rooms decorated in light and dark stones to produce, not wholly successfully, a marine cave appearance. Here there are some interesting historical items and some unusual curios – all well worth seeing.

Isola Pescatori

The second island is **Isola Pescatori**, sometimes known as Isola Superiori which, by constrast to Isola Bella, is almost drab. The island takes its popular name from the chief trade of the islanders (fishing), and was the first of the group to be inhabited. It seems to have changed very little over the centuries. The visitor can wander freely in narrow, sun-starved alleys, past drying fishing nets, and visit the delightful, though much altered, eleventh-century church. The little island has long been a favourite with artists, particularly writers.

Isola Madre

The third island lies right across the Borromean Bay, **Isola Madre** actually being closer to Pallanza, from where it can also be reached, than it is to Stresa. Though the biggest of the three islands, Isola Madre is occupied only by a single villa, and its gardens compete with those of Isola Bella on a botanical basis, though not at all in terms of lavishness. The island has been landscaped into five terraces, though this fact is frequently lost to the visitor, as the northern end appears totally natural and even the southern end has

Isola Pescatori

Isola Bella

terraces so wide that they get lost in the distance.

The eighteenth-century villa is simple but charming, and stands beside its own chapel where there are tombs of the Borromeo family. Inside, it is again simple and elegant, a great contrast to the villa on Isola Bella.

Back to Stresa

Back on the mainland, stroll along Stresa's waterfront again, this time towards the southern end of the town. The larger quay where the lake steamers put in is a busy spot with yet more public gardens beside it. Carry on, and reach the entrance to **Villa Pallavicino**. The nineteenth-century villa is not open to the public, but its parkland is (there is a car park opposite the entrance).

The park extends to about 40 acres (12 hectares) and is largely natural with sweeping grass, tall trees, flowers and a natural stream. At several points there are more formal gardens, but even these, perhaps because of the setting, do not detract from the naturalness. The park is teeming with wild animals! But it is all quite safe. It has been turned into a small zoo with the minimum of caging. It really is rather pleasant to just amble about between the llamas and the antelopes and it is excellent for children.

Stresa Music Festival

Stresa is famous as a conference and congress centre, and also for its **international music festival** held annually during the last week of August and the first three weeks of September. Though events are chiefly held in the town, the festival is now of such importance that concerts have spilled over into nearby towns and even across the lake to Luino.

The Verganate

From Stresa, and also from Baveno, roads lead up into the mountains that border Lake Maggiore and separate it from Lake Orta. Known as the Verganate this area was once mysterious, its people secretive, and there was little interchange between them and the lake dwellers. Today it is still a little-visited area, but a drive through it is worthwhile, the mountain villages having great charm and offering excellent views over the lake.

On the slopes of the Mottarone and Monte Zuchero, the neighbouring peak, a series of marked walks have been laid out, varying in duration from about $1\frac{1}{2}$ to $5\frac{1}{2}$ hours. A leaflet on them is available from the Baveno Tourist Office.

On the road beyond Levo there is an excellent view down into the Borromean Bay, though the best is obtained from **Motta Rossa** 689m (2,260ft) reached by a not-too-arduous climb from Carpugnino. The summit of the Mottarone can also be reached (well, very nearly – the car park is just below the top) by car, though the last stretch of the road is privately owned and a toll is levied.

The road to the Mottarone starts from **Gignese** where there is a most curious museum. The local industry in this hillside area was umbrella-making. The finest umbrellas, parasols and umbrella-makers came from around here, both products being exported around the world. The museum is devoted to the industry and to the history of the umbrella. Near the village is the **Pope's Stone**, an erratic monolith (i.e. a glacier-deposited single stone) of 55,000cu ft (1,550cu m) which must weigh about 8,500 tons. Quite a size for a boulder.

Giardino Alpino

Near Gignese, on the road to Alpino (the road that leads on to the Mottarone) are the Giardino Alpino (the Alpine Gardens) with many species of plant. Ambrosini, the founder of the garden, produced a small book in which he gave a poem, folklore tale, or story about each species he had planted. The gardens are the perfect antidote to the overwhelming displays of Isola Madre and Isola Bella and an absolute must for those interested in the species they have spotted in Val Grande. And the views from the gardens are awesome.

From Gignese it is possible to follow a road around Monte del Falo and down to Lake Orta, and also to take a road southward to Massino Visconti, above Lesa, but first, back to the lake.

South of Stresa

South of Stresa is **Belgirate** with a mixture of old houses and newer, elegant villas, some with historical connections from the time of the Risorgimento: Garibaldi stayed here, as a guest of Giovanni Cairoli, in the broad fronted Villa Bono Cairoli. The Belgirate Sailing Club is the oldest on Maggiore.

At **Lesa** there are the ruins of a **medieval castle**, and **Villa Cavallini**, which has superb gardens though not open to the public. Villa Stampa is open, and holds a small museum of memorabilia of the author Alessandro Manzoni who spent many holidays here. Lesa is an old port, and a walk along its lake front is very pleasant.

On the way to **Solcio** the road crosses the back of a headland, emerging beside the lake again near the small bay named after the village.

From the bay, travel to **Meina** along a road tightly held between the blue of Maggiore and the greens and multi-colours of the trees and flowers in the roadside villas. Meina is a pretty village with a large number of elegant villas, one of which, the neo-classical **Villa Feraggiana**, is quite superb.

The villa is set in its own park, and from it a road leads up into the mountains allowing access to **Massino Visconti**, which can also be reached

---

Massino

Massino is a village of great charm, some of its older parts being a great joy to wander through. There is a monument to the area's *lusciatti*, the umbrella-makers, and just north of Massino Visconti a track leads off to **San Salvatore** high up on the hillside. There, at the track end, is a welcome restaurant, expansive views, and the **church of Madonna della Cintura**, built in 1499 on the remains of a Romanesque church, some of which survives in the campanile. The church itself is not outstanding, but all around it are cells for monks, constructed in the thirteenth century, some still with their original frescoes. Not surprisingly, this spot is listed as one of Novara province's principal architectural treasures.

---

from Lesa. It was from here that the Visconti family came and their 'home' castle can still be seen, though little now remains of the original twelfth-century building following a fairly thorough dismantling and rebuilding in the fourteenth century.

In the opposite direction from San Salvatore is **Nebbiuno**, a pleasant village from where a road leads up Monte Cornaggia to **Poggio Radioso** at 2,035ft (620m). From here there are good views, but they are much improved if Monte Cornaggia, 3,025ft (922m) is climbed. The ascent, 1 mile distant, 980ft high (1.5km, 300m) takes about $1\frac{1}{4}$ hours, but is worth the effort.

From Nebbiuno the mountain road continues through Pisano to **Invorio**, where there are the remains of a Visconti castle of the fifteenth century. From there it is only a short distance to Gozzano and Lake Orta, or Arona.

Arona

Arona is the next place on the lakeside from Meina. It is the largest town on the Piemonte side of Maggiore, a size in part due to its important position at the point where the railway from Switzerland via the Simplon Tunnel meets railways from Turin, Milan and Genoa. Its prosperity has resulted in a lot of modern building which has not added substantially to the town's elegance, but some of the older parts of the town, while not being of great interest, make up for this lack of character.

On the right, coming into the town, is the *rocca*, a natural fortress which makes an elegant backdrop to harbour views, topped by the ruins of a medieval Borromean family castle. The Borromean family history is tied up with the history of the town (and with that of Angera which lies just across the lake at one of its narrowest points), the

San Carlo Boromeo

Carlo Borromeo was born in Arona Castle in 1538. He was a cardinal at twenty-two and archbishop of Milan by twenty-six, though these appointments were as much to do with his uncle being Pope Pius IV as anything he had accomplished in his life up to those times. But from his appointment to Milan onwards he was a diligent worker for the Christian faith, a builder of churches and a rooter-out of heretics. He was also a brave man, taking huge personal risks to bring comfort to the sick and dying during an outbreak of plague.

Many years after his death he was sanctified, although it was often said during his lifetime that he was too ugly to be anything but a saint: those who would like to check on this can view a portrait of him in the church of the martyrs, San Gratiniano and San Felino, which stands in Arona's Piazza San Graziano.

In 1679 a later Borromeo, Federico, himself archbishop of Milan, decided that a statue should be erected to the saint. It stands a short distance from Arona, above the road towards Meina. In the original concept it was to be of marble, and to include fifteen chapels dedicated to San Carlo. It is in fact copper, and there are three chapels, only one completed. The statue is certainly impressive, for sheer size alone – it is 76ft (23.5m) tall and stands on a granite plinth 39ft (12m) high. It is well constructed and has a patina of venerability. But it is not fine sculpture and the patina is mostly of doubtful origin.

Visitors can climb up inside the statue to reach viewpoints in unexpected parts of the saint's anatomy, but on a hot summer's day the expedition is similar to spending time in an oven.

family having been lords of the town from the late fifteenth century, taking over from the Viscontis.

The Borromean family produced several great men and also a saint, San Carlo Borromeo (*see* box above), whose huge statue can be seen a little way from the town, up a steep road to the left from the lakeside road on the way to Meina.

In the town itself, in the **Palazzo de Filippi**, is the **Civic Museum**, with an interesting collection on the town's history, and the mineralogy of the local area.

Excursion from Arona

From Arona the short trip to **Paruzzaro** is worthwhile, to see the **church of San Marcello**, an eleventh-century Romanesque building with an excellent campanile and a fine series of fifteenth- and sixteenth-century frescoes. The road to the village touches one boundary of the **Parco Naturale i Lagoni di Mercuragio**, a nature reserve set up around the wooded slopes that surround a tiny lake.

The road that leaves Arona southward passes through **Dormelletto**, famous with sailors for its boatyards and with lovers of the turf for its racehorse stud farms, and then branches left, as the lake ends, for Sesto Calende.

The right fork goes to Novara, capital of the Piemontian province in which both Lake Orta and western Lake Maggiore lie. Also along this road at **Pombia** is a safari park with an aquarium. Another similar park, La Torbiera, can be found a short distance from the first, at **Agrate Conturbia**.

Nearing Sesto Calende, a road off right leads to **Castellato Sopra Ticino**, which has quite recently yielded very interesting Bronze Age tombs. Finds are in the Novara City Museum and in Turin's Archaeological Museum.

THE LOMBARDIAN SHORE

Crossing the Ticino river which drains Lake Maggiore into the Po, the route crosses into Lombardy, Italy's fourth biggest region, and the name most synonymous with the Italian Lakes.

Sesto Calende

The first Lombardian town is Sesto Calende (Sesto C is how it is termed on the *autostrada* signs going north from Milan). The name is thought to derive from Roman times when the town had a market on the sixth day after Kalends (the first day of a new month). Even in Roman times the town was old, numerous finds having been made here of the so called Golasecca culture (named after a village a little way south of Sesto Calende), a people in transition from the Bronze Age to the Iron Age. Some of the finds are held in the town museum, in Piazza Mazzini.

Angera

Northward is Angera, a pleasant town with one of the finest castles on any of the lakes. Today Angera is a commercial town, but under the Romans it was not only a commercial, busy trading port, but also a military town of importance. When the barbarian hordes streamed down the valley of the Ticino the town was destroyed but the strategic importance of the site, with its huge natural fortress, the *rocca*, led the Lombards to make it the centre of their

Angera Castle from Arona

Verbano province which included Maggiore and much else besides. Such was its importance that it was involved in battles for supremacy successively by the Franks, the Torrianis, the Viscontis and, finally, the Borromeo family.

The latter, who gained possession in 1450, survived the rule of Spaniards and Austrians, and the upheaval of the Risorgimento. Today the Borromeo family still own the castle that stands on the *rocca*.

Angera's Castle

The road to the castle is steep and passes a natural cave the 'Cava del Lupo' (the wolf's den), which was inhabited in prehistoric times and was the site of a Roman temple to Mithras. The castle itself has a fortified gateway that is probably partly a Roman watch tower, though modified by the Lombards. The Lombards made other additions, as did the Viscontis and the Borromeos, so it combines a mixture of ages.

The Maschio tower dominates the first courtyard, beyond which is the 'noble' courtyard and the Borromean residential *palazzo*. Here the **Ceremony Room** contains frescoes detached from the Palazzo Borromeo in Milan, including a series on *Aesop's Fables*, painted in the late fourteenth and early fifteenth centuries.

The **Justice Room** is fifteenth-century and is architecturally of great interest, with its elegantly vaulted ceiling and mullioned windows. This room also has fifteenth-century frescoes commissioned by Giovanni Visconti, Archbishop of Milan, and depicting in part, battles of the Visconti family. The ceiling bays are mainly of geometric design, the vault bases once having been decorated with the signs of the zodiac. Sadly only two signs, as one pair, survive. There is no furniture in either room and, strangely, that improves the appearance, allowing the mind to concentrate on the architecture.

The Doll Museum

As a complete contrast to its warlike beginnings, Angera's castle now houses a museum of Italian dolls, with a superb collection dating from the early nineteenth century through to the early years of the twentieth century. There is also a collection of toys, and another of children's clothing from the 18th-20th century.

From the castle the views are superb, and it is easy to see why the *rocca* was so sought after as a defensive position. On the far side of the lake the **statue of San Carlo** can be seen (a mixed blessing – the view from statue to castle is superior). At night the castle and *rocca* are illuminated and that is a sight worth travelling many a mile to see. When the lake is calm go around to Arona – the sight of the *rocca* reflected in the mirror of the lake, is worth the drive.

Angera was the birthplace of Pietro Martire, the chief contemporary documenter of Columbus' expedition to the New World, and on the tiny Isolino Portegora in its bay, the monk Arialdo was murdered for daring to defend Christianity against the excesses of an archbishop of Milan. That happened in 1066, as the Normans were invading England. Some items of these, and other aspects of the town's history, can be seen at the **Town Museum** in Via Marconi. Elsewhere in the town a walk will be well rewarded, particularly in the shade of the double row of chestnut trees on the lake front.

From Angera

From the town, **Monte San Quirico**, 1,350ft (412m) can be climbed in about 45 minutes. The mountain is the summit of the ridge on which Angera's castle stands, on a lower plateau. From the top the views to the lake and castle are excellent.

The peak stands above the headland of **Ranco**, a village that can be reached from Angera by taking a minor road rather than the main road that goes directly to Ispra. At the village there is a small museum of transport, with steam locomotives, stage coaches, bicycles and much more.

Ispra is a small town still growing on the prosperity brought by the Euratom centre, on the road to **Lake Monate**. Also behind the town, on the slopes of the Motto di Cisano, are the scars of quarries, white in the sun.

Beyond Ispra the road gives a pleasant drive through small villages to **Reno**, from where the famous **church**

The Blessed Alberto and Santa Caterina del Sasso

In the twelfth century a man from Besozzo (inland from here) known as Alberto Bessozi made a living locally by a variety of unlawful means – for example, smuggling and high-interest money lending. One day while out alone in a boat on the lake he was surprised by a sudden storm, his boat capsized and he was in imminent danger of drowning when he promised God that, if his life was spared, he would dedicate it to prayer and penance for his sins.

Miraculously he was thrown onto a ledge of the steep cliff near Reno and there he spent the rest of his life – almost forty years – being kept alive by food local folk gave him (lowering it to him in a basket), or which he raised from boats, and by water from a spring.

When plague threatened the local community Alberto prayed for them and they were spared, showing their gratitude by building, on the hermit's ledge, a **chapel to Santa Caterina** who had answered his prayers. There, later, Alberto was buried. In the fourteenth century a Dominican monastery was added to the chapel.

Further evidence of the miraculous nature of the spot was given in the mid-seventeenth century when a substantial rock fall from the cliff above the sanctuary was prevented from crushing the hermit's tomb by three bricks. When the dust had cleared, the bricks were found to be holding the weight of numerous huge blocks, all jammed into a stable position. Not until many years later were the blocks finally removed.

of **Santa Caterina del Sasso** can be reached. Reno is a beautiful village set on a small bay formed by two headlands, one on which the church stands, and one at Cerro further north.

After many years of stabilising and renovating the sanctuary church of Santa Caterina it was finally re-opened in 1987 allowing the visitor to enjoy the peace of the site, marvel at the frescoes, some of which are very well preserved, see the remains of the Blessed Alberto's winch, and also view his body, miraculously preserved from decay, though not surprisingly looking a little mummified.

It should be noted that descent to the sanctuary is via a long series of sometimes tricky steps, with only the shady views and lizards for company. The climb back up is, of course, no easier. The site is to be added to the list of stops of the lake steamers, so access will be easier for those who find climbing difficult. But at all costs do visit it.

Inland from Reno, at **Leggiuno**, there is an interesting Romanesque church which incorporates parts of a Roman temple, including two columns supporting the portal.

Cerro del Lago Maggiore was a favourite resort of the writer Manzoni. It is a pretty village with an excellent view into the Borromean Bay across the lake. Within the village there is a very interesting museum, dedicated to the local ceramics industry.

Laveno

Laveno is a small lakeside town with an industrial area – known as Mombello – behind it, beside the Torrente Boesio. It was here that many of the potteries represented at the museum in Cerro were located.

Legend has it that the town is named after a Roman general, Titus Labienus, who either led an expedition against the Gauls from the town, or alternatively, fought the decisive battle of the campaign here at the Boesio crossing. During the Risorgimento there was action here again when the forces of Garibaldi fought the Austrians, who were in control of the castle whose ruins can still be seen in the park laid out on the Punta San Michele, on the northern headland of the small bay in which Laveno lies. A memorial to those who died stands at the lakeside.

At Christmas in Laveno a most unusual nativity is set up, not in the church as might be expected, but beneath the waters of the lake. Marble figures are set up on the lake floor by divers, and on the night of Christmas Eve the statue of the baby Jesus is lowered. The reason for this event is not well understood, but the floodlight nativity attracts many visitors.

Cerro and the Pirate

In medieval times a local pirate, captured after a long reign of terror, was sentenced to be hanged, the execution to be carried out on the beach at Cerro del Lago Maggiore. Asked if he had a last wish before the execution was carried out he requested a glass of wine. To their consternation his executioners found there was no inn at Cerro. When he was told that they could not fulfil his last wish the pirate gave the village a look of disgust. He turned to the hangman, said 'Better hell than this town of abstainers' and went quietly to his doom.

Laveno

The car ferry from Intra docks at Laveno – those approaching across the lake get a splendid view of the **church of San Giacomo and San Filippo,** a very recent church built on a grand scale with a fine dome. The church dominates the town which makes it a very busy place in summer, but also ensures that there are always sufficient places in the roadside cafés.

Take a Bucket to Sasso del Ferro

The best way to see Laveno is to ride up almost to the top of the Sasso del Ferro, the 3,485ft (1,062m) peak which dominates the town. The ride, on Sasso's *funivia*, is quite an experience, the visitor stands in a cylindrical, two-person bucket that is open to the air. The journey offers spectacular views and an equally sensational feeling of exposure. At the right time the view downwards is enhanced by the butterflies which find the grassy swathe cut through the woods below the cables – presumably to aid maintenance – a haven.

The *funivia* top station is at 3,145ft (959m), and from there a path goes to the actual summit – allow about half an hour. However, there is little point in the walk as it does not improve the view substantially. Monte Rosa is visible beyond the Mottarone, and a substantial part of the lake can also be seen.

Beyond Laveno

From Laveno the road is galleried for some distance, and when the visitor emerges from the gallery the view ahead is dominated by the **Rocca di Calde**, one of the most distinctive and impressive sights on the eastern shore.

The *rocca* was once topped by a castle, built in the tenth century and defended against Otto I when he came this way. It was destroyed by the Swiss in 1513, and it is easy to see why any invading army would be concerned about leaving a castle in such a position.

Away from the lake, the *rocca* slopes gently down to **Castelveccana** where the campanile of the **church of San Pietro** points sharply skyward. The church has a rare marble altar.

To reach **Luino**, either continue along the lake road (the quick way) or go inland via **Musadino** and **Brezzo di Bedero**. At this last village there is a fine lake view and a church of some interest. From Brezzo the inland road goes back down to the main road at Germignaga which is now almost continuous with Luino, from which it is divided by the Tresa river which drains Lake Lugano into Maggiore.

Luino

Luino is the chief town of the Lombardian shore of Maggiore, with a large railway complex in keeping with its light-industrial status. The town is believed to have been the birthplace of Bernardino Luini the painter. An *Adoration of the Magi* widely attributed to him can be seen in the **church of San Pietro**, beside the town cemetery in the eastern, uphill, section of the town.

Another son of the town was the Blessed Giacobino Luinese, a Carmelite who founded a monastery and to whom miracles are attributed. In his birthplace he founded the **church of Madonna del Carmine**, which stands beside the lake road on entering the town. In the church there are frescoes attributed to scholars of Luini.

At the town's centre is **Piazza Garibaldi** – there is an excellent market, particularly for leather, on Wednesdays – with a monument to the great man – the first ever erected to him in Italy and completed before his death. After his defeat at Custozza, Garibaldi raised a small army here to continue the struggle against Austria. The enthusiasm of local men for this renewal of the struggle, and the erection of this first Garibaldian monument, are deeds of which the town is justly proud.

Many aspects of the town's history, and a fossil collection, can be seen in the **Town Museum** in Palazzo Verbania.

A visit to the home studio of **Sergio Tapia Radic**, a Chilean sculptor now a resident of the town, is also worthwhile. Sergio lives in the southern suburb of Germignaga. Sergio works in terracota and bronze. His sculptures have attracted attention all over the world, and in Italy he has been hailed as a new master in the old tradition. Exhibitions of his work can be seen throughout the area during the summer months.

From Luino

From Luino it is just a short distance eastwards to Switzerland. The frontier follows the Tresa river to a point just short of the village of Fornasette and so gives a fascinating drive from Luino to Ponte Tresa, the road following the river all the way. After the second tunnel, Switzerland is on the other side of the river from the road.

Alternatively, go from Luino to **Dumenza** or **Runo**, each nicely placed villages, and climb the peaks of the Clivio or the Lema to stand on a ridge with one foot in either country. From the summit of Monte Lema, 5,320ft (1,621m), a chair-lift descends to Miglieglia in Switzerland. The climb is long and fairly strenuous – leave aside half a day.

From **Due Cossani**, where there is a good view of Monte Lema for potential walkers, a road leads to **Agra**, a beautiful mountain village well worth a visit. From just beyond the village there is a most beautiful view of northern Lake Maggiore.

The alternative road from Due Cossani leads to **Curiglia**, it is an interesting road, occasionally too narrow, occasionally too tightly curved. On the way is a more life-like, but no more handsome statue of San Carlo Borromeo. The reward for the journey is the scenery *en route* in the Val Veddasca. Curiglia is very picturesque, and from it **Monteviasco** can be reached, but only on foot. It is said to be 1,000 steps to Monteviasco, though it feels much further. The reward is a completely unspoilt village in magnificent surroundings.

The lake road from Luino goes to **Maccagno**, the last lake village with probably the best campsite on the lake. The upper part of the village is very pretty, and from it the Val Veddasca can be followed to the Swiss border at Indemini.

From Indemni a short walk – only about 425ft (130m) – leads to the summit of **Monte Cadriga**, 4,265ft (1,300m) with good panoramic views, including northern Lake Maggiore and little Lake Delio below (in the pass between Monte Cadriga and **Monte Borgna**, 3,800ft (1,158m). The latter peak does limit the view from Cadriga, and a better view of Maggiore is obtained by climbing Borgna from Lake Delio, reached by branching off the Val Veddasca road. The climb is longer than that to Monte Cadriga, but very worthwhile. On the road to Lake Delio the sanctuary of San Rocca also offers a fine view of the lake.

Maccagno was one of the earliest inhabited places on Maggiore, and it was there that Count Mandelli, the feudal lord, gave food and shelter to Otto I when he arrived in 962 to fight Berengar. In return for this Otto made the village a self-governing fief, with the power to mint its own money. The village is divided into two, Inferiore which is reached first, and Superiore with its quiet square. There are also remains of a tower from a later period of history.

The Maccagno Climbing Centre

Climbers will be entranced, and non-climbers amazed, by the extraordinary **Cinzanino Climbers' Studio** close to Maccagno. Here the natural cliffs have been turned into a climbing wall by adding fixed belays, and artificial walls have been added (in one place up the constructed walls of a bridge) to produce a massive outdoor arena.

Beyond Maccagno there is only one more village before Zenna and the Swiss border. That village is **Pino sulla sponda del Lago Maggiore**, which has the longest place name in Italy.

THE SWISS SHORE

ASCONA
Museum of Modern Art
Open: March-December,
Tuesday-Saturday 10am-
12noon, 3-6pm. Sunday 4-6pm
☎ 091 7805100

LOCARNO
Castello Visconti
Piazza Castello, Open: April-
September, Tuesday- Sunday
10am-12noon, 2-5pm.
☎ 091 7563180

THE PIEMONTE SHORE

ALPINO
Alpine Garden
Open: April-October Tuesday-
Sunday 9am-5pm
☎ 0323 61687

AGRATE CONTURBIA
La Torbiera Safari Park
Open: Spring/summer, daily
10am-7pm; autumn10am-
5pm; closed winter.
☎ 0322 832135/136

ARONA
Museum
Open: Tuesday 10am-12noon,
Saturday & Sunday 3.30-
6.30pm. At other times by
request. ☎ 0322 48294/243601

Rocca (Castle remains)
Open: April and May, daily
2-5pm; June-October,
10am-7.30pm.
☎ 0322 931300

Statue of San Carlo Borromeo
Open: all year, daily 9am-
12.30pm, 2-6.30pm (4.45pm
from November-March).
☎ 0322 249669

CANNERO RIVIERA
Malpaga Castle
Not open to the public,
but boat trips to view can
be made from Cannero.

GHIFFA
Hat Museum
Open: April-October, Saturday
& Sunday 3.30-6.30pm.
☎ 0323 59174/59186/59209

(cont'd overleaf)

A sculpture of Sergio Tapia Radic whose studio is at Luino

The church of Santa Caterina del Sasso on Lake Maggiore

(cont'd from previous page)

GIGNESE
Umbrella Museum
Open: April-September,
daily except Monday10.30am-
12noon, 3-6pm.
☎ 0323 208064

GURRO
Museum
Open: April-mid-October, Saturday
& Sunday, 10am-12noon, 2-5pm.
Also open Tuesday-Friday, July-
mid-September. ☎ 0322 76100

LESA
Museum
Open: July and August, daily 9am-
12noon, 3-6pm.
☎ 0322 76421

PALLANZA-VERBANIA
Paesaggio (Landscape) Museum
Open: April-October, Tuesday-
Sunday 10am-12noon, 3.30-
6.30pm.
☎ 0323 556621

Villa Taranto
Open: April-October daily 8.30am-
6.30pm or sunset. Gardens only
open to public.
☎ 0323 404555/556667

POMBIA
Zoo Safari del Lago Maggiore
Open: all year, daily 10am-5pm;
11am-4pm in winter.
☎ 0321 956401

SANTA MARIA MAGGIORE
Chimney Sweep's Museum
For information ☎ 0324 95061.

STRESA
Isola Bella
Open: Mid-March-October daily
9am-5.30pm. ☎ 0323 30556

5-minute boat trip from Stresa
commencing 6.35am, April-
September. Last boat leaves Bella
7pm, but 7.35pm from 1 June
onwards.

Isola Pescatori
10-minute boat trip from Stresa.
April-September, commencing
6.35am. Last boat leaves
Pescatori 6.55pm, but 7.30pm
from 1st June onwards.

Villa Pallavicino
Open: Mid-March-October, daily
9am-6pm (closes 12.30-2pm in
March and October).
☎ 0323 31533

Funivia (cablecar) **to Il
Mottarone**
Open: all year daily 10am-6pm;
7pm in July and August.
☎ 0323 30295

STRESA/VERBANIA
Isola Madre
Open: Easter-October daily
9am-5.30pm.
☎ 0323 31261
Half-hour boat trip from Stresa
from 7.20am, April-September.
Last boat leaves Madre at
6.40pm. Please note that visitors
cannot land on the island unless
they purchase an entry ticket.

THE LOMBARDIAN SHORE

ANGERA
**Borromeo Castle &
Doll Museum**
Open: Easter-October daily
9.30am-5pm.
☎ 0331 931300

Museum
Open: all year, Monday-Tuesday
3-5pm, Thursday 10am-12noon,
3-7pm and Saturday 3-7pm.
☎ 0332 931133

CERRO DEL LAGO MAGGIORE
Ceramics Museum
Open: all year, Friday, Saturday &
Sunday 10am-12noon, 2.30-
5.30pm, Tues-Thurs 2.30-5.30.
☎ 0332 666530

LAVENO
Funivia (cablecar)
to Sasso del Ferro
Open: April-September, daily
9.30am-6pm, 7pm on Saturdays,
Sundays and holidays; October-
March, Saturday, Sunday and
holidays 9.30am-5pm.
☎ 0332 668012

LUINO
Museum
Closed for restoration at time of
writing.
☎ 0332 532057

RANCO
Transport Museum
Open: all year, Tuesday-Sunday
10am-12noon, 2-4.30pm.
☎ 0331 975198

RENO
**Sanctuary of Santa
Caterina del Sasso**
Open: all year, daily 8.30am-
12noon, 3-6pm.
☎ 0332 647172

SESTO CALENDE
Museum
Open: Monday-Thursday 9am-
12.30pm, 2.30-4.30pm, Sunday
3-6pm, Saturday by request.
☎ 0331 928150/928160

LAKE STEAMERS

Full service on Lake Maggiore linking Arona, Angera, Meina, Lesa,
Belgirate, Stresa, Carciano, the Borromean Islands, Baveno, Verbania-
Pallanza, Villa Taranto, Intra, Laveno, Ghiffa, Porto Val Travaglia,
Oggebbio, Cannero, Luino, Maccagno and Cannobio, continuing to
Brissago, Porto Ronco, Ranzo, Gerra, Ascona, San Nazzaro, Vira,
Magadino and Locarno, all in Switzerland.

There are also small local services linking Carciano and Verbania-
Pallanza with the three Borromean Islands and the Villa Taranto.

Because the service crosses the border between Italy and Switzerland (which zig-zags in a curious way to stay in the middle of the lake
and at right-angles with the shore) there are customs and border
officials, so passports must be carried and duty-payable goods must
be declared.

Arona to Locarno and back takes about six hours if the outward
journey is on the normal ferry with its restaurant service, and the
return by hydrofoil.

The lake's only car-ferry links Verbania-Intra with Laveno, the
crossing taking around twenty minutes. For information on all of the
steamers ☎ 0332 233200.

VARESE

The large, modern city of Varese is built on flat land below Monte Campo dei Fiori. It is of ancient origin, probably Celtic, though little that remains outside the town museum is older than the sixteenth century. Today the city prospers as a provincial capital with a large amount of light industry and manufacturing (especially shoe making) and a range of good restaurants and fine shops to attract the visitor.

Varese is known as the 'garden city', a name that derives as much from the public gardens within the city boundary as from its position at the mouths of some very green and fertile valleys.

The heart of the city was also the heart of the old city, dominated by the 236ft-high (72m) campanile known as **Del Bernascone**, after its architect (Giuseppe Bernascone). The campanile, whose attractiveness lies in the ever-changing design patterns as it rises, is thought to be among the finest examples in Lombardy. Work on it started in the early seventeenth century, but it was not finally completed until 150 years later. The ironwork bell-wheel mechanisms peeping out from the stone pillars of the bell cell are particularly interesting.

Beside the campanile is the **basilica of San Vittore**, built in the late sixteenth/early seventeenth century to a plan by Pelligrini. The façade is much newer, a late eighteenth-century neo-classical addition. Inside there is a fine collection of artwork – paintings, sculpture and some very elaborate wood-carving. The work in the **chapel of the Rosary** is by Morazzone, from

Baptistery of San Giovanni

Beside the basilica of San Vittore is the baptistery of San Giovanni, an Italian national monument, which is the oldest building in the town. It is a fine, simple, but dignified stone building. The present structure dates from the twelfth and thirteenth centuries, though it stands on the site of a previous church. Inside there is an interesting eighth-century immersion font, with a single-stone basin carved in the thirteenth century. Also from that time is one of the finest Lombardian series of frescoes in existence.

the early seventeenth century, while the frescoes in the **chapel of Santa Marta** are, mostly, a century older.

Close to the complex beneath the campanile is the old town with its arcaded buildings, now mostly converted to shops and cafés. This area once housed the *Broletto* (town hall), but now the city's municipal centre has been transferred to the magnificent **Palazzo Estense**, another national monument which stands at the head of the equally magnificent Estense Gardens. The palace, built in baroque style in the mid-eighteenth century, was the summer and autumn home of Francesco II of Este, the Duke of Modena. It now houses the city fathers in grand style, but the visitor is allowed the freedom of the façade and the Italian-style gardens to its front.

Within the gardens, on the opposite side from the palace, is **Villa Mirabello**, in less sumptuous style and housing the town's museum. Here there are several quite different collections: archaeological items, including some from the Lake Varese site; a picture gallery, including detached frescoes from Castelseprio; a Risorgimento collection (Varese was an important centre – Garibaldi defeated the Austrians at Biumo, now within the city boundaries, in May 1859); and the butterfly collection of Francesco Tamagno, a tenor.

To the north, in **Biumo**, are the two **Villas Ponti**, now used as a congress centre. The larger villa is late nineteenth century, built in what is termed 'eclectic' style, i.e. bits from everything; the smaller is neo-classic. The villas stand in a large park that is open to the public. Here, too, is Villa Menafoglio Litta Panza, a beautiful 18th century villa housing a fine collection of comtemporay art.

Sacre Monte

Close to Varese is Sacre Monte, reached by going north from the Palazzo Estense for about 6 miles 10km. A document exists from 922 noting the existence of a church to Santa Maria on Monte Vellate, although both before and after that time the site was of considerable strategic importance and was fortified.

In the early fifteenth century Sant' Ambrogia came, bringing to the spot an ancient wooden statue of the Virgin, known as the 'Black Virgin', which legend ascribes to the apostle Luke. Pilgrimages were made to the Sacre Monte following this, and a nunnery was set up. The pilgrimages declined until San Carlo Borromeo renewed them, bringing a fresh impetus to the sacred site.

In the seventeenth century, fourteen chapels were erected along a Via Crucis leading to the **church of Santa Maria del Monte**, which illustrated Christ's life in painting and statuary. All the chapels are interesting, but general opinion holds that the seventh, with frescoes by Morazzone, is the finest.

At the top of the Via Crucis, beside the church, is the little village of **Sacre Monte**, from which the views are magnificent. The church still holds the 'Black Virgin' and has a silver altar rail by the sculptor Ludovico Pogliaghi who died in the village in 1950. His villa is now a museum devoted to his work, and contains a plaster cast of the central door of Milan's cathedral for which he was also responsible, and his own art collection.

Also in the village is the **Baroffio Museum** with artwork which had been in the church, and the art collection of the founder, Baron Baroffio.

The old village of Biumo, to the south of the park, is also worth visiting, its ancient heart looking much as it must have done when Garibaldi came this way. Across the city to the south, at Bosto, the eleventh-century **church of San Imerio** is worth a look on the way to the Milan *autostrada*.

CAMPO DEI FIORI

Beyond Sacre Monte the road continues up Monte Campo dei Fiori, the hill of the fields of flowers, which has several peaks. Near the first summit, Monte, (3,600ft, 1,098m) is the Grand Hotel, built in the early years of this century in fine art nouveau style. Sadly it is now closed and neglected.

From the hotel, the summit is easily reached (about 230ft/70m of ascent). The three crosses are now dedicated to those who have fallen in all wars. From the summit known as the 'Panoramic Balcony of Lombardy' the view is magnificent, stretching to Monte Rosa and the Bernese Oberland as well as Varese town and the local lakes. A higher summit can also be easily reached, and here there is an observatory which is open for guided tours, but these must be booked in advance.

THE LAKES OF VARESE

To the west of Varese is a trio of small lakes that can be seen in one circular outing. Travelling west from Varese the main road, the N394, bound for Laveno, goes through Gavirate. En route there is: the Varese golf course, at Luvinate, with a club house that started life in the eleventh century as a Benedictine monastery – surely one of the most romantic club houses in the world; Barasso, whose church has a fine painting by a pupil of Luini; and

Comerio, famous in caving circles for the caves in Monte Campo dei Fiori behind the town, and with a fine Romanesque church.

LAKE VARESE

At **Gavirate** the visitor reaches Lake Varese, the largest of the trio of lakes but sadly the most polluted of them too. So badly polluted that swimming is banned and a full-scale ecological rescue exercise is under way. The lake is 5.5 miles (9km) long, and at its broadest, into the bay beside Cazzago Brabbia, is 2.25 miles (3.5km) wide. Those dimensions mean the lake is about the same size as Lake Orta, and so has considerable scope as a tourist attraction once it has been 'restored'.

Gavirate was once famous for its fishing, but this has now declined. It is an interesting town with a local museum in Via Voltorre dedicated to pipes.

Continue along the same road to arrive at **Voltorre** itself where, beside the **church of San Michele** whose massive campanile boasts one of the biggest bells in Italy, there is a most interesting eleventh-century brick cloister of an old Cluniac monastery.

At **Calcinate del Pesce** there is a gliding club that offers demonstration flights, an excellent, though not cheap, way of seeing the local landscape. Beyond Schiranna, the site of the lake's rowing club, a large sports complex has been built, including two swimming pools, and from which boats can be hired.

On the southern side of the lake, the views across the water to Monte Campo dei Fiori are excellent as we make for **Biandronno**, behind which is a fourth lake, tiny and almost overgrown with weed. From the village, boats cross to **Isolino Virginia**, a national monument site of enormous

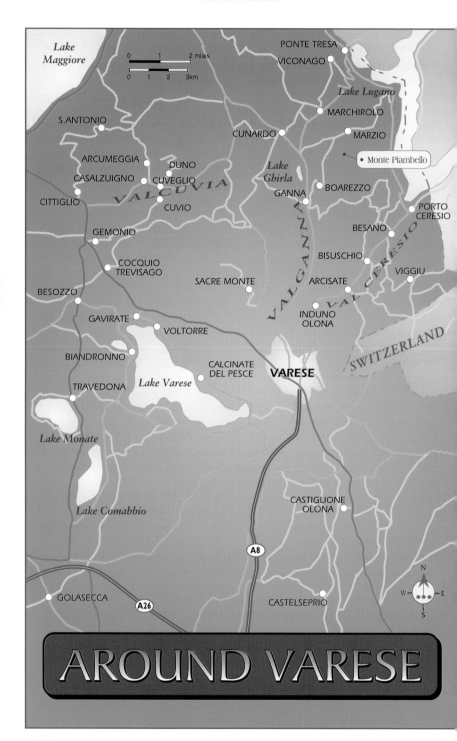

importance to the study of the Neo-lithic and Bronze Ages.

The island is, in part, built up on the remains of pile-built lake dwellings, which have been constructed over a period of centuries. Many of the items discovered here, together with displays on the dwellings and the cultures which created them, are on display in Varese. In the summer months, on Saturday and Sunday afternoons, the **Varese Museum** organises tours to the island. The museum and Tourist Offices have details.

Right: One of the frescoes on the buildings of Arcumeggia

Below: Palazzo Estense, at the heart of old Varese

LAKE COMABBIO

South from Biandronno the emerald green Lake Comabbio (no swimming here either), is reached. The lake is 2 miles (3km) long and 0.5 mile (1km) wide. Vareno Berghi on its eastern shore is an industrial centre, but does have one splendid building, the **Villa Borghi.**

On the road that leads south from the town to Corgeno, the visitor enters the huge **Ticino Nature Park,** which, in its southern section around Pavia, is very good. In the northern section, which touches Lake Comabbio and Sesto Calende and extends almost to Lake Monate, the park is less well defined and less interesting.

South from here is **Golasecca,** a name already familiar in the context of the prehistoric remains in the Novara province. The name of the ancient culture derives from the village. A museum of the better finds from the sites can be found in Sesto Calende at the southern tip of Lake Maggiore.

LAKE MONATE

Visitors reach Lake Monate by the main road along the western shore of Comabbio. It is the smallest of the lakes, (1.75 miles, 2.75km long by 0.5 mile, 1km wide) and in it there have been found a number of important pile dwellings from the Bronze Age. At the lake's western tip is Cadrezzate, from where there are fine views towards Maggiore as well as over the small lake. At **Travedona,** at the lake's northern end, the thirteenth-century Romanesque church has a fine series of frescoes.

Northward is **Besozzo** where a medieval tower has been incorporated into a more modern villa (though this is not open to the public) and also the combined villages of **Cocquio-Trevisago** where there is a museum dedicated to the work of the artist Innocente Salvini, a local Impressionist.

VALCUVIA

The Valcuvia is one of the greenest, most unspoilt valleys near any of the large lakes, and though it is very short, approximately 7.5 miles (12km) long, it is worth the effort to visit.

The route begins at Cittiglio. (Although there is a road the other side of the valley starting at **Gemonio** it is not as good, but **Gemenio** itself is, having an eleventh-century Romanesque church, with fourteenth- and sixteenth-century frescoes, which is a national monument). The first spot in the valley from Cittiglio is **Casalzuigno** where the Villa Della Porta Bozzolo, a magnificent sixteenth-century mansion, and its equally superb gardens and parkland are open to visitors. From Casalzuigno a narrow, windy lane leads up through some magnificent woodland to **Arcumegia,** one of the most remarkable of local villages.

The road to Arcumeggia can be followed further, to **Sant' Antonio,**

Arcummegia – Village of Frescoes

At Arcummegia contemporary artists have painted frescoes on the outside walls of the village houses. Each year new paintings are added, so that the village has become an open-air exhibition of contemporary Italian art. The artists have also produced panels for a Via Crucis on the grassed churchyard.

where there is a good view across Lake Maggiore, and from there down to the lake. To regain Valcuvia, go back down the winding lane. The tightness of the curves does at least allow the driver to look down the hillside to see what is coming up.

Back in the valley the scenery remains attractive as the road reaches **Cuvio**, with **Cuveglio**, an old Visconti *palazzo*, having a crenellated Romanesque bell-tower. Above Cuveglio, is **Duno**, with a small church dedicated to Italy's doctors. Beyond these Valcuvia ends, roads going right for the Valganna or left to follow Val Travaglia to Luino.

VALGANNA

The Valganna is followed by the main road, the N233, which goes northward from Varese towards Ponte Tresa and Switzerland. From Varese the road runs at first through open country, until the valley is joined. Valganna here is narrow, with steep, verdant walls. At one point a grotto has been carved out from the cliff top, and a moss blanket covers it, constantly dripping.

The road passes two small lakes, **Ganna** and **Ghirla**, each named after its neighbouring village and both very popular with the locals for winter skating. Lake Ghirla, the larger of the two, is also a summer resort, with swimming and windsurfing. In **Ganna**, the first village reached, the excellent frescoed remains of the eleventh-century monastery of San Gemolo now house a small museum to the history of the monastery and the area.

From Ganna a side road leads uphill to **Boarezzo**, from where the views are excellent, and which, like Arcumeggia, has contemporary frescoes. Though the overall effect is not as impressive as at

Arcumeggia, some of the frescoes are very good, particularly the still-life of Aldo Ambrosini and the intricate abstract work of Albino Reggiori.

A Mountain Walk

From Boarezzo it is possible to climb **Monte Piambello**, 3,700ft (1,129m) for expansive views over Lake Lugano. There is a track to the summit, but it would be a very difficult drive, and those with no time for the walk (2-3 hours are required) can go to **Marzio** where the view across Lake Lugano is equally good.

Beyond Ghirla, a developing holiday resort, the road divides. Going left the visitor passes **Cunardo**, in a fine position, and drops down to Luino. Going straight on the road descends through the equally open and pleasant Val Marchirolo to **Ponte Tresa**. From **Viconago**, above Marchirolo, there are fine views over Lugano and Switzerland. The village is a fine one, with old houses and two very good churches.

VALCERESIO

The Valceresio heads north-east from Varese to Porte Ceresio on Lake Lugano, through many interesting places, the first being **Induno Olona**, where there are good paintings in the parish church and fourteenth-century frescoes in the oratory of San Pietro. The town also has a fine museum with exhibits on the natural history of the valley. Here too, or rather at the

(cont'd on page 76)

VARESE

Baroffio Museum
Sacre Monte
Open: May-September,
Thursday, Saturday & Sunday
9.30am-12.30pm, 3-6.30pm.
At other times by request.
☎ 0332 777472.

Observatory
Monte Campo dei Fiori
Guided tours (individuals or
parties) must be booked in
advance.
Contact Tourist Information
Office, Varese.

Pogliaghi Museum
*Via Beata Giuliana,
5 Sacre Monte*
Closed for refurbishment at
time of writing.
☎ 0332 226040.

Town Museum
Villa Mirabello
Open: all year, Tuesday-
Saturday 10.30am-12.30pm,
2-5pm, Sunday 9.30am-
12.30pm, 2-5.30pm. Closed
holidays. ☎ 0332 281590

Villa Menafoglio Litta Panza
Biumo Superiore
Open: All year, Tuesday-
Sunday 10am-6pm
☎ 0332 283960.

Cycle race near Lake Varese

A view across Castiglione Olona, a village of art treasures

Ville Ponti
Biumo
Gardens only all year,
daily 8am-8pm.
For information
☎ 0332 295111.

THE VARESE LAKES

CALCINATE DEL PESCE
Gliding Club
Weather dependent!
For information ☎ 0332
310073.

COCQUIO-TREVISAGO
Salvini Gallery
Open: April-October, Saturday
& Sunday 3.30-6.30pmpm.
☎ 0332 602161

GAVIRATE
Pipe Museum
Open: April-October, by request
at building.
☎ 0332 743334

ISOLINO VIRGINIA
Villa Ponti
Open: April-October, Saturday
& Sunday 2-6pm. Tours
available. Contact Varese
Museum or Tourist Office
for details.
☎ 0332 281590

VALCUVIA

Arcumegia
Avoid times when village
is crowded (fêtes etc) as
parking will be impossible.
For information
☎ 0332 283604.

CASALZUIGNO
Villa Bozzolo
Open: February-mid-
December, Tuesday-Sunday
10am-1pm, 2-6pm; October-
December, Tuesday-Sunday
10am-1pm, 2-5pm.
☎ 0332 624136

(contd' overleaf)

(contd' from previous page)

VALGANNA

GANNA
Museum
S Gemolo Abby, 3 Via Ugo, Perego. Open: March-October, Sunday 3-6pm.
☎ 0332 994532

VALCERESIO

BESANO
Fossil Museum
Via Prestini. Open: April-September, Tuesday-Friday 10am-12.30, 2-6pm. Sat, Sun 11am-12.30pm, 2.30-6.30pm. October-March, Tuesday and Thursday 9.30am-12.30pm. Sunday 2.30-5.30pm.
☎ 0332 919200

BISUSCHIO
Villa Cicogna Mozzoni
8 viale Cigcogna. Open: April-October, Saturday 9.30am-12noon, 2.30-7pm and every afternoon in August.
☎ 0332 471134

INDUNO OLONA
Natural History Museum
4 Piazza Giovnni XXIII
Open: all year, Wednesday & Friday 9pm-12midnight, Sunday 2.30-5.30pm.
☎ 0332 840611

VIGGIU
Butti Gallery
All year: Tuesday & Friday 2-6.30pm, Wednesday, Thursday & Saturday 10am-12noon, Sunday by request.
☎ 0332 486510

SOUTH OF VARESE

CASTELSEPRIO
Archaeological Zone
Open: All year, Tues-Sun 9am-7.30pm (5pm Nov-Feb).
☎ 0331 820438

CASTIGLIONE OLONA
Museum/Church Complex
Open: all year, Tuesday-Sunday 10am-12noon, 3-6pm.
☎ 0331 858048

---

hamlet of **Frascarolo,** is the beautiful Villa Medici di Marignano, a Renaissance building sadly not open to the public.

Beyond is **Arcisate** where, in 1848, a handful of Garibaldi's troops held off 5,000 Austrians for over four hours. From the village a fine wooded road leads off to **Viggiu,** a pleasant village with good views of the Valceresio. Here there is a museum to the work of the artist Enrico Butti, with a collection of his sculpture plaster casts and a collection of the work of local artists. The village churches are also worthy of note. Beyond Viggiu roads lead to the Swiss border.

The last town before Valceresio reaches Lake Lugano is **Besano,** a small town famous for the fossils of the Triassic era found locally, some of which can be seen in a small museum in the town. Also noteworthy is the **church of San Giovanni** with good frescoes and fine views of Lake Lugano.

Villa Cicogna Mozzoni

Back in the main valley the next village is **Bisuschio**, notable for the Villa Cicogna Mozzoni, a sixteenth-century building which is a national monument. The villa is a beautiful building with an arcaded, frescoed ground floor, elegant rows of square cut windows and a shallow roof. Inside it has sixteenth-century frescoes by the Campi school, some excellent antique furniture and rare ornaments. The villa is surrounded by fine Italian-style gardens with ponds behind stone balustrades, fountains and a statue-filled, niched wall.

SOUTH OF VARESE

South from Varese, the 'Lake Country' is quickly left behind. One short journey is worthwhile however. Leave Varese on the N233 towards Milan.

At **Castiglione Olona** is one of Lombardy's finest collections of art treasures. The whole village seems as quiet as it must have been in the early fifteenth century when Cardinal Branda Castiglioni, Papal Legate, Bishop of Piacenza and a local man, constructed the complex of religious buildings which is still largely complete. There is Castiglioni's *palazzo* with his own room and a fine archive; the house he built for his parents; a beautiful, domed church; a baptistery with wonderful frescoes by Masolino da Panicale – *Herod's Feast* is widely renowned as a medieval masterpiece; and a collegiate church, also with frescoes by Masolino. There is also a small museum with items on the building and the cardinal.

In the town there is a fine fifteenth-century town hall and in the streets of the centre, every first Sunday of the month, is the Fiera del Cardinale (the Cardinal's Fair), a secondhand and antique fair.

Nearby is **Castelseprio**, a Roman fortress town that became a Lombard stronghold and was destroyed by the Viscontis in 1287. Today an 'Archaeological Zone' contains the remains of the original town and castle walls, and a medieval monastery. The new town also has a beautiful seventh-century church, to Santa Maria 'Foris Porta', with Byzantine frescoes.

Finally, close to Castelseprio, at **Torba**, are the remains of a very early Benedictine monastery. The complex includes a fifth-century tower, though the church beside it dates from the ninth century. The tower is decorated with frescoes which have been dated to the seventh century.

Parco Ciani, Lugano

L ake Lugano is a fox-shaped piece of water, with its nose at Ponte Tresa, ear at Agno, paws at Porto Ceresio and Capolago, and a huge tail all the way to Porlezza. From nose to tail the lake is 22½ miles (36km) long. It is always narrow, the maximum width (not measured into the many bays) being only about 1¼ miles (2km) just south of the bridge at Melide. The greater part of its shoreline is in Switzerland.

The city of Lugano is the lake's largest and one of the leading cities in the Swiss canton of Ticino, despite the fact it was once under the influence of Milan, having been caught up in the wars between Como and Milan in the early Middle Ages.

The Swiss took the city and the neighbouring country from Milan in 1512, and have held it ever since, as the land freed from Austrian rule in the Risorgimento was the entire claim by the new Italian state, which never made any serious attempt to annexe Italian-speaking Swiss territories.

Italy holds the north-western shoreline and the eastern tip of the lake together with the enclosure of Campione. However, to deal solely with the Italian territory is, despite the title of the book, unnecessarily pedantic, so Swiss Ticino will be briefly explored, with reference made to other places of interest there at the end of this chapter.

SWISS LAKE LUGANO

From Porto Ceresio the eye is drawn northward to **Morcote**, the village at the very point of a large finger of land that points southward into the lake from Lugano city. From across the lake the village, reflected in the water and held against the cone of Monte Arbostera, is very picturesque, an impression that is amplified when the village – known as the 'pearl of the lake' – is reached.

Morcote is a glorious place: a mass of narrow, interweaving alleyways between houses of great character; a fine old church; a cemetery heavily guarded by cypress trees; an open park with trees and shrubs; the harbour; and the lake views. Do not miss the **church of Santa Maria del Sasso** a fourteenth-century building with sixteenth-century frescoes and a tall campanile, or **Scherrer park** with its profusion of trees.

Swissminiatur

At **Melide** those with insufficient time can see Switzerland in miniature, all the essential features modelled at 1:25 scale. This delightful site is threaded by over 2 miles (3km) of model railway.

There is another fine park at **Carona**. Nearby, the summit of **Monte** **San Salvatore** (2,990ft/912m) can be reached via a cable car from Lugano. From the summit the views are magnificent, taking in – if the weather is kind – the Matterhorn, the Apennines, and the local lakes. Elsewhere on the peninsula **Gentilino** can be visited where, in the cemetery of the **church of San Abbondio**, the grave of Hermann Hesse, the writer, can be seen.

LUGANO

Lugano, at the foot of the Monte San Salvatore, lies at the back of a small lake bay, an elegant place, vying with Como as the finest lake city. Within the city there are fine buildings. The *Duomo*, the cathedral church of San Lorenzo, has fine fourteenth-century frescoes, but is best known for its impressive façade in Lombard-Venetian style, with three portals that some say are by the Rodaris and others say are by local sculptors.

Bernardino Luini in Lugano

The **church of Santa Maria degli Angioli** in Piazza Bernardino Luini is a simple, plain building, originally built for Franciscan friars and dating from the late fifteenth century. It is famous for its frescoes executed by Bernardino Luini at the end of his life when he was a guest of the friars. Luini was Leonardo's best student, and the *Passion* here, a huge work, is thought to be his masterpiece, almost the equal of that of Leonardo himself. The other two works are also excellent, one being a clear tribute by student to teacher.

From the cathedral narrow streets lead to the central square, **Piazza della Riforma**, close to which giant plastic chess pieces offer a game on a grand scale for visitors.

South-east from the chess pieces, the tree-lined lake front road leads to the **Parco Ciani**, a public park in which stands the **Villa Ciani**, holding the city's very good art collection. A century ago the villa, built on the site of the city's medieval castle, was the headquarters of Guiseppe Mazzini, one of the main political leaders of the Risorgimento. From here propaganda pamphlets were issued, and in the park (at that time the villa's private garden) a statue by Vincenzo Vela, of a mourning woman – called *La Desolazione* – was said to have had great significance when erected, representing occupied Italy.

On from the park (a good way by foot), in **Castagnola**, is **Villa Favorita**. Once housing the Thyssen-Bornemisza 'Old Masters' collection, the villa is now closed to visitors, though the gardens are occasionally open.

Beyond Lugano

From Castagnola **Gandria** is reached, the last Swiss village on the lake's eastern reach and the equal of Morcote for picturesque setting and unspoilt appearance. There is nothing to rival Morcote's park and the church is not quite as good, but there is more character here. There are also excellent fish restaurants and an interesting Customs Museum that has to be reached by boat. The 'Customs' here relates to smuggling, as the village's position on the frontier and on the lake meant that the customs officials were once kept very busy.

Above Gandria towers **Monte Bre** (3,035ft, 925m), a peak that is climbed by *funivia* from the village that names the mountain – **Bre**. From the summit the views – both those of the lake and of the Bernese Oberland and Valais Alps – are breathtaking.

South of Lake Lugano there are two distinct regions of Switzerland, the **Mendrisiotto**, and **Val Muggio**. The former is an interesting area with a fine peasant culture that finds voice in a series of museums dedicated to its lore and art, while the latter is a gentle mountain valley.

First comes **Bissone**, a village just yards away from Italian Campione, with a preserved seventeenth-century Ticino house (Casa Tencalla) sadly not open to visitors at present. Beyond is **Capolago** from where a rack and pinion railway runs up **Monte Generoso** (5,680ft/1,701m).

ITALIAN LAKE LUGANO

At the south-west corner of Lake Lugano there is a 7½-mile (12km) section of the lake shore that lies in the Varese province of Italy, from Ponte Tresa (opposite Luino on Lake Maggiore), to Porto Ceresio.

Ponte Tresa is a frontier town, and another Ponte Tresa lies across the river Tresa, flowing out of Lake Lugano, in Switzerland. A five-arched red granite bridge over the Tresa river separates Italian Ponte Tresa from the Swiss village of the same name. The bridge has a steady stream of traffic in both directions as the locals cross and recross to buy things which are cheaper over the border.

Younger visitors might consider that one good reason for crossing is a visit to the chocolate factory in **Caslano**, a

(cont'd on page 84)

Above: Elegant façades in the city of Lugano

Below: Porto Ceresio, on the Italian shore of Lake Lugano

An Italian Enclave in Switzerland – Campione d'Italia

In the eighth century the local overlord gave, in perpetuity, the land which is now Campione to the **church of Sant' Ambrogio** in Milan. Remarkably, when the Swiss annexed Milanese holdings on the shores of Lake Lugano they respected the original covenant and made no attempt to take the village that had grown up on the church's holding. During the struggles of Austrian rule over parts of northern Italy and the wars of the Risorgimento, Switzerland made no attempt to absorb the village. And so, despite the fact that the village – now grown into a town – is entirely surrounded by Switzerland, it remains resolutely Italian.

Of necessity Campione uses the Swiss postal system and all the shops and restaurants accept Swiss money, but this is very much an Italian town. A scheme a few years ago to link the town with Italy by building a cable car from it to Sighignola, a small village near Lanzo d'Intelvi, failed when money and enthusiasm ran out so it is likely that Campione's unique position, reachable only from Switzerland, will continue for many years.

The town now makes the most of its position by having a casino which extracts the hard-earned cash of the Swiss who cross the lake from Lugano and further afield to enjoy its gaming tables and cabarets.

Visitors to Campione are left in little doubt about the unusual nature of the town when they are greeted by a huge arch and elaborate fountain, a distinctly ceremonial entranceway.

The town is famous historically as the home of the Maestri Campionesi, the Master Builders of Campionesi, who were a part of the Maestri Comacina and will be mentioned again in connection with Como. The Maestri were architects, builders and sculptors, most renowned for their work on Modena Cathedral and the church of San Ambrogio in Milan, but whose work can be appreciated here in the church of San Pietro, which dates from the early fourteenth century.

More interesting still is the Church of **Madonna dei Ghirli** (Madonna of the Swallows) at the western end of the town, a fine medieval building best seen from the lake, with work in both Gothic and Baroque styles. It is to the Gothic period (the fourteenth century), that the internal and external frescoes for which the church is famous, belong.

short distance north of Swiss Ponte Tresa. Here visitors can watch the process of chocolate making and taste the finished product.

Porto Ceresio, the next village on the Italian shore, is a beautiful little port, tucked into a sheltered, square-cut bay of Lugano with excellent views along the dog-legged lake and across to Morcote.

From Porto Ceresio it is necessary to cross into Switzerland in order to reach the next part of Italian Lugano, **Campione d'Italia** being an Italian enclave within Switzerland.

EAST FROM LUGANO

Italy is reached beyond the village of Gandria and the first Italians are met at the frontier hamlet of Oria, though the first village is San Mamete, beautifully placed at the mouth of the unfrequented Valsolda. The valley can be penetrated for a short distance by car, but it soon becomes the territory of the walker, superb hill country. **Oria** is famous in Italy for being where Antonio Fogazzaro, an author not well known to the English-speaking world, lived. Across the lake the Val d'Intelvi can be seen, opening through the ridge of mountains separating Lugano and Como, and to the side of the road driving on to Porlezza, Monte del Pizzoni dominates the view.

Porlezza is a pretty town and seems very Italian to those who have arrived from Switzerland. From it, continue along one of three roads. Going north to Corrido the road enters the Val Rezzo, climbing up through vineyards to meadows, beech woods and rocks. At Buggiolo a side road leads to **Seghebbia**, at 3,770ft (1,149m) the highest of the mountain hamlets and a convenient starting point for walks along the ridge from Cime di Fiorina

to Monte Garzirola that forms the border between Italy and Switzerland. The first peak is the better one to climb, the top being only at 5,935ft (1,809m), which offers a reasonable afternoon's walk and magnificent views from the top.

Porlezza

The town's name is derived from its Roman origins. Then it was *Portus Retiae*, the gateway to the *Retiae* (the people of the country beyond). In the Middle Ages Porlezza was famous as a home for artists – one, Guglielmo della Porta, was the best loved pupil of Michelangelo. It is worth exploring the town, but do not fail to visit the ruins of the church of San Maurizio, lonely beside the road to the Val d'Intelvi. Here are campaniles and some ruined walls.

VAL CAVARGNA

Beyond Buggiolo the road rises further and then drops down into Val Cavargna, a beautiful, rugged, but heavily wooded, valley – certainly the best in this area near the Swiss border. **Cavargna** itself is a picturesque village and has a church built in 1970, with contemporary artwork. The campanile is seventeenth-century however. Above Cavargna is the 'Holy Wood', so called because it protects the village from winter avalanches.

Cavargna is the seat of the **Museo della Valle**, the museum of Val Cavargna. There are several rooms here:

in one the work of a valley blacksmith is illustrated; another has items from the sanctuary of San Lucio which stands 1,500ft (457m) above the village on the Italian-Swiss border; while others deal with the agriculture of the valley and the local trade of woodworking.

From Cavargna, travel down the valley, a somewhat winding journey with occasional very windy sections, but one where each turn brings new scenic delights. There are several villages in the valley: **San Nazzaro Val Cavargna** with the best of the views; **San Bartolomeo Val Cavargna**, the biggest village with a rebuilt church that still contains some fine medieval art work; and **Cusino**, where the campanile seems to be held up by faith alone.

Leave the valley at **Carlazzo** at the valley's entrance, once fortified and still with a farmhouse called 'The Castle'. The peak behind the village, **Monte Pidaggio** (5,010ft,1,528m) is reached by a straightforward, but very long climb to a good panoramic position. From Carlazzo either return to Porlezza, or join the second road from the town that passes Lake Piano, originally attached to Lake Lugano but separated from it by landslides and silting. The lake has abundant fish and a quiet air, with blue mountains reflected in its blue waters. The road is joined by the one from Carlazzo and Val Cavargna at Piano, from where it leads on through several pleasant hamlets to Menaggio and Lake Como.

At **Cardano** on this road, is the very fine Villa Beagatti Valsecchi, from the early part of this century, set in beautiful gardens, though sadly not open to the public.

Val Sanagra

From Cardano the road enters Val Sanagra and the pretty mountain hamlets that comprise **Grandola ed Uniti**. Here there are some excellent villas and, in the upper reaches of the valley, some fine walking.

The third road from Porlezza rounds the northern tip of Lake Lugano to reach Claino-Osteno, a joined pair of villages and the only ones on the road on the southern shore of this reach of the lake. Claino-Osteno stands at the mouth of **Val d'Intelvi**.

Val d'Intelvi

Val d'Intelvi is a fine, airy series of valleys with delightful villages, many with superb churches by the Maestri Comacini, the medieval builders and sculptors.

As an important link between the lakes of Lugano and Como it was heavily fortified, surviving almost unscathed when it sided with Como in the Ten Years' War. During the wars of the Risorgimento its position was again important and it was active against the Austrians. Today the valley takes advantage of its position and its beauty and is an important tourist area. In winter there is skiing on the Pian della Noci above Pellio d'Intelvi and near the villages of Lanzo d'Intelvi and Casasco d'Intelvi.

Exploration of the valley starts at **Claino-Osteno**. The village of Osteno was the birthplace of the Bregnos, sculptors well known for their work in Venice. There is a marble Madonna and Child in Osteno's church of San Pietro and San Paolo by Andrea Bregno. Also at Osteno is a fine *orrido*, which is best viewed by boat, and an interesting natural cave, the Grotte di Rescia.

Above Claino-Osteno is Laino from where **Ponna** can be reached, two small hamlets with excellent views. At the upper hamlet, Superiore, is a museum in the form of a house furnished as a valley house would have been in the late nineteenth century, and including the first electric lights used in the valley, dating from 1910.

Laino lays claim to the most elegant church in Val d'Intelvi, a sixteenth-century building with local artwork. Near Laino are the two villages, Inferiore and Superiore, of **Pellio d'Intelvi**, from which the road to Lanzo d'Intelvi is followed, passing through **Scaria** with a fine frescoed church to San Nazaro and San Celso and, below it, museums of sacred art and of fossils, each chiefly from the valley.

Beyond Scaria lies **Lanzo d'Intelvi**, a beautifully sited, popular village with multi-green meadows and conifer forests. In the village there is a fine square and interesting houses, one of which – in Via Mascheroni – has a fine eighteenth-century fresco over an ancient doorway.

A round trip from Lanzo to Pellio can be made over the **Pian delle Noci**, which is a golf course in summer, as well as being used for winter skiing. From Pellio, go towards **Argegno**,

Panoramic Views

From Lanzo, **Sighignola** can be reached. From here, close to the ruins of the failed attempt to build a cable car to Campione, there is a magnificent view of Lake Lugano and the Swiss mountains, including Monte Rosa, the Matterhorn and the peaks of the Bernese Oberland. Almost as good is the view from Belvedere to the north from where a cable car descends to Santa Margherita on the southern shore of Lake Lugano.

reaching a tangled mass of hamlets, all of them worthy of note, but through which no straightforward itinerary can be devised. **San Fedele d'Intelvi** has the best Romanesque church in the valley, **Pigra** has one of the best panoramas of Lake Como, from **Casasco d'Intelvi** roads lead up into the mountains offering fine walks and **Schignano** is beautifully sited with fine views over Lake Como.

From Schignano a road follows one side of the Telo river out of Val d'Intelvi to Argegno, but the main valley road is now on the other bank, from **Castiglione d'Intelvi**, a fine place with ancient ruins and old houses. That road too drops into Argegno.

Lanzo d'Intelvi

SWISS LUGANO

Note: not all of the following places are mentioned in the text, but they are included here to give further ideas for interesting things to see.

BRE
Wilhelm Schmid Museum
Open: All year, Thursday-Sunday 10am-12noon, 2-6pm.
☎ 058 8666910.

CARONA
Botanical Park
Open: all year at any reasonable time.

CASLANO
Chocolate Factory
Open: all year, daily 9am-5.30pm; 4.30pm on Saturday and Sunday.
☎ 091 6118856

GANDRIA
Customs/Smuggling Museum
Open: April-October, daily 1.30-5.30pm.
☎ 091 9239843

LUGANO CITY
Museo Cantonale d'Arte
Villa Malpensata, Riva Caccia
Open: all year, Tuesday-Sunday 9am-7pm; closes at 5pm in winter.
☎ 058 8666908

Natural History Museum
Via Cattaneo
Open: Tuesday-Saturday 9am-12noon, 2-5pm.
☎ 091 9115380

Villa Ciani
City Park
Open: Tuesday-Sunday 9am-12noon, 2-6pm.
☎ 058 8667201

(cont'd overleaf)

Ponte Tresa

(cont'd from previous page)

Museum of Non-European Cultures
Villa Heleneum, Via Cortivo, Via Cortivo 24 Castagnola
Open: March-October,
Wednesday-Sunday 10am-5pm.
☎ 058 8666960

LIGORNETTO
Villa Vela
Open: April-November, Tuesday-Sunday 2-5pm.
☎ 091 6407040

LUGANO TO MONTE SAN SALVATORE
Funivia (cablecar)
Open: mid-June-mid-September daily 8.30am-11pm, mid-May-mid-June & last half September 8.30am-5pm, October and Easter-mid-May 9am-6.30pm.
☎ 091 9852828

MELIDE
Swissminiatur
Open: March-October,
daily 9am-6pm.
☎ 091 6401060

MENDRISIO
Art Museum
Piazza S. Giovanni
Open: All year Tuesday-Sunday 10am-12noon, 2-5pm.
☎ 091 6467649

MERIDE
Museum
Open: daily 8am-6pm.
☎ 091 6463780

MONTAGNOLA
Hermann Hesse Museum
Open: March-October, Tuesday-Sunday 10am-12.30, 2-6.30pm.
November-Feburary, Saturday-Sunday 10am-12.30, 2-6.30pm.
☎ 091 9933770

MONTE BRE
Funivia (cablecar)
Open: April-October, daily 10am-6pm or dusk. Closed Sunday in April-mid-June.
☎ 091 9713171

MONTE GENEROSO
Rack and Pinion Railway
Open: May-October, daily 10am-6pm or dusk.
☎ 091 6481105

MONTE LEMA
Funivia (cablecar)
Open: March-mid-November, daily 9am-5pm.
☎ 091 6091168

MORCOTE
Scherrer Park
Open: Mid March-October, daily 10am-5pm (6pm July and August).
☎ 091 9962125

RANCATE
Gallery Züst
Open: March-November, Tuesday-Sunday 9am-12noon, 2-5pm.
☎ 091 6464565

STABIO
Museum
Open: All year, Tuesday, Thursday, Saturday and Sunday 2-5pm.
☎ 091 6416990

ITALIAN LUGANO

CAMPIONE D'ITALIA
Casino
Restaurant opens from 12noon, gaming rooms open from 3pm.
☎ 091 6401111

CAVARGNA
Museum of Val Cavargna
Open: All year Sunday 2-5pm.
At other times by request.
☎ 0344 63162

CLAINO-OSTENO
Grotte di Rescia
Open: Easter-September, daily 2-6pm.
Those camping at 'Campeggia Rescia' may ask for permission to enter at any time. Others may phone ☎ 0344 72520.

Orrido
For information ☎ 031 840143.

PONNA D'INTELVI SUPERIORE
Peasent Museum
Open: by request.
☎ 031 267494

SCARIA
Museum of Sacred Art/ Museum of Fossils
Open: July and August, daily 3-7pm.
☎ 031 840143

LAKE STEAMERS

There is a full ferry service on the lake, an end-to-end journey having the delight of numerous crossings into and out of Switzerland. The formalities noted for Lake Maggiore also apply here.

The ferry links Ponte Tresa, Lavena, Figino (Switzerland) and Porto Ceresio, crossing into Switzerland to reach Morcote, Brusino Arsizio, Melide, Poiana, Capolago, Bissone, Campione (Italy), Paradiso, Lugano, Castagnola, Caprino and Gandria, then crosses back into Italy to visit Santa Margherita, San Mamete, Claino-Osteno and Porlezza. For information on the steamers ☎ 091 9715223.

Lake Como is the third biggest of the northern lakes, with an area of 55sq miles (148sq km) and has the longest perimeter, a shore line of over 106 miles (170km). The glacier that cut out its hollow, the Adda, divided around the promontory ridge south of Bellagio, forming two arms. These arms, extending to the towns of Como and Lecco, give the lake an inverted Y-shape, and explain the lengthy perimeter. It is the most enclosed of the major lakes and many think it is the finest, its northern reaches showing to perfection the V-cut hollow of its glacial birth.

THE CITY OF COMO

HISTORY OF THE CITY

Como is situated at the southern end of the western arm of the lake's upturned Y. There is no outflowing river from this arm, which helps to maintain a wholeness to a city whose first founding was probably at the end of the Bronze Age, around 1000BC. Little is known of the early town, recorded history starting when the Romans took it, probably from the Gauls, in 196BC. Como was then rebuilt by Julius Caesar, who repopulated it with about 5,000 settlers, including 500 Greek noblemen whose influence can still be detected in the names of some lakeside places.

The site was already strategically important before the Romans, the lake being navigable and offering easy access to Val Bregaglia and Val San Giacomo, both of which offered passes over the Alps to northern Europe. Recognising this importance, the Romans linked the city with Milan, building the Royal Road, Via Regia, that continued northward to Chiavenna. At a later stage, probably when the city was ruled by Queen Theodolinda, the name was corrupted to Via Regina (Queen's Way), a name that lives on in Strada Regina today.

Later in its history the town was an important centre in the growth of Christianity, and its churches commemorate important martyrs and bishops – Fedele, Carpoforo, Abbondio and Felice.

The town also had its share of strife from which this border country suffered so much. It was almost destroyed in the Ten Years' War with Milan, recovering thanks to the efforts of Barbarossa, but being plagued by civil wars after the death of his grandson, Frederik II.

At one point in its history it was actually sold to the Visconti family who held it for a century. At this time, and later under the Sforzas, the city was very prosperous, a prosperity based on silk and woollen industries. However, the prosperity did not last, the city fell under Spanish rule in 1535 following the Franco-Spanish Wars. Spanish rule, which lasted almost two centuries, was harsh – this was the time of the Inquisition.

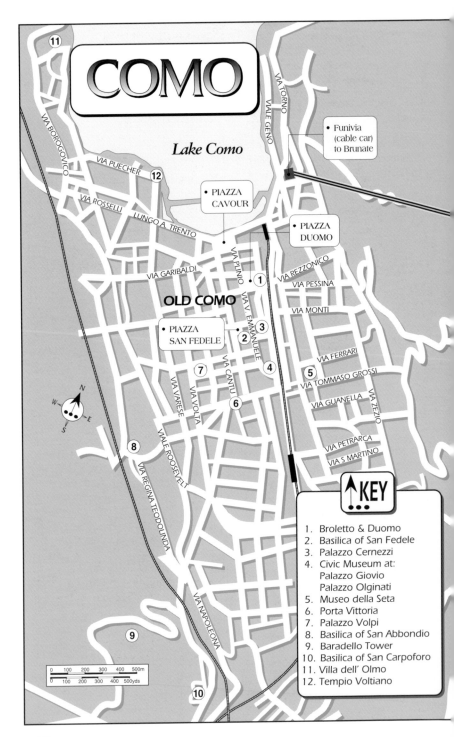

COMO

Lake Como

- Funivia (cable car) to Brunate

- PIAZZA CAVOUR

- PIAZZA DUOMO

VIA TORNO

VIALE GENO

VIA BOROGOVICO

VIA PUECHER

VIA ROSSELLI

LUNGO A. TRENTO

VIA GARIBALDI

VIA PLINIO

VIA REZZONICO

VIA PESSINA

VIA MONTI

OLD COMO

- PIAZZA SAN FEDELE

VIA V. EMMANUELE

VIA CANTU

VIA VARESE

VIA VOLTA

VIA FERRARI

VIA TOMMASO GROSSI

VIA GUANELLA

VIA ZEZIO

VIA PETRARCA

VIA S MARTINO

VIALE ROOSEVELT

VIA REGINA TEODOLINDA

VIA NAPOLEONA

N W E S

① ② ③ ④ ⑤ ⑥ ⑦ ⑧ ⑨ ⑩ ⑪ ⑫

0 100 200 300 400 500m
0 100 200 300 400 500yds

KEY

1. Broletto & Duomo
2. Basilica of San Fedele
3. Palazzo Cernezzi
4. Civic Museum at:
   Palazzo Giovio
   Palazzo Olginati
5. Museo della Seta
6. Porta Vittoria
7. Palazzo Volpi
8. Basilica of San Abbondio
9. Baradello Tower
10. Basilica of San Carpoforo
11. Villa dell' Olmo
12. Tempio Voltiano

The silk and woollen industries declined drastically, barely surviving until relief came in 1714 with the arrival of the Austrians. The city's fortunes improved immediately, an improvement which was maintained through the Napoleonic period, and which gave the city the self-confidence to battle courageously during the Risorgimento.

Como rose up with Milan in 1848, setting the scene for the battle of San Fermo, fought just to the west of the city in 1859, when the forces of Garibaldi defeated those of the Austrian Marshal Urban. When Garibaldi's troops marched in triumph following their great victory, it was through the Porta Vittoria in the old town walls that they came.

With the coming of the Italian kingdom, Como's prosperity increased again. Today it is a flourishing city, with around 100,000 inhabitants. The city's prosperity, tourism apart, is still based on the silk and textile industries, together with some light engineering and manufacturing. Como is also the capital of the Lombardian province that bears its name.

A Tour of Como

There is much of interest in the city, and it is well worth an exploration. Approaching from Piazza Cavour, probably by way of Via Plinio, **Piazza del Duomo** is reached.

Piazza del Duomo

The *piazza* is entered by the western end of the cathedral building to which is attached the **Broletto**, the old court of justice, and attached to that is the campanile.

Both of these buildings are excellent, the unfaced stone of the tower with its delightful eyebrow roof over the one-eye-clock, and the smooth faced,

Como's *Duomo*

The difference between the two ends of the building is not wholly due to the attached buildings, however, Como's Duomo having been built over four centuries, and representing one of the most important examples of architecture in transition. The western façade is late Gothic, with elegant sweeps of polished marble between equally elegant long windows and fine arrays of statues. In the niches on either side of the doors are statues by the Rodari brothers of the Plinys, Elder and Younger, both of whom found fame in Rome from origins near the city. The Rodaris were also responsible for the sides of the cathedral, including the northern doorway – the Porta della Rana or Frog Door.

The eastern end of the cathedral marks the transition in style from Gothic to Renaissance, the apses being of the later period. Surprisingly, the final dome is later still, not having been completed until the mid-eighteenth century. The whole is breathtaking and it is no surprise to find that it has been described as the most beautiful building in Italy for illustrating the fusion of styles.

The interior maintains the standards of the exterior. The inside of the dome has both beauty and symmetry, and the works of art – paintings and tapestry – would grace the walls of any museum or art gallery.

arched Broletto with its especially elegant balcony, but they do interrupt the splendour of the cathedral building itself. It has to be said, of course, that both tower and Broletto pre-date the building whose symmetry they obscure. As a comparison walk the cathedral's length to view the eastern end, where the apses and dome can come as a great surprise.

Piazza San Fedele

Continue the walk through Como by going through the Piazza del Duomo and along Via Vittorio Emanuele, followed by a quick right, then left turn, to reach Piazza San Fedele, a highlight of the walk.

The *piazza* was the centre of the old walled town of Como and was, at that time, the corn market. Some of the houses that enclose the square are still supported by pillars, and date back perhaps 400 years. That is an interest-

The Maestri Comacini

Literally the Masters of Como the Maestri were a collection of tightly knit corporations of architects, stone-masons and decorators who, from the seventh century through to the seventeenth, were renowned throughout Europe as builders of the highest calibre. Their best work is now believed to be represented in the Intelvi valley that runs down to Lake Como at Argegno, around Lake Lugano and in Swiss Ticino as well as here at Piazza San Fedele, though examples are known from as far afield as Poland and Russia.

The cathedral and broletto in Como's Piazza del Duomo

On special occasions the old lakeside steamers are brought back into service – Piazza Cavour, Como

ing thought as you sit beneath their shade and gaze across the patterned cobble to the **basilica of San Fedele**. The church is now thought to be one of the finest examples of the work of the Maestri Comacini, though to see their best work it is necessary to continue along Via Vittorio Emanuele to the church which stands opposite the **Palazzo Cernezzi**, a seventeenth-century palace, now the town hall.

Going left from San Fedele would bring the visitor to the **Civic Museum**, housed in two palaces. The **Palazzo Giovio** is the Archaeological and Art Museum, with many items from pre-historic Como and the surrounding area, including an Iron Age chariot, a boat from Lake Monate and a fine Roman bronze sword. The art is chiefly from the sixteenth to eighteenth centuries, but there are also some very fine, and much earlier, frescoes.

The second palace, **Palazzo Olginati**, holds a museum of the Risorgimento named for Giuseppe Garibaldi, hardly surprising in view of Garibaldi's triumphant entry into the city after the battle of San Fermo. The Como area was of considerable importance in this region, and the museum reflects its often heroic contribution to Italian unification.

Continuing eastwards from these museums the **Museo della Seta**, dedicated to the city's silk industry, is reached.

Old Como

Alternatively, turn right from San Fedele and enter old Como, the remaining section of the old walled town. Here there are narrow alleys, held in shadow by tall stone houses with shuttered windows, from which the visitor occasionally emerges into small, blindingly sunlit squares.

Alessandro Volta, whose museum can be visited, was born in the street that bears his name, while Pope Innocent XI was born in his named street, just the other side of the old town wall. On that wall there are three original towers, none more impressive than that of **Porta Vittoria**, the central one, which stands at the head of the Via Cantu. This is 130ft (40m) high with huge scalloped windows and a most impressive arched entrance. The towers all date from the latter half of the twelfth century.

Nearby, in Via Diaz, the city's art gallery in **Palazzo Volpi** has works from the fourteenth to eighteenth centuries and frequent exhibitions by contemporary artists.

Not far from the Porta Vittoria is the **basilica of San Abbondio** on a site where the city's first cathedral once stood. The present church was built in the mid-eleventh century and was once the church of a Benedictine monastery, the cloister of which is still visible. Again the church is the work of the Maestri Comacini, building here at a time when their work was influenced by Nordic art, perhaps due to travel of the masters or to northern monks in the monastery. The church is more austere than some of their other work, almost to the point of being severe, but it does have a recognisable apse and, though here as a symmetrical pair, campaniles.

Beyond the church is a hill, and the tower on top of it dominates most views of the city. This is the **Baradello Tower** (*see* box above) which, together with a small section of curtain wall, is all that remains of a castle built by Barbarossa in the mid-twelfth century. From the tower, 115ft (35m) high, the view of Como and the first arm of the lake is excellent.

At the foot of the hill is **San Carpoforo** the last of Como's trio of magnificent basilicas. This one is believed to have been built on the site

A Dreadful Death

Legend has it that in 1227 a local lord, Napo Torriani, was defeated in battle by the Viscontis. The Milanese captured Torriani and his family and put them in a cage hung on the outside of the Baradello Tower. Exposed to the elements and inadequately fed his family died one by one until only Napo remained alive. He is then said to have smashed his head against the tower wall to end his misery.

of a temple to Mercury, and has a Christian history going back 1,500 years. Its style is very early Romanesque, its earliness revealing itself in its irregularities, the poor quality of much of its stone, and the almost complete absence of decoration. But there is an apse, and the campanile is clearly of the same style as the pair on San Abbondio.

Near the lake are two buildings of great contrast but equal interest, the sumptuous **Villa Olmo**, first of the great villas that characterise Lake Como, and **Tempio Voltiano**, built to house a museum to Alessandro Volta (*see* box opposite).

Villa Olmo

Villa Olmo (sometimes written Villa dell'Olmo) is named after a forest of elm trees which, according to Pliny the Younger, grew on this spot. The earliest building was in the twelfth century when a monastery was built by the Umiliati Order. The present villa was built in the late seventeenth century by the Odescalchi family, though it was

Alessandro Volta

On 28 February 1745 Alessandro Volta was born at 10 Contrada di Porta Nuova, Como (the house was later renumbered 62 and the street renamed in his honour). Despite having no formal training in physics, Volta was publishing important papers on electricity and magnetism by the time he was 20. He became a schoolmaster in Como, but in recognition of his work was made Professor of Physics at Padua University in 1778.

After retirement he returned to Como where he died in 1827. After his death many of his pieces of apparatus, together with his manuscripts, were gathered together and exhibited in Como. Sadly a fire in 1899 destroyed a great number of the exhibits though most of the manuscripts were saved. Over a period of many years the pieces of apparatus were reproduced and in 1927 these, together with the surviving material, were housed in the specially built Tempio Voltiano. The temple is of almost classical design, the interior having polished marble columns and a mosaic floor, and the exhibits are held in glass cases. There are also books on, and paintings of, the city's great son. The volt, the electrical unit with which everyone is familiar, is named after Volta.

There is also a statue of Volta in Piazza Volta, close to Piazza Cavour.

more than a century before it was finally finished.

In the late nineteenth century the villa was owned by the Viscontis, who pulled down a pair of much criticised side wings and restored much of the original. Since 1927 the villa has been owned by the city.

Today the formal gardens that lie between the villa and the lake, and the wooded parkland to the rear of the villa, are open to the public. The villa itself can also be visited and is used for concerts, conferences and exhibitions. Its interior has fine stucco and gilt work and a large number of statues. Externally it is solid and formal, though the arched centre section with the colonnade surmounting it is very elegant.

BRUNATE

Back in the city there will be time to look at the range of locally made silkwear for which the city is famous, before taking the *funivia* to **Brunate**.

On the journey, and at the top, there are fine views of the city and lake, if you can find a gap between the tall conifers!

For the more energetic there is a footpath from the village, or better, from the end of the lane through San Maurizio, to the summit of **Monte Boletto**, 4,055ft (1,236m). The views from here are wonderfully expansive, taking in on a good day Monte Rosa and Milan, as well as giving a very good view of the glacial valley of Lake Como.

Those travelling by road from Como to Brunate pass a **Temple Sacrarium** dedicated to all nautical sports in the name of the Madonna del Prodigio.

WESTERN LAKE COMO

Leaving Como on a road that leads in only 4 miles (6km) to Switzerland, the **Museo Rivarossi**, in Via Pio XI, is reached. This new and interesting museum has many scale models of trains and cars.

A turn off right from this road follows the western arm of the lake towards Cernobbio. Almost immediately the route begins to pass the villas for which this western arm of Lake Como is so famous, though unfortunately most are not open to the public.

Beyond Tavernola the road crosses the Breggia, a *torrente* not a *fiume* (a torrent not a river), draining the Val di Muggio and in spring, heavy with melt-water. Beyond is Cernobbio.

CERNOBBIO

After Como and Lecco, Cernobbio is one of the biggest towns on Lake Como, an industrial town, well situated up the hillside between the trees. There is a good beach here, a pleasant, small port, and in the old part of the town, close to the lakeside square a delightful collection of picturesque houses and narrow alleys grouped around the ancient church.

Close to Cernobbio are two fine garden parks. **Villa Erba** is now a conference and exhibition centre, but is worth visiting for its immaculate and peaceful parkland overlooking the lake. **Villa Il Pizzo** has only recently been opened to visitors, but keen gardeners will also want to add it to their agenda. The land here was covered by olive trees and vines when first purchased in the fifteenth century. It was improved over the years but what the visitor now sees was the work of Villoresi, a famous garden architect of the seventeenth century. Please note the villa is only open to groups.

Above Cernobbio rises **Monte Bisbino**, which at 4,350ft (1,325m) offers truly spectacular views of the lake, and is easy to reach along a winding road through Rovenna, a village that clings precariously to a low ridge of the same peak. The summit of

Villa d'Este

All walks aound Cernobbio seem to lead towards the Villa d'Este, one of the most famous Lake Como villas and now the grandest of its hotels. The villa was built in the late sixteenth century for Cardinal Gallio, Secretary of State to Pope Gregory XIII, and this is what can still be seen, with some minor alterations required by its use as a hotel. In the eighteenth century the villa was owned by the local Austrian commander-in-chief and so probably played its part in the intrigues of Austrian occupation. Later it was occupied by Caroline of Brunswick, wife of the British Prince of Wales, George Frederick, later George IV.

The hotel has now possibly become the grandest encountered on this tour of the Italian Lakes. With its beautiful gardens and an interior that is a treasure house of art, it would seem to be the absolute height of luxury, though whether it would be possible to shake off the feeling that you were sleeping in a museum is questionable. The gardens include a shallow, stepped waterfall which crosses the bridge visitors on the road north of Cernobbio drive under, and the curious castellated look-outs on the cliff above the same road. The swimming pool is worth a mention too, advertised as unique in Italy, it is a floating swimming pool!

LAKE COMO

SWITZERLAND

Lake Mezzola

• Pian di Spagna

Valtellina

DOMASO
GRAVEDONA

COLICO

DONGO
MUSSO

PIANELLO D.LARIO

DORIO

CREMIA
REZZONICO

DERVIO

ACQUASERIA
BREGLIA

PREMANA

BELLANO

TACENO

MENAGGIO
CROCE
GRIANTE
TREMEZZO

PARLASCO
VARENNA

CORTENOVA

VALSASSINA

PRIMALUNA

BELLAGIO

CASTELLO

SPURANO
SALA COMACINA
PIGRA
ARGEGNO

LENNO
IS.
COMACINA
LÉZZANO

GUELLO

CIVENNA

OLIVETO

MANDELLO
D. LARIO

BARZIO

• Monte
Grigna

Lake Lugano

BRIENNO
• Monte
Bishino
TORRIGGIA
LAGLIO

NESSO

• MAGREGLIO

• Monte
S. Primo

SORMANO

Lake Lecco

VALSASSINA

ABBADIA LARIANA

BALLABIO

• Cori di
Carizo

MOLTRASIO
CERNOBBIO

TORNO
MOLINA

BLEVIO

ASSO

CANZO
*Lake
Annone*

LECCO

*Lake
Garlate*

BRUNATE

ERBA

GARLATE

OLGINATE

COMO

A9

*Lake
Alserio*

*Lake
Pusiano*

99

Bisbino has a refuge hut and a chapel to which pilgrimages are still made, and offers the possibility of a panoramic view with one foot in Italy and one in Switzerland.

NORTH FROM CERNOBBIO

Back at lake level the visitor can now choose an upper road that swiftly bypasses Moltrasio, Carate Urio and Laglio, but makes the most of the lake views before dropping into **Torriggia** where the lake is at its narrowest – a few hundred metres separates it from Careno.

But what will be missed? In **Moltrasio** there is another fine collection of villas, each with its own historical interest. In particular, **Villa Passalacqua**, a fine late eighteenth-century building once known as the Palace of Moltrasio, and in which the composer Vicenzo Bellini stayed. The villa is in private hands, but occasionally open for concerts.

Also at Moltrasio is a delightful little Romanesque church, dedicated to Santa Agata, built towards the end of the eleventh century, with a fine campanile.

There is a chance too for excellent walking in the wooded shade of the upper reaches of the town, or near the gorge that splits the town in half and offers a fine show in spring or after heavy rain.

Carate Urio was once two separate villages. From the second village, Carate, there is a walk all the way to the top of Colmegnone (4,535ft/1,383m), though to actually reach the top would take considerable time and effort.

Laglio also has a good walk, taking about 1½ hours, up to the 'Bear's Den', a cave from which have been excavated a number of fossil bones, including those of cave bears. Exhibits from the cave can be seen in the museums of Como and Milan, and also in the Laglio village hall.

Beyond Torriggia the new upper road goes on to **Argegno**, where the Intelvi valley (described in Chapter 5) reaches Lake Como. Val d'Intelvi is drained by the Telo river, which flows under an ancient, single-arched bridge in a crowded, but still wooded, part of the town.

When approaching from the Val d'Intelvi, Argegno is a pretty town, an array of red tiled houses – the half-round tiles so familiar to all visitors to northern Italy (but perhaps best associated with Venice) – in a wooded inlet of the lake. It is worth a tour, a bustling holidaymaker village with a *funivia* to Pigra and fine views of the lake.

Beyond Argegno the lake is dominated by **Isola Comacina**. The island, Como's only island, is quite small, only 875 by 437yd (800m by 400m) and can be reached via a short ferry ride from Sala Comacina, Ospedaletto or Spurano. The visitor finds a church dedicated to St John (which explains the occasional alternative name of Isola San Giovanni), an excellent restaurant and a large number of ruins. For the rest, the island is a wilderness of trees and shrubs.

On shore, the towns benefit from the island's shelter, the quiet bay between island and mainland once having been known as '*zocca de l'oli*', the oil container, because of the growth and importance of the local olive trees.

At **Ospedaletto** is one of the most photographed of all the lakeside campaniles, a late Gothic turret having been grafted onto the Romanesque belfry of the **church of Santa Maria Magdalene**. The church's annexation

The Festival of Comacina

It is difficult when viewing Comacina to imagine that the scatter of ruins among the trees mark the place where one of the richest towns on the lake once stood. Then it was Crisopoli, the City of Gold – sometimes, quite wrongly, given as Christopoli, the City of Christ.

In 1128, during the Ten Years' War between Milan and Como, Crisopoli sided with Milan. Como was defeated and ransacked. It took years for the city to regain its wealth and influence, but eventually it did, and its rulers had not forgotten the part played in its defeat by Crisopoli. In 1169 Como's armies invaded the island, the inhabitants were slaughtered and the city burnt. So total was the destruction that Crisopoli was never rebuilt.

Until very recently, on the evening of the Saturday following St John's Day (24 June), the destruction was commemorated in the most spectacular of all the lake festivals. This started with small oil-filled containers floating on the lake close to the island, their flames representing the invasion fleet. Next, the island exploded with the red flames of Roman candles signifying the blood of the slaughtered folk of Crisopoli. The flames changed to white, signifying the burning of the city and the spectacle finished with a magnificent firework display. This elaborate light show stopped just a few years ago, but such has been the outcry that it is likely to start again very soon.

One aspect of the festival remains: on the Sunday, a religious procession starts on the mainland. It continues by boat to Isola Comacina where it threads its way through the trees to reach the ruins of the old basilica. An open-air mass is then said, one that symbolises the unification of all the folk of Lake Como.

to a hospice – a *hospitalis* – by a rich local family gave the village its name. At **Spurano**, if you have enjoyed the Ospadaletto campanile, take a moment to look at the eleventh-century church belfry. The contrast is overwhelming.

At **Ossuccio** the church contains a third-century Romano-Christian altar. The village also has a long avenue climbing the hill past fourteen chapels (some are minor works of art) dedicated to the Madonna of the Rosary, leading to the sanctuary of the Madonna del Soccorso. The whole of it was built between the mid-seventeenth and early eighteenth centuries.

High above the sanctuary (about 1,310ft/400m, and fairly steep and strenuous – allow 2 hours at least) is the **basilica of San Benedetto** in **Val Perlana**, regarded as the best preserved Romanesque church in Como province. The church can also be reached from the massive abbey at **Acquafredda** – itself reached by road from Lenno and worth a visit – but again there is a walk of about two hours, though in this case a less strenuous one.

From Ossuccio the **Balbianello Point**, or Back of Lavedo, pokes out into the lake. Beyond the point, at **Lenno**, is the start of the Tremezzina, the Azalean Riviera, where the fertile soil allows luxuriant growth to a profusion of shrubs and trees. Here there are orange trees, lemons and olives.

Magnolias and laurels cover the hill slopes and there are, of course, azaleas. Lenno was the site of Comoedia, a villa belonging to the Elder, and Younger Plinys, where, they said, you could 'fish from your very bed'. Some of the excavated remains of the villa are in Como Museum. **Azzano**, the next village, is where Mussolini and his mistress were summarily executed in 1945.

Pliny, Elder and Younger

Pliny the Elder was born at Como in 23AD. He was a Roman statesman and scholar most notable for his *Natural History*, an encyclopaedia of the natural world. Pliny was killed while observing the eruption of Vesuvius in 79AD which destroyed Pompeii. Pliny the Younger was the Elder's nephew. He was a senator and is famed for his writings on the Roman state. Ironically he also wrote a description of the eruption which killed his uncle.

Villa d'Este, Cernobbio

One of Lake Como's most important festivals is held on Isola Comacina in late June

though the road is just as pleasant all the way to Menaggio, from where it is about 8 miles (12km) to Lake Lugano, that journey starting with a twisting road to Croce which is a good viewpoint. The nearby golf course must be one of the most romantic courses anywhere.

A little higher, and further north, the village of **Breglia** offers a short walk to the point of San Domenico and an even better view, taking in the whole northern end of the lake. Those with sufficient time and energy can continue to the summit of Monte Bregagno for a tremendous panorama of both lakes – Lugano and Como – and the pre-alpine peaks. But, at a distance of 4 miles and a height of 4,590ft (6km and 1,400m) the walk should not be undertaken lightly.

Tremezzo is a fine lakeside town, some of its remaining wealth of villas having been converted into regal looking hotels. In one of these villas Verdi stayed while finishing his score for *La Traviata*. A tree-lined avenue, celebrated by the visiting Longfellow as a leafy colonnade, links it with **Cadenabbia** where the lake attains its maximum width, the two arms linking at last, beyond Bellagio, a fact which explains why it is a terminus for Como's main car ferry, ferries linking Cadenabbia with Bellagio and Varenna.

Above Cadenabbia, a little way north, is **Griante**. In *The Charterhouse of Parma* Stendhal changes (or misspells) the village's name to Grianta and notes it has a sublime view of the lake, a description which still holds.

Beyond Cadenabbia, with its row of fine hotels, the Tremezzina ends,

Fishing at Argegno

Villas Balbianello and Carlotta

Villa Balbianello was built as a palazzo, placed at the end of the finger of land near Lenno to take advantage of the impressive views down towards Como and across to the Bellagio spur. The villa later became a rest home for Franciscan monks and is justly famous for the statue of St Francis offering a welcome to lake-borne visitors. The statue, with the landing stage (the villa can only be reached by boat from Lenno or Campo) and long stone stairway up through the brilliant shades of the flowers and shrubs to its side, is reckoned to be the most photographed spot on Lake Como. The present building, a rebuilding and extension of the original, is from the late eighteenth century, built for Cardinal Angelo Durini.

At Tremezzo is **Villa Carlotta**, the most famous of all Lake Como's villas. The 'C' above the entrance is not for Carlotta, as many visitors believe, but for Clerici, the family for whom the villa was built in the early eighteenth century. What we see today is due to the Counts Sommariva who owned the villa for the first half of the nineteenth century. The last Sommarivan owner sold the building to Princess Marianna, wife of Adalbert of Prussia, who gave it to her daughter Charlotte (or Carlotta, hence the name) when she married the Prince of Saxe-Meinigen. It has been in the hands of the Italian State since early this century.

Inside, the villa is a shrine to the plasterers' and painters' art. Every ceiling is a masterpiece. In addition to the paintings and the ornamental work, be sure to see the marble table and sculptures, particularly that of Antonio Canova. Outside, Sommariva made the most of the area's fertile soil: there are around 150 species of rhododendron and azalea, many grouped in 'Azalea Avenue'. Here too, are a giant sequoia, wisterias, cypresses, camellias, trees and shrubs from Japan and Australia, in all over 500 species. There is 'Great Avenue', with towering specimens of tropical and sub-tropical trees, a fern valley, a rock garden and a host of citrus fruit trees and bushes.

MENAGGIO

Menaggio is more of a bustle than the places visited so far. This atmosphere is no doubt due to its position, at a point where access to Lugano and Switzerland is straightforward, and it is this that contributed to its troubled, as well as prosperous, past. It was fortified, but sieged and taken in the Ten Years' War, and almost destroyed a century later, when it was again on the wrong side of a feud. It also had its problems with both Spaniards and Austrians.

Menaggio is a good place to stroll, the trading influence making window shopping worthwhile, and it is also a good centre for exploration, both of the road to Lugano (dealt with in Chapter 5) and also the little villages on the first terrace above the town. As an example, try the walled streets of Laveno. Try also the beautiful valley of the Senagra stream.

The town also has an excellent beach, equipped with a swimming pool, and a car ferry to Varenna on the eastern side of the lake. Beyond Menaggio the elegant Como villas and garden countryside are left behind for the moment as the lake becomes progressively more confined by higher peaks on the way north. The peaks sweep up to over 8,200ft 2,500m and are often snow-topped. Indeed, the mountains on each side of the lake are centres for skiing.

BEYOND MENAGGIO

The road disappears into a tunnel beyond Menaggio, re-emerging almost opposite Bellano. Ahead now is **Acquaseria**, with an old stone quay, beyond which a road up into the hills reaches **Santa Maria di Rezzonico**, a collection of old hamlets, little touched by the course of time and certainly worth a visit.

At **Cremia** there is another collection of interesting hamlets stretching up the hill from the shore village of San Vito, with a small beach, to **Vezzedo**, almost lost among the streams and hills. Beyond is **Pianello del Lario**, with a most interesting museum.

The Boat Museum

The museum at Pianello del Lario, housed in a nineteenth-century mill, is devoted to the history of the boat on Lake Como, with well over a hundred boats in the large number of exhibition halls. Equally fascinating is a collection of boat building tools from across the ages.

It is appropriate, in view of the presence of the museum, that Pianello del Lario should also be home to the Como Sailing Club, the lake's oldest club. As with the other lakes, the northern reaches have the best and most dependable winds. Those on northern Como change with a regularity that can almost be used for clock setting, and their steadiness assists anyone learning to sail. The club runs schools of varying length, as well as holding races.

Beyond Pianello is **Musso**, dominated by the **Sasso di Musso**, a natural fortress, its sides scarred by quarries that have yielded marble for Como Cathedral and Milan's Arch of Peace, among others. On top of this natural barrier there once stood a castle, one-time home to Il Medeghino, a fierce pirate. Recognising its awesome use to an enemy, after it had been vacated by the pirate the castle was razed. Today only the sasso remains.

Il Medeghino

Gian Giacomo Medici was born in Milan, but exiled here as a youth for the killing of another boy. At the time of Milan's war against the French and Spanish, Il Medeghino, as Medici became known, organised a murder for the city's governor, receiving as reward governorship of Musso's castle. From it he terrorised the lake, his reign coming to an end only when he sold the castle to Milan, choosing just the right moment to escape, both rich and free from retribution. When he died he was even buried in Milan Cathedral, where the visitor can still see his memorial.

Dongo, next along the coast, is most famous for having been the site of the capture of Mussolini, a fact which sadly undermines its delightful position and very pretty old section. Today Dongo has a small museum dedicated to the Italian resistance movement.

The Death of Mussolini

On 27 April 1945 a German motor column was halted at Dongo by Italian partisans and a search of the lorries revealed a large number of Italy's Fascist leaders, including Benito Mussolini together with his mistress Clara Petacci.

The Fascist leaders were held at Palazzo Monti, now the town hall, which overlooks the town square, a building whose bland exterior is at odds with an interior that is quite regal. At a drumhead trial in the village the following day thirteen of the leaders were convicted and immediately executed by shooting. Mussolini and Clara Petacci were immediately driven south, but at Azzano a partisan leader decided that the public trial of the former leader would be a further humiliation for Italy and ordered their execution. The same day Mussolini and Clara Petacci were shot and their bodies taken to Milan to hang upside down in disgrace.

In medieval times Dongo was one-third of the 'Tre Pievi', the three parishes, chief of which was **Gravedona**, the next stop on the route. The Tre Pievi had a warship with a crucifix mounted on it which, it was said, made the ship invincible. It is certainly true that the villages pirated a gold-laden ship of Barbarossa's and later defied him successfully enough to obtain special terms in the Treaty of Constance. The last village of the Tre Pievi, Sorico, can be visited as Lake Como reaches its northern end.

Gravedona has the last villa worthy of note on the western shore, **Palazzo Gallio**, built for Cardinal Tolomeo Gallio about 1500 on the remains of an old castle. The palace was known as Gallio's 'Villa of Delights', but today is the head-office of a local council. It is open to visitors during office hours on an informal, by request basis.

Do not miss, either, the **church of Santa Maria del Tiglio**, built in the twelfth century, on the site of a fifth-century Roman church. Part of the earlier church's mosaic flooring is still visible, and there is an awesome crucifix carved from a single block of wood.

Behind the Tre Pievi are a number of hamlets strung out along roads that thrust cautiously between the hills to the west. This is summer walking rather than winter skiing country, in the valley of the Albano, or on the flanks of Monte Cortafon (5,540ft/1,688m) or Monte Duria (7,430ft/2,264m). The villages too are worthy of note – Garzeno, Dosso del Liro, Livo – old stone houses grouped around interesting churches. On the Gravedona to Travisa road, do not fail to stop for the marvellous panorama of the northern lake.

Beyond **Domaso**, recognised as *the* centre for windsurfing on Lake Como, there are a couple of villages – **Gera Lario**, last stopping point of the lake steamers, and **Sorico** – before reaching the Mera river inflowing from Lake Mezzola. At Gera Lario another series of roads leads off to ancient villages in the hills, while at Sorico there is a church dedicated to St Mirus who landed here after crossing the lake on his cloak – shades of San Giulio and Lake Orta.

Lake Mezzola

The lake is 2 miles by 1¼ miles (3km by 2km) and has, at its northern end, an historically interesting church that can only be reached by water. The lake, and the marshes of Pian di Spagna formed between the two inflows (the Adda and Mera rivers) into Lake Como, is an important site for migrating birds. Those interested should not fail to visit Varenna's **Museum of Ornithology**, which includes many exhibits on the migrations.

Right: Old ice-cream cycle, Gravedona

Below: Domaso

EASTERN LAKE COMO

COLICO

The first town at the northern end of the eastern shore is Colico, which is also the first town where the lake steamer stops on its way to its terminus a short distance south at the Abbey of Piona. The town, nestling beneath conical Monte Legnone (8,560ft/ 2,609m), is surprisingly new, though there have been settlements here sporadically over the centuries.

Only with the partial reclamation of **Pian di Spagna**, now a nature reserve, and the passes north and east ceasing to be highways of war, did any reasonable chance exist for settled buildings. Beyond, two spits of land, reaching forwards like the pincers of a crab, enclose a small portion of Lake Como, creating **Lake Piona**, beloved of sailors.

107

Abbey of Piona

On the tip of the southern pincer is the isolated Abbey of Piona. The abbey was founded by the Cluniac order in 1138, though it was built on a site that was already ancient, possibly even pre-Christian. Earlier this century the abbey was taken over by the Cistercians, an order famous for their liking of sites in remote, but scenically beautiful, country. The building has a beauty to match its setting, note especially the cloisters – dating from the mid-thirteenth century – a blend of Romanesque and Gothic architecture in stone and brick. The church is the oldest part of the abbey, though the campanile is eighteenth-century, replacing the original.

town, but is a good centre for exploring the northern lake and Val Varrone, and Valsassina through the mountains to the east. These excellent valleys will be explored later, the present route continuing instead southwards to **Bellano**.

BELLANO

The town (which is, after Mandello, the largest on the eastern lake shore) is an active holiday centre, but with some splendid old sections. The lakeside pathway passes two monuments to famous sons – Sigismondo Boldoni, a seventeenth-century scientist, and Tommaso Grossi, a nineteenth-century writer – neither being widely known in the English-speaking world. Another Bellano Boldoni, Pietro, was responsible for introducing the silk trade to Como.

Be sure also to see the **church of San Nazzaro and San Celso**, a really beautiful building with a symmetrical façade

Returning to the main road southward, pass through **Dorio**, a well sited village, to **Corenno Plinio**. This village is named, it is believed, from Corinth and from Pliny the Elder, who liked this area. The lake is quite narrow here and the castle was important in its day, but the little that remains is private. The church is dedicated to St Thomas à Becket. Elsewhere there is much that is of interest. There are some beautiful old houses, and the town square has three fourteenth-century marble tombs – as the outside walls of the church and castle!

Next is **Dervio**, which now shows little of the fortifications that grew around it because of the local headland which makes this the narrowest spot of the lake. Today the town is remarkably industrialised for a small lake

The Orrido of Bellano

Close to Bellano is one of the best local examples of an *orrido*, a gorge cut through the mountainside by the Pioverna, a stream that brings down melting snow in spring, and rain in any season. The gorge has been cut deep, but not wide, and is viewed from a collection of ladders and ropeways that allow the visitor to get really close. The gorge holds the sound of rushing water and confines the spray too, making for a really unusual visit that only the Cascata del Varonne near Riva on Lake Garda can match.

of contrasting colours, a magnificent circular centrepiece and a rose window with terracotta surround. There are other fine buildings in the town, on some of which is carved the Visconti emblem, the viper.

VARENNA

On from Bellano the views from the road are excellent, culminating in the first sight of the Bellagio peninsula, and the beautiful car-ferry town of Varenna is soon reached. Its houses cling to the foot of a hill on which are the ruins of a castle, said to have been the last home of Theodolinda, Queen of the Lombards, who died in the early seventh century, and which has its own torrent stream, the Esino.

Varenna has a long history, the name being, it is thought, of Celtic origin. The old quarter is the most picturesque. Here are steep, narrow lanes, with occasional archways, all of which eventually end at the lake. One of the town's famous sons was G Pirelli, who founded the now huge industrial company famous for tyres and calendars.

Many visitors come here, not only for the old quarter, but for the more luxurious surroundings of the two famous villas or, perhaps, for the museum devoted to the birdlife of the lake. Those who have come from Colico and Lake Mezzola, particularly during the annual migrations, will certainly want to see the **museum** where the hundreds of species that have been seen on the lake are displayed, together with other displays on bird migration.

Villa Cipressi, in Via 4 Novembre, is well sited for the best of the views from the Varenna promontory across the lake and to Bellagio. Its terraced gardens go right down to the lake edge to gain maximum benefit from the position, and are a riot of colour in summer.

Villa Monastero

Although Villa Cipressi is well positioned, Villa Monastero is the highlight of Varenna (and some may say, of Como's eastern shore). It was built in 1208 for Cistercian nuns and was dedicated to Santa Maria Magdalene, but was later sold to a private owner.

Following World War I the building was acquired by the Italian Government and housed the Italian Centre for Hydrobiology and Lake Geomorphology. Today it is still a scientific (chiefly physics) base, playing host to annual summer schools and meetings that have attracted the best scientists from all over the world.

The villa has stone staircases, with columns and statues, which lead up from elegant shrubberies; an arcaded terrace beside the lake; arched windows and balconies; and a lovely view across the water. Monastero is truly a beautiful place and not to be missed.

Close to the town the Castello di Vezio ia an ancient fortress offering one of the best views of the lake.

FIUMELATTE

At Fiumelatte, a little south of Varenna, is a torrent stream which is the shortest in Italy (and surely in Europe), which was noted by Leonardo da Vinci. The village name derives from this stream – milk river – which emerges from a cave on the hillside and disappears just over 800ft (250m) further on, in the lake. The stream starts quite suddenly in spring as the snows melt, and runs until autumn, occasionally as the torrent of its name, occasionally as a trickle. The village has another stream lower down which runs continuously, the cave stream being, as it were, the overflow.

LAKE LECCO

Below Fiumelatte is Lake Lecco, as the eastern arm of Lake Como is sometimes known. At **Castello** the ruins of an old castle form part of the village houses; at **Lierna** Bronze Age remains have been discovered.

Then comes **Mandello del Lario**, a fine town which is seen to perfection from across the lake when the rocks of the Grigna make a spectacular backdrop. It is an industrial town, but is increasingly developing its tourist potential. Within the town, the lakeside church of San Lorenzo dates from the ninth century, although since this was a re-building there must have been a Romano-Christian church. Mandello is the home of the Moto Guzzi Motorcycle Factory and a museum of the bikes which attracts bikers from all over Europe.

Above the town, the village of **Maggiana** has 'Barbarossa's Tower' – tradition has it that he stayed here in 1158.

South again, the views are increasingly dominated by rocky, as opposed to grass-covered, peaks. Beyond Abbadia Lariana, named after a long-gone Benedictine abbey, the western side of the lake is dominated by the crags of Monte Moregallo, while those of Monte Coltignone, crowd in on the east.

Lecco

Lecco, at the southern end of the eastern arm of Lake Como, is a large town, second only to Como itself, but still has an old-fishing-port quarter and surroundings of such scenic splendour that its modernity is easily forgiven. Of its particular attractions special note should be made of the Visconti Bridge that has been renovated to look much

The *Aliscato* nearing Como

as it did when Azzone Visconti had it built over the Adda in 1336. Originally it had drawbridge sections on both ends, but with modern traffic it was not thought reasonable to restore these!

Pliny and the River Adda

In his *Natural History* Pliny the Elder claimed that the waters of the River Adda flow the entire length of the lake without mixing with lake water.

Within the town there are statues of Garibaldi, who liberated the area, and Lecco's most famous son, Alessandro Manzoni, a writer whose best-known book, *The Betrothed*, deals with the Spanish occupation of Lecco in the seventeenth century. The villa, known as 'Il Caleotto,' in which Manzoni spent much of his early, and parts of his later life, is now a shrine to the writer. Known now as **Villa Manzoni**, it is in Via Amendola, which can be reached by continuing in a straight line after crossing the Visconti Bridge into Lecco.

Due north from Villa Manzoni (follow Via XI Febbraio from Largo Caleotto) is the town's museum, housed in the **Palazzo Belgioioso**, a palace built by Cardinal Locatelli in the seventeenth century. Apart from the building, which is worth the visit in itself, there are items from the town's early history, a hall on the development of fishing in the lake and a natural history section.

An overall picture of town and lake, together with the smaller lakes that

Alessandro Manzoni

Alessandro Manzoni was born on his father's estate close to Lake Como in 1785. He was sent to boarding school when he was five and it is said that his mother never visited him, deserting the family when Alessandro was seven to live with another man in Paris. Though it is claimed that this was a defining moment in the young boy's life, he did join his mother in Paris when he was twenty, living in the city for many years.

Manzoni had begun writing poetry by the age of 16 and was writing in earnest during his stay in Paris. He married in 1808 and two years later moved back to Italy, living in Milan. Though he continued to write, his most famous work, *I Promessi Sposi* (The Betrothed), was not published until 1827. It was an instant hit, both in Italy and throughout Europe. Sir Walter Scott claimed it was the finest book ever written and it is now considered to be the greatest Italian novel of the nineteenth century. Though Manzoni edited the book several times, he did not write anything else of any significance.

Troubled by increasingly poor health, by the death of his beloved first wife and seven of their nine children, and then by the death of his second wife, he lived unhappily in Milan until his death in 1873. He was given a state funeral and Verdi wrote his Requiem to commemorate the first anniversary of his death.

crowd in on Lecco, can be gained by riding the cable car from **Versasio**, above the town, to **Piani d'Erna**, at 4,360ft (1,329m). The view eastward, away from the town, towards the rocky peaks of the Resegone, is equally good. The walking on and from the plateau is excellent.

VALSASSINA

Lecco is a good place from which to explore the Valsassina, the valley which threads its way behind the Grigna, allowing the visitor to reach the lake again at Varenna (via Esino Lario), Bellano (via the Val Muggiasca), or Dervio (via the Val Varrone). All start, however, by leaving Lecco for **Ballabio**, from which a twisting road leads up to Piani Resinelli, a winter sports centre and, with its mountain huts, a centre for summer climbing.

Beyond Ballabio the road crosses the Balisio pass and enters Valsassina itself. The valley has been widely described as the finest in the pre-Alps, a continuous mixture of scenic delight from rocky grandeur to pastoral green. It also has a long and important history. Bronze Age man lived here, though the metal which has brought lasting fame is iron. This was mined in the upper reaches of the Val Varrone, but was worked in Valsassina, the trade only having stopped when ore extraction became too expensive. Then the trade went to the more easily reached Lecco, where it flourishes today.

At this rocky end of the valley is **Barzio**, another important winter sports centre and an equally fine summer holiday centre. Cable cars take visitors up to the Piani di Bobbio or the Piani di Artavaggio where, in winter, there are a good number of blue and red ski runs, and in summer fine high-level walking.

Down the valley, a road off left leads to Pasturo where one of Manzoni's heroines lived, while further on at **Primaluna**, there is a very fine museum on the ethnography of the valley. Exhibits deal with iron-making and the range of farming carried on here. There is also a collection of local minerals.

The valley widens now, the view extends, and all around is a sea of greens to complement the lake's blues. **Cortenova** is set among fields, belying its remaining, though small, interest in the iron industry, and here a side road leads off for Varenna. On this road, at **Parlasco** and several points beyond, are exhilarating views over Lake Como, as the road winds round to **Esino Lario**, the 'Pearl of the Grigna'. Esino Lario is an excellent starting point for walking in the Grigna mountains and from it a road winds down to Varenna.

The Via Crucis

In the sixteenth century this village was famously prosperous, and it retains a wealth of architectural beauty. A recent addition, as late as 1941, is a Via Crucis, with fourteen shrines and sculptures, leading up through firs and larches to the church on its hill. From the church both Como and Lugano lakes can be seen. Also here is a museum with items of local history, and also of the geology and mineralogy of the Grigna group.

The Valsassina continues from Cortenova, passing the thermal springs of Tartavalle Terme, and reaching

Taceno where a left turn follows the Pioverna stream through the Val Muggiasca. The stream drops finally though Bellano's *orrido*, while the visitor endures a more winding but controlled descent to the town.

Going right at Taceno, the road reaches **Margno**, from where a cable car rises to Pian delle Betulle at 4,780ft (1,456m), another winter sports area with good summer walking. Nearby are two tiny villages, Crandola Valsassina and Vegno, in superb positions. The **Val Varrone** is reached near **Premana**, the archetypal valley village still famous for its iron working, the 'ladies' costume', an echo of Venetian influence and its dialect, and also a reminder of its Venetian past. From Val Varrone a series of fine villages and tremendous views are laid out along the road that winds down to Dervio.

SOUTHERN LAKE COMO

Lake Como's shape creates a triangular peninsula of land at its southern end, the point being at Bellagio, the base sitting on the road from Como to Lecco. The exploration of this area is awkward, requiring some doubling back if everything is to be seen. The route notes all the important sites, but in recognition of the difficulty of traversing the area in one tour, the peninsula will be explored by travelling from Como to Bellagio, following the Vallassina to Erba, then the road into Lecco.

COMO TO BELLAGIO

The peninsular triangle, sometimes called the **High Brianza**, has been created by a ridge of hard rock running south from Bellagio. This high land, steep but not rocky and almost continuously wooded, hems in the road

on the right, so much so that the road engineers had to tunnel through a couple of times en route to Blevio, the first village on this western shore of the Como lake arm.

Blevio

Blevio lies opposite Cernobbio, but the sun lies behind the hills here, and there is little similarity. However, it must be said that the position does offer sun in summer and the most beautiful sunsets. There is a row of elegant villas on the lake front, and their gardens are a tribute to the summer sun.

Torno & Beyond

The next village is **Torno** where the shore takes a right-angled bend, the turning of which offers a marvellous view north (which the Villa Pliniana further on was built to capture). In the thirteenth century a monastery here led to the establishment of a woollen industry, and the town became very prosperous. Much of the surviving old town has remained as it was, a wealth of old houses, narrow lanes, archways and two excellent churches.

The better is the **church of San Giovanni**, with an excellent Renaissance doorway in marble. Those who see a resemblance to Como's cathedral doorway are correct, the statuary here being by the Rodari school if not actually by the Rodaris. It is an irony that Como provided both builders and destroyers of the town. Inside, the church has much of interest, including a sixth-century memorial stone and a reliquary, shown only three times each year, that holds a piece of a Holy Nail.

Beyond Torno the road has beautiful tree-laden cliffs to the right, blue water and the villas of the western shore to the left. A road from Faggeto del Lario reaches three villages set among the trees, hanging off the cliffs. **Palanzo**, the last village, has the ruins of an old castle, while at **Molina**, the first, a waterfall drops noisily into a rocky gorge.

North of Pognana Lario, where Roman tombs were discovered, the road climbs a little way up the hill with an improvement in the lake views. Several picturesque villages are now passed before **Nesso** is reached, itself a picturesque, but much larger village.

Nesso

Nesso's castle did not survive a battle between the Sforzas and Il Medeghino, though a single wall with three turrets can still be seen in the oldest, most picturesque, part of the town. Here too is the *orrido* (gorge) of the Torrente Nesso, best viewed from a bridge over the stream near the lake shore.

The mountains above Lake Como are ideal for walking

A quiet moment at Gravedona

From Nesso a road climbs into the High Brianza, passing through several well-sited villages, reaching the winter sports area of Pian del Tivano, and then descending to Vallassina.

Lezzeno

Back on the shore road the lake has an elbow at Punta della Cavagnola, beyond which are a series of villages belonging to the commune of **Lezzeno**, the village of that name being the largest and last.

The views across the lake to Isola Comacina and Punta del Balbianello are memorable, and equally spectacular are the light plays in the lake cave, Buco dei Carpi, which can be reached only by boat. The cave is named for the carp which, together with other lake fish, take refuge there, but is more famous for its reflections of the setting sun.

Lezzeno is also home to **Club Morgan**, the most famous water-ski club on the lakes, where several national and European champions have been trained, and of the restaurant **Crotto del Misto**, partly built into an old cave and specialising in lake fish.

Onto Bellagio

The shore is overhung now by broken cliffs all the way to **Bellagio**, the 'Pearl of the Lake', thought by many to be the loveliest town not only on Como but in Europe. The town stands just behind the tip of the triangle of land.

The Point that Divides the Wind

The sharp point of land that pokes out into the lake just beyond Bellagio is known as **La Punta Spartivento**, 'the point that divides the wind'.

Before the town comes **Villa Melzi d'Eryl**, which sets the tone for Bellagio itself. The house cannot be visited, but externally it is a masterpiece of Neo-classical architecture – even the chimneys are exquisite! The gardens were landscaped by the moving of many tons of earth, though now, as with the best landscape gardening, that is not obvious.

BELLAGIO

The defences which Bellagio's position almost compelled its possessor to build are now gone – they have been dismantled more than once in the town's history. What still remains is an intricate network of lanes, some steep, some cobbled, that rise from the lake shore. The **church of San Giacomo** has work from an eleventh century Romanesque construction and a later Baroque expansion.

Bellagio from the lake ferry

Villa Serbelloni, which now belongs to the Rockefeller Foundation, is built on an ancient site. The present building fell into disrepair, even to the extent of having its name transferred to a hotel that stands on the other side of the point from it. It is now restored, though the visitor can only visit its gardens, which are terraced in grand Italian style. Visitors with an interest in sailing will also find a new museum dedicated to marine navigation fascinating.

Beautiful though the villas are at Bellagio, it is the old, cobbled village and the views which haunt the memory.

BEYOND BELLAGIO INTO THE VALLASSINA

South from Bellagio the route follows the Vallassina, but an alternative would be the shore road to Lecco. This is dominated by the Grigna across the lake, with some good closer views of the mountains of the High Brianza as Lecco is approached. At **Oliveto Lario** the olive groves that give the village its name offer a pleasant, softer contrast.

The uphill route starts by climbing quite steeply to **Guello**, a village sitting on a wooded shelf, from where there are two roads forward. To the right, the western road can be followed for one of the best views of Como, from the summit of **Monte San Primo**, 6,175ft (1,882m) The summit can be reached from Alpe di Ville, but does involve a climb of around 2,625ft (800m) so allow three hours.

The eastern road from Guello takes the visitor through **Civenna** which was once, with Limonta below it, an independent state, rather as Campione d'Italia is today. This existence, for more than 1,000 years, was only ended 200 years ago. Thereafter the village

---

The Cyclists' Chapel

Beyond Civenna at the high point of the road, is a church dedicated to the patron saint of cycling, and a monument to cyclists. Those who arrive on cycles must find it a delightful resting spot, particularly if they have toiled up the hill from Bellagio.

---

became a popular holiday resort, as the number and wealth of its villas amply testifies.

THE VALLASSINA

South again, enter the Vallassina, a valley of green meadows and scattered woods of chestnut, birch, beech and various firs and pines, set among which are **Magreglio** and **Barni**, justifiably well known as holiday centres. The first has a camp site, and is a reasonable, though not well equipped, winter sports centre.

Before Asso, one of the chief villages of Vallassina, a road off left leads to **Lasnigo** with its beautiful church, while one to the right leads to Sormano and the road that drops steeply into Nesso. **Sormano** itself is beautifully sited, an open sunny village.

Asso

Asso, which gives its name to the valley, is an ancient village. There was a Roman settlement here, as an inscribed stone set into the tower which is itself all that remains of the tenth-century castle, shows. Today Asso is a busy, light-industrial town, worthy of an exploration.

Canzo

From Asso a road left drops down to the Lecco arm of Como, but the route carries on to **Canzo**, another town with a prosperity based on light industry and tourism.

Canzo too was fortified, the remains of the castle now forming part of the Albergo Castello, the **Castle Hotel**, which also acts as an unofficial museum of the town. High above the town, to the east, are the Corni di Canzo rock masses set in the green alpine meadows. Below is a remote chapel dedicated to San Miro, a twelfth-century hermit, who was said to be able to control water, producing the odd spring at the Villa Pliniana and bringing or ending rain.

Erba

Two roads lead to Erba, one passing the tiny **Lago del Segrino**, exquisitely set among the trees, the other following the Vallassina river. Due to its position, this large industrial town was fortified from its earliest history, though its defences have now been dismantled. Those interested in its history, from earliest times to the Risorgimento, should visit the town museum which has some good exhibits, and a walk around the town goes past some fine villas.

Around Erba

South of Erba is **Lago di Alserio** the first of three lakes on the route back to Lecco. The second lake, **Lago di Pusiano**, has a tiny island, named for the cypress tree and is surrounded by pleasant villages each with an elegant array of villas.

The third lake, **Lago di Annone**, is the largest and has a tongue of land, Isella, extending into it, reminiscent of Sirmione at Lake Garda. At the very tip of Isella is a camp site that must be in the ultimate position for the water lover. The view from here of the village of **Annone** with its tall campanile is superb. At one time a bridge linked Isella and the shore at Annone, but this was never rebuilt following its destruction by the Spaniards in the seventeenth century. Today traces of it can still be seen below the water.

Beyond Lago di Annone are two more lakes, south of Lecco, **Garlate** and **Olginate**, each worthy of a visit. The village of Garlate at the southern end of the lake bearing its name is interesting for its museum of silk.

Buco del Piombo

Close to Erba lies the Buco del Piombo, named for the lead ore which has been found there. The huge cave has not been fully explored, but paleolithic remains have been found, together with evidence that it was used as a refuge by the locals right up to the eleventh century. Local legend has it that 1,160 peasants found shelter within the cave to escape the wrath of Barbarossa.

COMO CITY

Pinacoteca Palazzo Volpi (Art Gallery)
84 Via Diaz
Usually open all year ,Tuesday-Friday 9.30am-12.30pm, 2-5pm, Sunday
10am-1pm.
☎ 031 269869

Baradello Castle
Open: Thursday, Saturday & Sunday 2.30-6pm.
☎ 031 592805

Civic Museum (Archaeological and Risorgimento Museums) Palazzo Giovio and Palazzo Oliginati,
Piazza Medaglie D'Oro,
Via Vittorio Emanuele II
Open: Tuesday-Saturday 9.30am-12.30, 2-5pm, Sunday 10am-1pm; closed holidays.
☎ 031 271343

Funivia (cablecar) to Brunate
Open: all year, normally 6am-10.30pm, cars every 30 minutes.
☎ 031 303608

Rivarossi Museum
157-8 Via Pio XI, Sagnino
Open: by request.
☎ 031 541541

Silk Museum
3 Via Valleggio
Open: all year, Tuesday-Friday 9am-12noon, 3-6pm.
☎ 031 303180

Temple Sacrarium
Via per Brunate
Open: all year Saturday & Sunday 2.30-6pm. At other times by request. ☎ 031 305958

Temple Voltiano
Viale Marconi
Open: April-September Tuesday-Sunday 10am-12noon, 3-6pm, October-March Tuesday-Sunday 10am-12noon, 2-4pm.
☎ 031 574705/271343

Villa Melzi d'Ergl, Bellagio

Herbal liqueurs and remedies are made and sold by the monks at Piona Abbey

Villa Olmo
Via Cantoni
Park and gardens open: 8am-11pm (summer), 9am-7pm (winter) daily except holidays. Villa open 9am-12noon, 3-6pm, but sometimes closed for conferences.
☎ 031 252443/271343

THE WESTERN SHORE

ARGEGNO
Funivia to Pigra
Open: all year, daily 9am-dusk. For information ☎ 031 265592.

CERNOBBIO
Villa Erba
Open: all year, Saturday 2-6pm, Sunday 10am-6pm.
☎ 031 3491

Villa Il Pizzo
Via Regina
Open: April-October, daliy, 8.30-12.30, 2-5pm. Gardens open to groups only: ask at Tourist Information Office for details. The villa is open by request only and then to groups only.
☎ 031 511700/511262
or 02 876139

DONGO
Resistance Museum
Open: by request only.
☎ 0344 82572

GRAVEDONA
Palazzo Gallio
For information ☎ 031 265592.

LENNO
**Villa del Balbianello
(Il Balbianello)**
Gardens only Open: April-October, Tuesday, Thursday & Friday 10am-12.30pm, 2-6pm, Saturday & Sunday 10am-6pm. Can only be reached by boat from Lenno or Campo. The villa is open by request only.
☎ 0344 56110 or 02 4676151

PIANELLO DEL LARIO
Boat Museum
Open: Easter-October, Saturday & Sunday 10.30am-12.30pm, 2.30-6pm. Open daily from July-mid-September, same times.
☎ 0344 87235 or 87294

(cont'd overleaf)

(cont'd from previous page)

TREMEZZO
Villa Carlotta
Open: daily, April-September,
9am-6pm, March and October,
daily 9-11.30am 2-4.30pm
☎ 0344 40405

THE EASTERN SHORE

BELLANO
Orrido
Open: all year, Sunday 10am-
12noon 2-6pm. Everyday in
August, same times.
Note: If there has been
torrential rain the gorge may
be closed as the water rises
above the ropeways.
For information ☎ 031 265592.

COLICO
Abbey of Piona
Open: all year, daily 9am-12noon
2-6pm or sunset.
☎ 0341 940331

ESINO LARIO
Museum
Open: July & August, Wednesday
6-7pm, Friday 8.30-10pm, Sunday
10.30am-12noon, at other times
by request. ☎ 0341 860111.

LECCO
Palazzo Belgioiaso (Museum)
Corso Matteotti
Open: Tuesday-Saturday
9.30am-2pm.
☎ 0341 481247

Villa Manzoni
Via Amendola
Open: Tuesday-Saturday
9.30am-2pm.
☎ 0341 481247

MANDELLO DEL LARIO
Motorcycle Museum
Via E. Parodi 57
All year: guided tours at 3pm and
4pm, Monday-Friday. No charge,
but knowledge of Italian handly.
☎ 0341 709111

PRIMALUNA
Museum
Open: July and August, Saturday
& Sunday 4.30-6.30pm.
☎ 0341 980253

VARENNA
Ornithological Museum
Closed for restoration at time of
writing, ring for details.
☎ 0341 830367

Vezio Castle
Open: All year, daily 10am-5pm
(or dusk). Open until 8pm from
April-September. ☎ 0335 465186

Villa Cipressi
Open: March-September,
Monday-Friday 9am-6pm,
Saturday & Sunday 9am-7pm.
☎ 0341 830113

Villa Monastero
Open: daily, April-October,
9am-6pm. ☎ 0341 830129

VERSASIO, NEAR LECCO, TO PIANI D' ERNA
Funivia (cablecar)
Times vary, ☎ 031 265592
for information.

THE SOUTHERN SHORE

BELLAGIO
Museum of Navigational Instruments
Piazza Don Miotti

Open: Easter, May-October,
Tuesday-Sunday 10am-1pm.
☎ 031 950309

Villa Melzi d'Eryl
Open: Gardens and villa chapel
only March-October daily 9am-
6pm. ☎ 0339 6446830

Villa Serbelloni
Open: April-OctoberGardens only
open. Pre-booking essential, daily
tours at 11am and 4pm
☎ 031 950204

ERBA
Town Museum
Via Foscolo
Open: All year;
Tuesday 9am-12noon
Wednesday 2.30-6pm

Friday 2.30-6pm.
☎ 031 3355341

Buco del Piombo
Open: April-October Saturday 2-
6pm, Sunday 10am-6pm.
☎ 031 629599

GARLATE
Museum of Silk
All year: Sunday 10am-12noon 2-
6pm, all other times by request.
☎ 0341 681306

LEZZENO
Buco dei Carpi (Carp Hole)
For information ☎ 031 265592.

NESSO
Orrido
For information ☎ 031 265592.

LAKE STEAMERS

Diesel and hydrofoil ferries link a very large number of ports on Como's
shores, particularly on the Como arm, and the western shore of the
Colico arm. Como itself is a terminus and from it ferries visit Tavernola,
Cernobbio, Blevio, Moltrasio, Torno, Urio, Carate, Laglio, Faggeto Lario,
Pognana Lario, Toriggia, Careno, Nesso, Brieno, Argegno, Colonno, Sala
Comacina, Lezzeno, Lenno, Tremezzo, Cadenabbia and Bellagio.

Continuing to Lake Colico, as the upper arm of Lake Como is some-
times called, the ferries reach Menaggio, Varenna, Bellano, Acquaseria,
Rezzonico, Dervio, Cremia, Pianello del Lario, Musso, Dongo, Gravedona,
Domaso, Gera Lario, Colico and a terminus at Piona.

In the Lecco arm of the lake the ferries leave Bellagio for Lierna,
Limonta, Oliveto, Mandello del Lario, Abbadia Lariana and finish at
Lecco. In addition, boats cross to Isola Comacina from several ports on
the mainland close to the island.

A return trip from Como to Piona, via Bellagio, will take about six
hours, more if Bellagio itself and Piona Abbey are visited. Such a trip can
take advantage of the restaurants on the ferries and is quicker if full
advantage is taken of the hydrofoil service.

As an alternative to the ferry for sightseeing, Lake Como also has a
flying boat service, regular tourist flights taking off from the lake close to
the city of Como. The flights are not cheap, but they guarantee an
exciting ride.

Lake Como has four car ferries criss-crossing the waters near Punta
Spartivento, beyond Bellagio. They link Menaggio with Bellagio and
Varenna, Cadenabbia with Bellagio and Varenna, and Bellagio with
Varenna. Each crossing takes from 15 to 30 minutes. For information on
all of the steamers ☎ 031579211.

Piazza Vecchia, Bergamo

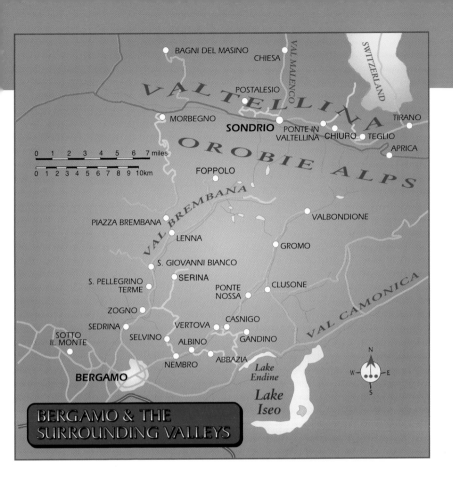

BERGAMO & THE SURROUNDING VALLEYS

The city of Bergamo (or rather the cities of Bergamo, since there are two distinct cities, the upper and lower), stands at the junctions of the Val Seriana and the Val Brembana – though neither of the two valley rivers actually runs through the cities. It is an ancient place – there was a Celtic settlement here even before the establishment, around 200BC, of the Roman *Bergomum*.

BERGAMO

From any position that offers a view of Bergamo, it is the upper city – **Bergamo Alta** – that attracts the eye. This is true even from the lower city – **Bergamo Bassa** – but it is there that the tour will begin.

BERGAMO BASSA

Bergamo Bassa is a spacious city, with broad avenues and open *piazze*. At its centre is **Piazza Matteotti**, with gardens and memorials, and running parallel to it, the **Sentierone**, linking Piazza Cavour and Piazza Vittorio Veneto.

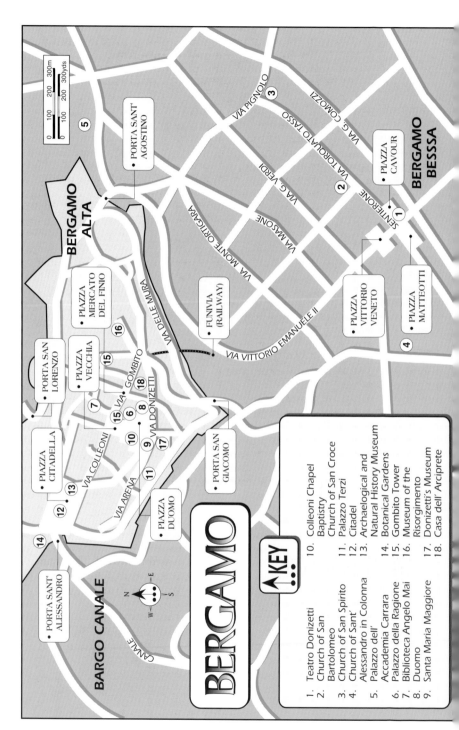

BERGAMO

KEY

1. Teatro Donizetti
2. Church of San Bartolomeo
3. Church of San Spirito
4. Church of Sant' Alessandro in Colonna
5. Palazzo dell' Accademia Carrara
6. Palazzo della Ragione
7. Biblioteca Angelo Mai
8. Duomo
9. Santa Maria Maggiore
10. Colleoni Chapel
11. Baptistry
12. Church of San Croce
13. Palazzo Terzi
14. Citadel
15. Archaelogical and Natural History Museum
16. Botanical Gardens
17. Gombito Tower
18. Museum of the Risorgimento
17. Donizetti's Museum
18. Casa dell' Arciprete

In **Piazza Cavour** is a monument to Donizetti, the eighteenth-century composer who was born in the city, while the **Teatro Donizetti** stands on the Sentierone. The monument has the composer listening to Melopea, on her lyre; the theatre, built at the end of the eighteenth century was named for the composer in 1898, the centenary of his birth. It holds 1,300 people.

Also in the Sentierone is the **church of San Bartolomeo** with a large altarpiece by Lorenzo Lotto, one of his major works. Other works by the painter can be seen in the churches **San Spirito** – in Via Torquato Tasso next to San Bartolomeo, and **San Bernardino**, a small church in the steep Via Pignolo to the north.

East of Piazza Matteotti is the **church of Sant' Alessandro in Colonna**, outside of which a column made of ancient stone fragments marks the spot where St Alexander is said to have been martyred in AD297.

The upper city is fully walled (the walls having been completed by the Venetians in the late sixteenth century when the city was the Venetian Republic's western bastion) and so entry to it can only be made through the ancient gates. To all intents and purposes, cars are excluded. Four gates exist, two on the Bergamo Bassa side, two towards the open country to the north.

In addition a *funivia* runs up from the lower city (follow Via Vittorio Emanuele II from Piazza Vittorio Veneto) and it is on the left after the road has curved rightward. This is an excellent way to approach the upper city. You climb on board the rack railway and when you get out you are several metres higher, and 400 years further back in time.

BERGAMO ALTA

Porta San Giacomo lies to the left of the *funivia*, while further along Via Vittorio Emanuele II is Porta Sant'

Donizetti

Gaetano Donizetti was born in Borgo Canale in Bergamo's Città Alta in November 1797, the fifth child of six in a poor family with no musical tradition. He joined a charitable school at which choirboys were trained in Bergamo Cathedral when he was nine and was immediately recognised as musically gifted. At the age of eighteen he was sent to study music at Bologna, returning to Bergamo when he was twenty. His first opera was performed in Rome when he was twenty-five and he was soon being commissioned to write works for opera houses all over Italy.

For twenty years Donizetti was the leading Italian composer, his reign ending with the performance of Verdi's *Nabucco* in 1842. By then Donizetti's health was already failing. He returned to his Bergamo home and remained there for the rest of his life, dying in April 1848. He was buried in the local cemetery, but his remains were moved to the church of Santa Maria Maggiore where a fine memorial had been erected to him. Donizetti's most famous works are *Lucia di Lammermoor* and the comic opera *L'Elisir d'Amore*.

View of the upper city from the lower city

Agostino. Using this last gate has the advantage of taking the visitor close to the **Palazzo dell' Accademia Carrara**, which no art lover will want to miss. Here are works by Raphael, Titian, Botticelli, and Rubens as well as paintings by local artists Maroni

The Upper City *Funivia*

The funicular railway which lifts visitors to the Città Alta's Piazza Mercato delle Scarpe was opened on 20 September 1887, an inauspicious opening as the dignititaries who made the inaugural ride were forced to walk back down when a wheel jammed and forced the railway to a halt. The funicular is just 787ft (240m) long – the left track is actually shorter than the right by 20ft (6m) because of the curve – and rises by 85m (279ft) a gradient of 52°.

The Bergamesque

The famous dance, the Bergamesque – danced by the company at the end of Shakespeare's *A Midsummer Night's Dream* – began in Bergamo, as did the *Commedia dell'Arte*, the improvised comedy with a strict cast of masked characters – Pulcinella, Columbine, Pierrot, Scaramouch, Pantaloon, etc.

and Lotto, and artists of the Venetian school. The gallery was founded in the late eighteenth century by Count Giacomo Carrara.

Across from the Accademia the Contemporary and Modern Art Galley has a permanent collection and exhibitions. Close by, in Via Pignolo, the Diocesan Museum, found in the beautiful Palazzo Bassi Rathgeb has a remarkable collection of sacred objects.

Beyond the Porta Sant' Agostino is a church to the same saint built in the thirteenth century, but deconsecrated following extensive fire damage. The Gothic façade is superb, though little else remains of the original. Today the church is used for occasional exhibitions.

Piazza Vecchia

The centre of the upper city is Piazza Vecchia, the Old Square, a wonderful place, thought by many to be without any equal anywhere. Both Frank Lloyd Wright and Le Corbusier claimed that the *piazza* was the finest Renaissance square in Italy. The square, at first sight, is tiled on a grand scale, but closer examination shows that each large 'tile' is of brick, the bricks going diagonally across the square 'tile'; a simple yet brilliant idea.

The **Palazzo della Ragione** was rebuilt in the mid-sixteenth century following a fire. It is a dark, brilliantly conceived building with a statue of the poet Torquato Tasso on a plinth to the side of its central portico. In the room above the statue there is a collection of detached frescoes, some from the original building and some from the Venetian Mayor's mansion, rebuilt in the fifteenth century, which also stands on a side of the *piazza*. The mansion is now part of the university.

Contarini Fountain

In the centre of the square is the Contarini fountain, presented to the city in 1780 by the Venetian mayor Alvese Contarini. Its lions, symbols of the Venetian Republic, demurely hold chains in their mouths. When on St Stephen's Day in 1796 the citizens of Bergamo tore the Venetian lion from the façade of the Palazzo della Ragione and smashed it, they had decided that the chains were those of slavery, and that they would bear them no longer. Today the *palazzo* has another lion.

127

To the side of the *palazzo* is the city's **campanile**, begun in the twelfth century, but not completed until the sixteenth. A lift climbs the tower and from the top there are superb views over the old city. Each evening the largest bell tolls a 180-chime curfew. In front of the campanile, access to the *palazzo* is up a beautiful covered stairway.

At the opposite end of the *piazza* from the *palazzo* is the library, the **Biblioteca Angelo Mai**, built in the seventeenth century as a new town hall, and only completed when the façade above the portico was added in 1928.

Piazza del Duomo

The Palazzo della Ragione separates the Piazza Vecchia from the **Piazza del Duomo**, its arcades providing a perfect frame for a view of the church of Santa Maria Maggiore and the Colleoni chapel.

Also in the square, not surprisingly in view of the name, is the city *duomo*, seemingly jammed in between its surrounding buildings. Externally – though it is very difficult to see the whole of the outside, even from the campanile – the cathedral is simple, a fine dome overtopping red tiled rooves and a dignified white front. The building was started in the mid-fifteenth century on the site of the old cathedral, but additions were made until the seventeenth century, and the dome and frontage were added only last century.

Inside, the cathedral is magnificent, with many fine artworks. Chief of these are a painting by Maroni, to the left after entering, one by Tiepolo at the far end, and the two altars, the northern with bas-reliefs of the seventeenth century, the southern with sculptured saints, of the eighteenth century.

Opposite the Palazzo della Ragione is the **church of Santa Maria Maggiore**, built in the late twelfth century by the citizens when they were exhausted by war, famine, drought and plague, and in need of spiritual assistance. It is a

The Colleoni Chapel

Built into the side of Santa Maria Maggiore is the Colleoni Chapel. Bartolomeo Colleoni, who died in 1476, was a remarkable man, a son of Bergamo, who twice captained Venetian forces against Milan, and twice captained Milanese forces against Venice, managing during the whole time not only to maintain his head but to make a small fortune besides. Colleoni gave money for a statue of himself in Venice, specifying a position in front of San Marco. He meant the basilica of San Marco but was given instead the school of that name, a play on words he was never to be aware of, as the statue was positioned after his death. It is now considered one of the finest equestrian statues in the world.

Another, also finished after his death, can be seen in the chapel that Colleoni had built here in Bergamo. The chapel was begun in 1470, designed by Amadeo, the most famous architect and sculptor of the day, and is a masterwork of intricate design and craftsmanship. Inside are the tombs of Colleoni, and of his daughter Medea, both of which are also by Amadeo.

simple building, the elaborate red and white marble porch over the entrance having been added 150 years later. Inside, the church is massively and sumptuously decorated, with so much to look at that it is beyond reasonable description. But do look out for the sixteenth-century Florentine and Flemish tapestries, the wooden choir and the monument to the composer Donizetti. The latter is a remarkable work with seven distraught children representing the seven musical notes, and the muse of music hanging her head.

On the fourth side of the Piazza del Duomo is a delightful polygonal **baptistery** built in the fourteenth century, which originally stood inside Santa Maria Maggiore, but which was taken down and accurately reconstructed here in the last years of the nineteenth century. Inside, it is a minor treasure house of bas-relief and sculpture by Campione masters.

Surrounding the two piazze are a large number of equally fascinating buildings, the oddly shaped and squat eleventh-century **church of San Croce**; the **Ateneo** built over an early water supply cistern which, a still-extant memorial tablet tells us, was completed in 1342; and the **Bishop's Court**.

A Short Tour

Old Bergamo is virtually an open-air museum. An exhaustive tour is beyond the scope of this book, but some general pointers are worthwhile. Inside the old walls a tree-lined road circles the city, and taking this from Porta Sant' Agostino leads to Porta San Giacomo and then on past the **Palazzo Terzi**, the most magnificent private palace in the city.

Beyond the seminary that dominates the south-western corner of the city is the **citadel**, built around a closed *piazza*. The buildings here are of the thirteenth century, with fine cloisters, and one houses the **Archaeological and Natural History Museum**. The thirteenth-century tower near the *piazza* is 'di Adalberto', the tower of hunger.

Ahead now is a green valley, a surprising but delightful discovery, beyond which is Porta San Lorenzo, through which Garibaldi passed in 1859. To the left is the final gate, Porta Sant' Alessandro, and the city's **Botanical Gardens**.

From Piazza Cittadella, Via Colleoni leads back to the old square, a magnificent, narrow, enclosed street of old houses and fine churches. Past the old square is Via Gambito, with the **Gambito Tower**, square cut and unadorned, marking the entrance to the beautiful Piazza Mercato del Fieno with its strange medieval tower-houses.

At the back of the square is the thirteenth-century convent of San Francesco, and to the side of it, the *rocca*, the remains of the city's fourteenth century fortress from which there are fine views of both the upper and lower cities. The convent houses the cities history museum.

Elsewhere in the city, the visitor can see the birthplace of Donizetti in Borgo Canale, just outside Porta Sant' Alessandro, while a museum devoted to the composer is in Via Arena.

Another famous man who came from Bergamo province, (though not actually from the city) was Angelo Giuseppe Roncalli, who found fame as Pope John XXIII, one of the most universally loved popes of modern times who died in 1963. His birthplace at Sotto il Monte lies a short driving distance west of the city, and the house has become a place of pilgrimage and homage.

(cont'd on page 132)

The Rocca, Old Bergamo

BERGAMO'S SURROUNDING VALLEYS

VAL SERIANA

Val Seriana, the valley of the Serio river, has one of the longest histories of any of the local valleys and is, as a result, one of the best to visit for a glimpse of Italy's architectural and artistic heritage. The valley's place in history is due to its metalliferous mines, and to its wide bottom and gently sloping sides that allowed easy farming on fertile soil.

Today the lower valley, that closest to Bergamo, is industrial, mainly the light industry of silk and cotton milling but with the heavier activity of a cement works occasionally visible. Higher up, the valley is still beautifully unspoilt, and there agriculture is still the mainstay, though tourism is now a major industry, especially in winter as the valley's winter sports facilities improve. In summer the alpine pastures offer excellent walking in cool surroundings – just the thing for relaxation after long hot days at the lake's edge – with wonderful views, occasionally to jagged ridges of peaks.

Nembro and **Albino**, the first valley villages reached from Bergamo, are a little industrial, but do not be put off and so miss the painting of the Crucifixion by Maroni in the church of San Giuliano in Albino. Maroni was born near the village, in the hamlet of Bondo Petello on the slopes above it. The hamlet can be seen by those who take the *funivia* from the top of Albino to the hill village of **Selvino**, a pretty, well sited village, rightly popular both in summer and now, more frequently, in winter.

By crossing the river at Albino a road can be reached that links the Val Seriana with the Val Cavallina at Lake Endine. This road passes **Abbazia** where there is a delightful twelfth-century Cistercian monastery. The half-cone apses with stone-tiled rooves are especially attractive.

Another road out of the valley, but here into a side valley, can be taken at Gazzaniga to reach **Gandino**, a very old, pretty village with a fine artistic history, and also the birthplace of Bartolomeo Bon, the sculptor, and the painter Castello. The town's past is well represented in its preserved **medieval gateway** and in its excellent early fifteenth-century **basilica**, with a baroque interior that includes a sixteenth-century bronze balustrade. The basilica's campanile is topped by a very eastern-looking spire, while its museum holds a collection of important documents and vestments.

From Gandino a chair lift can be taken to a high plateau that offers good skiing in winter and good walking in summer.

Vertova, in the valley, and **Casnigo**, on a road that branches off right after yet another bridge over the Serio is crossed, are each worth visiting for their churches. The one at Vertova is surrounded by a remarkable arcade that gives it a curious 'hen and chickens' look which belies its great interest, while that at Casnigo is a simple, elegantly arcaded, fourteenth-century building.

In the main valley, at **Ponte Nossa**, a very winding road links (eventually!) Val Seriana and Val Brembana, and a little further up the valley, **Clusone**, a major centre, can be reached by a short detour.

At **Clusone** the **Oratorio dei Disciplini**, beside the church, has fifteenth-century frescoes of the

Triumph of Death and the *Dance of Death*, the latter being a mixture of people and skeletons hand-in-hand. Also here is a fine astronomical clock by Pietro Fanzago, a local man, dating from the late sixteenth century.

The nearby village of **Rovetta** has a museum to the work of the Fantoni family, who were sixteenth-century sculptors.

Beyond the Clusone turn-off, the valley is dotted with pretty villages in beautiful positions and outlooks increasingly dominated by big mountains. **Gromo** has an attractive medieval tower and an equally good Palazzo Communale with three tiers of arcades. From the village there is what must be the most corkscrew road in the province up to the winter sports centre of Spiazzi.

The last village is **Valbondione**, where the valley is rugged, and from there it is possible to walk to the Cascata del Serio (*see* box overleaf).

Val Brembana

The valley of the Brembo has a curious geography which, before the advent of modern road engineering, meant that it was virtually cut off from the outside world. To the north, at its head, there are high peaks without passes,

and the ridges of these peaks run down not only the east and west sides of the valley, but weave east and west at the southern end as well, to produce a difficult exit for the river through the 'straits' as they are called.

Until about 1600 there were only two passes into the valley and neither of them was particularly easy. Not surprisingly the valley folk evolved a rich mixture of dialect, culture and architecture which, whilst it has not survived intact into the modern era, does at least colour the landscape, making the trip up the valley very worthwhile.

From Bergamo the road reaches the valley at **Villa d'Alme** where the river ends its sinuous curves through the straits. Over the river from here, at **Almenno San Bartolomeo**, the twelfth-century circular church of San Tome stands on the ruins of a Roman temple. Its unusual shape and its isolation make it a captivating building. Equally fascinating is the **Museo del Falegname**, the woodwork museum, devoted to the local craftsmen in wood.

Beyond, **Sedrina** is most famous for its series of bridges high above the river, linking the steep cliffs that form the

(cont'd on page 136)

The Waters of San Pellegrino

The history of the thermal springs at **San Pellegrino Terme** goes back to the thirteenth century, but it is really only in the twentieth century that they became famous and brought the prosperity that allowed the Grand Hotel and the casino, for example, to be built. The casino, with its square but elegant lines and its backdrop of trees, is a very fine building.

The thermal 'station' is open from May to September and visitors can buy a single 'cure' or a full course, though a full examination by a doctor is required first. The spa can be visited and the waters tried each morning and afternoon.

The Cascata del Serio

The *cascata* (waterfall), one of Europe's highest waterfalls (1,035ft/ 315m), is magnificently set in very rugged, almost inhospitable, country. The one problem is that as the water from the stream which feeds it is now used to power a hydro-electric power station, most of the time the waterfall is dry! The power station 'opens' the fall at certain weekends in July and August when the sight of the *cascata* being 'turned on' brings hundreds to this remote spot. Ask at the Tourist Office for up-to-date information on this year's schedule.

Before the falls are 'turned on'...

... and after!

Above: The village of Valbondione nestles in the Val Seriana

Below: San Pelligrino Terme

banks in the straits. Over the river the tourist can visit the **Grotte delle Meraviglie**, one of the limestone caves for which the valley is famous among speleologists. One cave hereabouts, the Buca del Castello, is one of the deepest in Italy.

Although **Zogno** is a commercial and industrial centre, it does have the **Museo della Valle**, a museum showing the history and development of the valley. Beyond is **San Pellegrino Terme**, the most famous of the valley's towns, and one of Italy's most famous spas, specialising in the treatment of kidney disorders (*see* box on page 133).

From San Pellegrino Terme, a side valley can be followed to **Serina**, a beautiful village with frescoed, arcaded houses and a huge church with many works by Palma il Vecchio, who was born here.

In the main valley is **San Giovanni Bianco**, with an equally magnificent church – an imposing collection of cylinders, half cylinders and squares with a pencil-thin campanile. The village sits at the mouth of the Taleggio valley, famous for its cheese, and has slim, elegant bridges over the rivers of both valleys as they meet.

Next in the main valley comes **Cornello dei Tasso**, just a huddle of houses around a fine campanile, hardly credible as a birthplace for household words. The Tasso family came from this village, a family that started a Europewide postal service in the late thirteenth century and who have given us both the name of the Russian news agency (Tass) and the word 'taxi', deriving from their exclusive, private vehicle service when they were postmasters to the Holy Roman Empire in the sixteenth century. Torquato Tasso, the poet whose statue is in old Bergamo, was from this family.

At **Piazza Brembana**, a beautiful spot with expansive views over green meadows and blue mountains, the valley splits. The western fork goes over the San Marco Pass and down into the Valtellina, whilst the eastern fork, the Val Brembana proper, goes on through a series of mountain villages to end at **Foppolo**, the most developed of all Bergamo province's winter sports centres and fast becoming one of the leading centres in Italy.

Using the village's chairlifts as a start, it is possible to climb the **Corno Stella** (8,595ft/2,620m). The climb is about 3,280ft (1,000m) and 2 miles (3km) in distance and should not be undertaken lightly, but the summit does offer one of the best alpine panoramas of the whole region, from the Bernese Oberland peaks across to the Ortler Alps.

SONDRIO AND VALTELLINA

The Valtellina has always been important in Italian history, for while most of the alpine valleys, and all of the passes, run north-south, the Valtellina (the valley of the Adda river) lies predominantly east-west. As a consequence many of the alpine passes end in the Valtellina, so control of the valley gave control of the many passes. In addition, the Adda flows into Lake Como, which gave the defenders of the valley quick access to the Lombardy plain.

Sondrio

Sondrio, half way along the Valtellina, is capital of a Lombardian province that bears its name, a mountainous province sharing a long border with Switzerland and including, arguably, the best of Italy's skiing resorts. The town lies each side of the Torrente Mallero (now enclosed in a trench that signifies its potential destructive force) which seems to cut the town in half. Above one bank is the **Masegra Castle**, last of a long line of castles on the site, all destroyed by various warring factions. Today the castle is in government hands and is not open to visitors.

The centre of the town is **Piazza Campello** where stands the town hall, the **Palazzo Communale**, a square cut sixteenth-century building, its lower façade interestingly textured. Also here is the parish **church of San Gerasio and San Protasio**. The site is ancient, but the eleventh-century church that stood here was demolished in the eighteenth century, and the present building was erected. The campanile was built at the same time.

North of the square is the oldest part of the town, well worth investigating, though many of the finest buildings date only from the eighteenth century, which is rather new by Italian standards. The **Palazzo Lavizzari** in Via Parravicini is an exception, an attractive building with a white marble doorway from the sixteenth century. It houses a museum devoted to the history of the Valtellina. It has some good exhibits including Etruscan and Roman finds, and paintings by local artists. A diocesan section has some fine religious works including a rare seventeenth-century copper cross.

The second museum is in Via Ragazzi del' 99, a natural history museum, with exhibits on the wildlife, geology and mineralogy of the valley. Just outside the town the fifteenth-century **church of the Madonna della Sassella** is set among the vineyards that grow the grapes for Sassella wine.

The Valtellina

Visitors will have already glimpsed the Valtellina as they crossed the Piano di Spagna which separates the lakes of Como and Mezzola. The valley is famous for its wines – Grumello and Sassella to name just two – the vines, which are frame grown, are to be seen everywhere. It also has great scenic beauty, the lower alpine slopes bearing woods of oak and chestnut, while higher there are rhododendron, fir and larch, and everywhere the usual diversity of alpine flora. It is also an area rich in minerals and has attracted crystal hunters for many years.

From the western end of the valley, after a side road heads north for Chiavenna and Switzerland, the first call is at **Morbegno**, a very pleasant town from which two alpine side valleys – the Val Gerola going south towards Monte Ponteronica and a valley leading to the San Marco Pass and Bergamo's Val Brembana – can be reached. Each of these valleys is delightful, with rugged hamlets set among some magnificent unspoilt scenery.

In Morbegno the eighteenth-century bridge, the Ponte di Ganda, is elegantly constructed, with a semi-circular arch. Also worth noting is the natural history museum with exhibits on valley birdlife and mineralogy.

Beyond Morbegno the main road, the N38, carves a fast route through the valley, avoiding all the valley villages on its way to Sondrio, Tirano and Bormio. Many of the villages which are avoided are worth seeing if time permits, though none is of really exceptional note.

In the **Val Masino**, going north from the main valley, is **Bagno del Masino** with thermal springs used for therapeutic purposes, and a centre for excellent walking on rough alpine terrain among massive granite peaks.

At **Postalesio** in the main valley there are earth pillars – pyramids of erosion

– the same odd, other-worldly pillars, each capped with a boulder, are seen again near Cislano, above Iseo.

From Sondrio the **Val Malenco** heads north. The valley is one of the richest in the world for both the variety and abundance of its mineral crystals, so any walk has the potential of a real find. Within the valley there are several cable ways allowing access to the High Alps and a fine view of the quarries that produce Malenco marble, a green serpentine.

At **Chiesa** there is a small museum with exhibits on the history and natural history of the valley. The upper reaches of the valley, which offer excellent winter sport, also offer magnificent views of the Bernina Alps at all times of the year.

Ponte in Valtellina

Ponte in Valtellina is one of the most important artistic sites in the valley. The **church of San Maurizio** is magnificient, with a Romanesque bell tower, a fresco by Luini and a bronze tabernacle. Elsewhere there are other excellent buildings, the **church of Madonna di Campagna** with a fine series of frescoes, and a monument to a local man, Guiseppe Piazzi, who discovered the first asteroid.

The town also has two museums, a small diocesan collection beside the church of San Maurizio, and one dedicated to the area, in Via Ginnasio.

Beyond Sondrio, back on the Valtellina road, is a succession of very pretty villages, each with magnificent settings. The road to Tirano was called one of the most beautiful in the world by a nineteenth-century English mountaineer and it is an undeniable claim.

At **Chiuro** the minor valley road climbs through vine-covered hills, with lovely views and a succession of small valleys each with a stream edged with water polished rocks.

Teglio is the old capital of the valley, indeed the village gave the valley its name. The Romanesque **church of San Pietro** has an eleventh-century campanile and **Palazzo Besta** is the finest sixteenth-century villa in the valley with a wonderful courtyard surrounded by two floors of arcades and frescoed walls. On the ground floor of the villa is a small museum with a collection of items from Valtellina's pre-history.

Near Teglio a side valley leads steeply to **Aprica**, Valtellina's major winter sports area and one of Italy's more famous resorts. Cableways give access to high plateaux and fine walking, and the town has a small museum of local artwork and natural history. From Aprica a road leads to Brescia's Val Camonica.

The tour stops at **Tirano**, where the road starts its climb to the Stelvio Pass. Tirano was, historically, an important valley town, and has villas built by the Viscontis and Pallavicinis amongst others. The town also has a small ethnographic museum.

From Tirano a road leads north, passing the **church of the Madonna di Tirano**, a famous pilgrimage church built in the early sixteenth century to commemorate a miracle of 1504. This has a very fine doorway and a rich interior. Just beyond the church is the Swiss-Italian border.

BERGAMO

Accademia Carrera
82 Piazza dell' Accademia
Open: All year Tuesday-Sunday
9.30am-1pm, 2.30-5.30pm.
Closed holidays.
☎ 035 399643

Archaeology Museum
9 Piazza Cittadella
Open: All year Daily except
Monday 9am-12.30pm, 2-6pm.
Closed holidays and Saturday &
Sunday from October-March.
☎ 035 242839

Botanical Gardens
Porta San Alessandro
Open: March-October, Monday-
Friday 9am-12noon, 2-6pm (5pm
in March and October). Saturday
& Sunday 9am-7pm.
For information ☎ 035 286060

Campanile
Piazza Vecchia
Open: April-October, Tuesday-
Friday 9.30-7pm, Saturday &
Sunday 9.30am-9.30pm.
November-March, Saturday &
Sunday 9.30am-4pm.
☎ 035 247116

The *Duomo*, from the companile in Piazza Vecchia, Bergamo

(cont'd overleaf)

(cont'd from previous page)

Church of Santa Maria Maggiore. *Piazza Duomo*
Open: April-October, Monday-Saturday 9am-12.30pm, 2.30-6pm, Sunday 9am-1pm, 3-6pm. November-March, Monday-Friday 9am-12.30pm, 2.30-5pm, Saturday 9am-12.30pm, 2.30-6pm, Sunday 9am-1pm, 3-6pm. ☎ 035 223327

Colleoni Chapel
Piazza Duomo
Open: March-October daily, except Monday 9am-12.30pm, 2-6.30pm; November-February daily except Monday 9am-12.30pm, 2-4.30pm. ☎ 035 210061

Diocesan Museum
Via Pighola 76
All year: Tuesday-Sunday 9.30am-12.30pm, 3-6pm. ☎ 035 248772.

Donizetti Museum
9 Via Arena
Open: June-September, Tuesday-Sunday 9.30am-1pm, 2-5.30pm, October-May, Tuesday-Friday 9.30am-1pm, Saturday 9.30am-1pm, 2-5.30pm. ☎ 035 399269 or 247116

Donizetti's Birthplace
14 Via Borgo Canale
Closed for restoration at time of writing. ☎ 035 244483

Gallery of Contemperany & Modern Art
Via San Tommaso 53
Open: April-September, Tuesday-Sunday 10am-1pm, 3-6.45pm, October-March, Tuesday-Sunday 9.30am-1pm, 2.30-5.45pm. ☎ 035 399528

History Museum
Convent of San Francesco,

Piazza Mercato del Fieno 6A.
Open: June-September, Tuesday-Friday 9.30am-1pm, 2-5.30pm, Saturday & Sunday 9.30am-7pm, October-May, Tuesday-Sunday 9.30am-1pm, 2-5.30pm. ☎ 035 247116

Natural History Museum
10 Piazza Cittadella
Open: All year Tuesday-Friday 9.30am-12.30pm, 2.30-6pm, 5.30 from October-March; Saturday & Sunday 9am-7pm. Closes at 5.30pm October-March. Closed holidays. ☎ 035 286011

Sotto il Monte
West of Bergamo
Pope John XXIII Museum
Open: all year, Tuesday-Sunday 8.30-11.30am, 2.30-5.30pm. ☎ 035 792956.
Pope John's Home
Open: all year daily, 8.30am-6.30pm (5.30pm October-March). ☎ 035 792956

VAL SERIANA

ALBINO TO SELVINO
Funivia (cablecar)
Open: all year, approximately hourly from 7am-6pm (shorter hours in winter). ☎ 035 289011

CLUSONE
Astronomical Clock
Open: July and August Guided tours on Thursday at 3pm. At other times by appointment. ☎ 0346 21113

Oratorio dei Disciplini
Open: by request at the Town Hall. ☎ 0346 21113

GANDINO
Museum of the Basilica
By appointment only. On 1st &

3rd Sunday of each month between 3-6pm.
☎ 035 745425/746115

ROVETTA
Fantoni Foundation
Open: July-September, Tuesday-Sunday 3.30-5.30pm.
☎ 0346 735523

VAL BREMBANA

ALMENNO SAN BARTOLOMEO
Church of San Tome
Open: May-September, Saturday 2.30-6pm, Sunday 10am-12noon, 2.30-6pm, October-April, Sunday 10am-12noon, 2-5pm.
☎ 035 640241

Woodworking Museum
Via Papa Giovanni XXIII
Open: all year, Saturday 3-6pm; Sunday 9.30am-12noon, 3-6pm.
☎ 035 554411

Grotte del Sogne
Open: by request only.
☎ 035 251233

Thermal Waters
Open: all year, 8am-12noon, 3.30-6.30pm.
☎ 0345 224455

SEDRINA
Grotte delle Meraviglie
Closed for restoration at time of writing. Ring for details.
☎ 035 251233

ZOGNO
Museum
Open: all year, Thursday & Sunday 3-6pm. ☎ 0345 91083

VALTELLINA

APRICA
Museum Open: by request only.
☎ 0342 746162

CHIESA
Museum
Open: July-August, Wedesday 5pm-7pm; September-June, Saturday 4.30-6.30pm.
☎ 0342 451150

MORBEGNO
Natural History Museum
Open: Tuesday, Thursday & Saturday 2.30-5.30pm.
☎ 0342 612451

PONTE IN VALTELLINA
Diocesan Museum
Attached to parish church of San Maurizio. Entry by request.
☎ 0342 482158

Ethnography Museum
Attached to school in Via Ginnasio. Entry by request.
☎ 0342 482158

SONDRIO
Valley Museum
Villa Lavizzari, 27 Via Quadrio
Open: Tuesday-Saturday 10am-12noon, 3-6pm.
☎ 0342 566269

Natural History Musem
Via Rogazzi del'99
Open: Tuesday-Saturday 2.30-5.30pm.

TEGLIO
Palazzo Besta
Open: May-September Tuesday-Saturday 9am-12noon, 2-5pm; October-April Tuesday-Saturday 8am-2pm. ☎ 0342 781218

TIRANO
Museum
Open: June-September, Tuesday-Sunday 10am-12noon, 3.30-6.30pm; October-May, Saturday 10am-12noon, 3-6pm.
☎ 0342 701181

8. Around Brescia

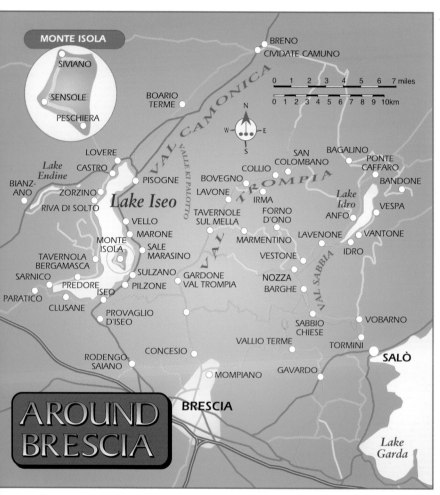

BRESCIA

The capital of the province that bears its name, Brescia is Lombardy's second city, with around 195,000 inhabitants. It sits at the mouth of the Val Trompia, built at the base of two of the last hills of the pre-Alps (here known as the Brescian Alps) as the mountains make their last sweep down to the Lombardian plain.

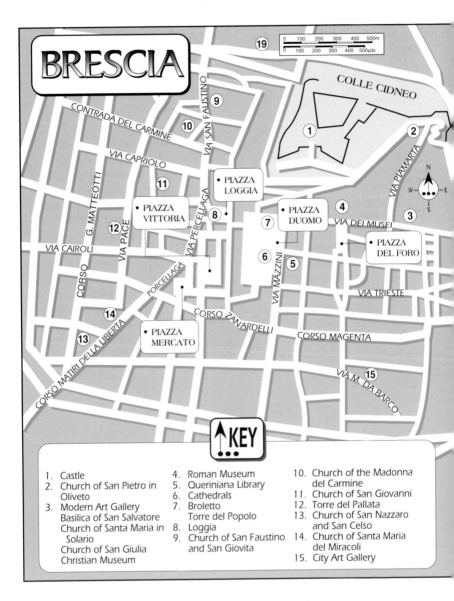

KEY

1. Castle
2. Church of San Pietro in Oliveto
3. Modern Art Gallery
   Basilica of San Salvatore
   Church of Santa Maria in Solario
   Church of San Giulia
   Christian Museum
4. Roman Museum
5. Queriniana Library
6. Cathedrals
7. Broletto
   Torre del Popolo
8. Loggia
9. Church of San Faustino and San Giovita
10. Church of the Madonna del Carmine
11. Church of San Giovanni
12. Torre del Pallata
13. Church of San Nazzaro and San Celso
14. Church of Santa Maria del Miracoli
15. City Art Gallery

WALKING TOUR

What is given here is an itinerary that allows the visitor to see what are, by common consent, the major Brescian buildings and art works, though those who explore the town will find that much of interest has, of necessity, been excluded.

The Castle

Starting at the top (on Colle Cidneo, the oldest part of the town), the castle is the first building to be visited. Although, at first glance, it seems to be a single structure, it is in fact a complex array of buildings dating from the first century. Roman remains of a temple and later fortification works are preserved, as are the remains of a fifth-century church to San Stefano. There is a Byzantine arch from the same period, and the Mirabella Tower is from the thirteenth century – though even this has been constructed on a Roman base. The castle itself was started by the Viscontis in the fourteenth century, with additions and modifications right through to the sixteenth century.

Within the castle buildings are two museums. One of these is devoted to the Risorgimento. The other is the **Luigi Marzoli Museum of Arms**, one of the finest collections of its kind in Europe, and a fitting reminder of Brescia's ancient industry, though the arms are not restricted to the medieval period.

The Grande Miglio

Brescia's **Risorgimento Museum** is housed in a part of the castle known as the 'Grande Miglio', the Great Mile – now almost the only link with the Mille Miglia, the 'Thousand Miles', a car race around Italy starting from Brescia which was famous in its day, finally being stopped in 1957 when car speeds had increased to the point where spectator and driver deaths had become alarming. Since 1977 a nostalgic re-enactment of the race has started, as the original did, in May from Piazza Vittoria. While a museum in the old monastery of Sant' Eutemia explores the race's history.

The castle stands in a large and very good park, landscaped into a garden. From the grounds go eastward across the hill to the **church of San Pietro in Oliveto** from where the view is excellent. The church, twelfth-century, is delightfully sited, surrounded by olive trees, and has two very fine sixteenth-century cloisters. From the church go south down Via Piamarta, which has the remains of the town's only surviving Roman gate, dating from the first century.

Via dei Musei

Go left at Via dei Musei, soon reaching the remains of a first century AD Roman theatre which once stood at the edge of the Roman forum. Beyond are the remains of the Capitoline Temple built in AD73 by the Emperor Vespasian but lost under a landslide and rediscovered only in 1823. Though heavily restored, what remains of the steps and colonnade is excellent.

The **Museo della Cittá** is housed in the convent of Santa Giulia. There was a Benedictine nunnery on this site from AD753 when Desiderius, the last King of the Lombards, or his wife Ansa, founded one dedicated to San Salvatore.

The present complex actually consists of several linked religious buildings, the whole being of such importance that it is on the UNESCO list as being worthy of special preservation. The **basilica of San Salvatore** has sections dating from the eighth century, including traces of Carolingian frecoes, but is most famous for its medieval crypt, stonework and excellent medieval cloisters. The twelfth century **church of Santa Maria** in Solario has superb sixteenth-century frescoes, as has the Nuns' Choir in the **church of Santa Giulia**.

The convent now houses collections covering the history of the city. The Roman section includes a bronze

Winged Victory – probably gilded in its original form – of the first century AD. The wings and draped clothing are beautifully worked, and it is intriguing to speculate what was once held in the outstretched hands.

There are also six bronze portraits of the emperor from the second and third centuries, as well as stone and mosaic work from the site.

The early Christian collection has many relics from the convent, all of great historical interest. Several pieces are, however, not only rare and priceless, but of immense beauty. The **Lipsanoteca** is an ivory reliquary dating from the fourth-century and restored to its original form in the twentieth century. The smooth slabs of ivory are included in place of missing slabs. The reliefs on the box show scenes from the Old and New Testaments. The lid is closed with a medieval lock.

The **Cross of Desiderius** dates from the time of the founder, or a little later, but includes a painted glass cameo from the third or fourth century. The cross is gold, inlaid with semi-precious stones and coloured glass, and is a major work of art. Equally beautiful is a series of ivory diptychs, each is two leaves of ivory hinged together: diptychs were given to officials appointed to high public office. One of the museum's examples dates from the fifth century.

These two main collections are supplemented with many others which, together with the churches themselves, make the Museo della Città one of the finest museums in the lakes area.

Piazza Duomo

From Via dei Musei it is a short step to Piazza Duomo in which stand the city's two cathedrals. North of the cathedrals, but still in the *piazza*, is the **Broletto**, the thirteenth-century town hall, above which is Brescia's oldest tower, the **Torre del Popolo** – the People's Tower.

The Broletto was replaced as town hall in the fifteenth century by the **Loggia** that stands in Piazza Loggia, due west from the Broletto.

The Two Cathedrals

Brescia has two cathedrals, the Old (the Rotonda or Duomo Vecchio) and New (Duomo Nuovo). The **Rotonda**, is late eleventh-century in Romanesque-Gothic style but with an interesting circular design, austere enough to pass for a fortress rather than a cathedral. It is an interesting building, not obviously beautiful but certainly imposing. Inside there are some interesting works of art, including a reliquary with sections of the True Cross and a Holy Thorn. But everywhere inside, the curved walls allow that imposing exterior to reach the mind.

The **Duomo Nuovo** is sixteenth-century (Baroque), constructed of white marble and with a now green lead dome. Though started in the sixteenth century the building was not completed until the dome was finished in 1825, though there is no lack of wholeness. Inside, the cathedral is cold, almost bleak, with few treasures.

Piazza Loggia

On the western corner of Piazza Loggia is the Loggia, a masterpiece of

Above: The Capitoline Temple, Brescia

Right: The Loggia, Brescia

Renaissance architecture. The contrast of the ground floor arches, first floor windows and the decorated balustrade gives the building a beauty that is enhanced by the use of white marble. The roof is new, built in the mid-eighteenth century to replace the original which was burned down in a fire of 1575.

The southern side of the square has what looks like an early, smaller version of the Loggia, the Monte di Pietà Vecchio. In the façade of this Renaissance building (of the sixteenth century) is a collection of inscribed Roman stones, so many in fact, that it could be viewed as an outpost of the Roman Museum.

147

Continuing from
Piazza Loggia

From the Loggia, go northward along Via San Faustino, to reach the **church of San Faustino and San Giovita**, dedicated to the patron saints of the city. Inside there are excellent paintings, but the church is known chiefly for the frescoes of Giando-menico Tiepolo depicting stories from the saints' lives.

Go back along the same street – at the patron saint's feast day it is a thronging mass of people – and enter Contrada del Carmine to see the **church of the Madonna del Carmine**, considered one of the finest examples of fifteenth-century Lombardian Gothic architecture. The church is in brick, a most striking material, studded with coloured ceramic, and this innovative use of materials is carried on inside where there is a piece of monumental sculpture known as a *Deposition*, in multicoloured terracotta, also dating from the fifteenth century.

South from the church, but best reached by returning down the Via San Faustino, is the **church of San Giovanni** in Contrada San Giovanni, a narrow street going south from Via Capriolo. The church contains a series of altarpieces by Moretto and Romanino, sixteenth-century Brescian artists, one of the true treasures of Brescian art.

Nearby, in Via Pace, is the **Torre della Pallata**, the Pallata Tower, which dominates the city at this point. The tower is thirteenth century, buttressed in the fifteenth century. A fountain at its base takes the edge off its bulk.

Now follow the Via Cairoli, a road with a large number of fine *palazzi*, chiefly of the eighteenth century, interspersed with lighter, arcaded houses from as early as the fifteenth century. Turning left into Corso Giacomo Matteotti, continue to the **church of San Nazzaro and San Celso**, a lovely eighteenth-century building containing paintings by Moretto, and a polyptych by Titian which is a true masterpiece. Close by, in Corso Martiri della Liberta is the **church of Santa Maria del Miracoli**, a fine Renaissance church in Botticino marble with excellent relief sculptures both inside and out.

A right turn from Via Percellaga, a continuation of Corso Martiri della Liberta, leads to the **Piazza Mercato**, flanked by sixteenth-century porticoes, with statues and an array of elegant buildings. Then go eastward to Corso Zanardelli, with the **Grand Theatre** to the left and the Tourist Office to the right, behind the pavement café.

Other Museums

Those not already satiated by museums might also like to visit the city's **Natural History Museum**, a new building in Via Ozanam, or the **Museum of Musical Instruments** in Via Trieste which has a good collection of guitars and violins, as well as other instruments. The **Association of Art and Spirituality** shows contemporary art with a religious theme, while the **Diocesian Museum** has a fine collection of older religious art. Finally there are two interesting photography museums, the '**Ken Damy**' which has contemporary works and the **National Museum** which has both contemporary and historical collections.

Straight on is Corso Magenta, and turns right and then left lead to Via Martinengo da Barco where the **City Art Gallery** is housed in the Palazzo Martinengo da Barco, a sixteenth-century building, restored a century later, behind the Lebanon cypresses. The art gallery contains work by Raphael and Tintoretto, as well as other great masters, and many masters of the Brescia school.

From Brescia three parallel valleys, running north-south, can be reached, two containing lakes. These are dealt with from west to east.

LAKE ISEO
& VAL CAMONICA

From Brescia the N510 main road goes direct to Iseo town and the lake that bears its name. Those preferring the *autostrada*, or arriving on it from farther afield, take the Palazzolo exit, head north and arrive at the lakeside village of Paratico from where a drive around the southern lake shore reaches Iseo.

The road from Brescia passes through **Rodengo-Saiano** where there is an architecturally important fifteenth-century Cluniac abbey with frescoes by Brescian artists and friezes in multi-coloured ceramics. The abbey is currently being restored by the Italian Government, and when complete will be a deserving addition to the list of 'places to visit'. Further on, at **Provaglio d'Iseo**, there is a Romanesque church with fifteenth-century frescoes, while above the village to the north is the church of the Madonna del Carno, interesting in its own right, and offering the first and one of the finest views of the lake.

LAKE ISEO

Lake Iseo is the fifth largest of the northern lakes, being 15 miles (24km)

long and 3 miles (5km) wide at its widest point. However, at that widest point the lake is almost filled by Monte Isola, the largest island in any of the lakes, or in any lake in Europe, at over 2 miles (3km) long and about 1.25 miles (2km) wide. The lake narrows down to only 0.5 mile (1km) towards the northern end, but those tempted to swim it should bear in mind that it is around 250m (820ft) deep at its deepest. Although it is possible to drown in only a few metres of water if things go wrong, these depths do seem to have a psychological effect.

Natural Scenery

At the southern end, as the lake ends onto the plain, there is a large peat bog, the 'Torbiere', famed for its water-lilies and marsh weeds. The marshland is a protected area for wildlife and is also important archaeologically, having yielded evidence of pile-mounted lake dwellings.

Elsewhere too, the lake surround is famous for its plant life, its sheltered position between two high mountain ridges helping to provide an ideal climate for plant growth. At the northern end, the high ridges on the edge of the lake actually fall into the water as high cliffs, producing some of the most spectacular scenery on any of the lakes.

A TOUR AROUND
LAKE ISEO

The tour starts at the village of **Iseo**, an outstanding holiday resort with, at the Sassabonek, a tourist centre which is the most impressive of any of the resorts visited. In addition to the normal rectangular swimming pool, there is a circular one which is irresistible. Elsewhere the village has much of interest, a twelfth-century church with a Romanesque campanile, and the remains of the Oldofredi Castle, now incorporated into a village community centre. There is also a small war museum here.

From Iseo a winding road climbs up the mountain ridge that borders the lake's eastern shore, crossing the Passo del Tre Termini and making its way through a series of pretty villages down into the Val Trompia. This route goes instead along the lakeside road to **Pilzone**.

PILZONE

The village is inland from a small headland liberally sprinkled with hotels and camping sites, but is itself small and quiet. Beyond the headland the view northward is dominated by Monte Isola, which can be reached by the lake steamer from **Sulzano**, an excellent sailing centre. The village has some lovely houses, gathered together in delightful streets, close to the lake edge with the wooded cliffs of Monte Isola making a compelling background to views of the lake.

At the back of the town there is a cobbled street leading off up the mountain, taking the visitor through a series of beautifully set small villages and, finally, at 3,165ft (965m), reaching the fifteenth-century **church of Santa Maria del Giogo**.

The view from the top of the ridge (which dips then rises again to Monte Rodondone) over the top of Monte Isola to the western shore and the northern section of the lake is excellent, and none the less satisfying for having been so easily achieved.

The village of Iseo on Lake Iseo

Sulzano

MONTE ISOLA

Those who take the short boat trip across the lake to Monte Isola are immediately surprised by its quietness, the reason for which becomes clear the moment they start along the street of Peschiera Maraglio. There are no cars!

Peschiera is a fishing village (only tourism representing a sizeable alternative industry on the island) and has that timeless air that characterises fishing

---

Monte Isola

Monte Isola is not an island in the accepted sense, consisting of one giant mountain, pushed 1,310ft (400m) out of the lake (the peak is 1,970ft (600m) above sea level), but the lake surface is itself at about 620ft (190m). In places the peak, which has a plateau summit, drops so steeply that the tree cover cannot always cling to the slope, and white streaks of cliff are exposed. Perched on top of the island peak, half hidden among the chestnut trees, is the **church of the Madonna della Ceriola**, a place of pilgrimage for centuries.

The view from the peak is, of course, expansive, but those with limited time (and energy) may choose to spend it instead on a walk from Peschiera Maraglio to Sensole, Siviano or on to Carzano, from each of which boats return around the island to Sulzano. From Carzano boats also cross to Sale Marasino, from where a return boat crosses the channel between island and mainland to reach Peschiera. This trip offers a close-up view of the steepest of the island's cliffs.

ports. Elsewhere the villages are similar, little collections of red-tiled houses on each side of narrow, cobbled streets, the villages linked by lanes that wind through chestnut woods, olive groves and vineyards. There is also a museum of Fishing.

At **Sensole** there are the ruins of a fifteenth-century Oldofredi castle, while **Siviano** has a Martinengo tower from the same period. Flowers have encroached on these places, on virtually every square centimetre of bare soil. In spring the island is yellow with broom, in autumn purple with heather and in between countless shades with countless flowers. Small wonder the island has been so loved by painters.

RETURNING TO THE MAINLAND

Back on the mainland the road leads to **Sale Marasino**, a pleasant village dominated by its beautiful eighteenth-century church. The church interior is as fine as its exterior. Near the lakeside there is the **Villa Martinengo** standing in excellent gardens which contain the remains of a first-century Roman villa.

From Sale Marasino a track leads up through the terraces on the hillside to the top of Punta Almana at 4,560ft (1,391m). Not surprisingly this is a good viewpoint, but the walk, at 5 miles (8km) and around 3,610ft (1,100m) requires enthusiasm and considerable time.

Beyond Sale Marasino there are excellent beaches and good camping sites up to **Marone**, where there are the ruins of an early Roman villa and, housed in the local library, a fine collection of photographs which are the work of a local photographer, Lorenzo Antonio Predali, taken during the first half of this century.

From the village a road into the mountains allows access to some excellent walking country, and also to **Zone**, a beautifully set village in a valley of beech and fir woods.

The Erosion Pyramids

The best of the sights on Lake Iseo near Zone are to be found just below the village of **Cislano**, at an obvious hairpin bend with limited parking to the right. Here are the *piramidi di erosione*. Uneven glacial erosion, caused by the layering of the strata, has created eerie pillars of earthy conglomerate some tens of metres high.At first glance they look like termite nests, but invariably they are topped by a granite boulder, precariously balanced. Though not unique in alpine Europe, this collection of pyramids is reckoned to be the best and offers one of the most unusual views that will be encountered.

Vello is another pleasant little fishing port beyond which the road excavates a way through the almost sheer cliffs of the Corna Trentapassi, emerging only briefly to offer a tantalising glimpse of the Bögn di Zorzino on the western lake shore.

Beyond is **Pisogne**, the gateway to Val Camonica, a town dominated by a fourteenth-century tower, the Torre del Vescovo, which is the town's symbol. There is a pretty square, with porticoed surrounds and the **church of Santa Maria della Neve** which is famous as the poor man's Sistine Chapel, such are the quality of the frescoes by the artist Romanino.

From Pisogne a road leads to the terrace of Fraine, with good views of the Val Camonica, and on up the **Valle di Palotto**, in the upper reaches of which there is a good winter sports area.

The Val Camonica now leads off towards the High Alps, to points beyond the scope of this book. This route will follow it only as far as Capo di Ponte and the **National Park of Rock Engravings**. But first it crosses the valley to go down the west side of Lake Iseo.

LAKE ISEO'S WESTERN SHORE

Lovere

On the western shore the first town is Lovere, second only to Iseo as a tourist resort on the lake. It is a delightful place, built on terraces so that it seems to tumble down the hill slopes into the lake. It is also very old – on Monte Cala are the remains of a Celtic fort from the fourth or third century BC. Not surprisingly, the rest of the town's buildings are considerably younger, though still old, and very interesting.

There are three towers, the Alghisi and the Soca from the thirteenth century and another from the fourteenth century, and a number of very interesting churches.

The **Palazzo Tadini** dates from the nineteenth century, a fine building holding the Galleria dell'Accademia Tadini, a small gallery of paintings, sculpture, ceramics and some arms. The *palazzo* is open to the public, both for the collection and also for a summer season of concerts. For those with good Italian there are also lectures.

The terraced nature of the town makes it ideal for walking – odd perspectives and angles are continuously

cropping up – and the area around the town is also good for exploring. Most visitors passing through eventually feel the tug of the Bögn, but before giving in to it, a short excursion, about 6 miles (10km), can be made to the tiny **Lake Endine**, tucked away in the **Val Cavallina**.

***

Lake Endine

This is a very secluded lake with a minimum of tourist amenities, but in a superb setting. Just the place for those who really want to be away from the mainstream, to discover Italy quietly and at their own pace.

***

Castro and Riva di Solto

Instead of following the main road to Lake Endine, turn off for **Castro** to find an ancient, once-fortified town sheltering under its long-empty *rocca*. There is a wealth of steep, narrow streets and an old, ruined tower. Beyond is the Bögn of Castro, the first of the two Bögns. The Bögns are huge sheets of limestone plunging vertically from the slopes of Monte Clemo into the lake. The second, the Bögn of Zorzino, creates its own enclosed bay. Some people believe the Bögns are best viewed from across the lake, but although such cliffs are foreshortened at close range, and the full form cannot be grasped, their size and power can be better appreciated.

Beyond the second Bögn is **Riva di Solto**, a picturesque fishing village beyond which the road is excellent, with views to Monte Isola and the slopes of Monte Creo, which advances on the road and eventually smothers it, forcing it to disappear into a tunnel.

The extraordinary erosion pyramids near the village of Zone are the finest example of their type in Europe

Heading South

Opposite Monte Isola is **Tavernola Bergamasca** with a few forlorn ruins of a fourteenth-century castle tower. From the village a road goes up into the hills, to the villages of **Parzanica**, only comparatively recently reached by road and still unspoilt, and **Vigolo** with good views of the lake. Good views are also available from the Punta del Carno, where the lake has an elbow. Near here is a natural well, known as the 'Giant's Pot'.

Beyond is **Predore**, noted for its vineyards and also for the numerous archaeological finds, chiefly Roman, made in the area. The town also has the ruins of a castle, and a curious tower which was cut in half in the fourteenth century.

Sarnico is a terminus for the lake steamer and will be well known to enthusiasts of motor boat racing. Factories here make good boats, and the lake at this point is used for international competitions and record breaking attempts. The town's architecture is a mixture, with the remains of old fortifications, a centre consisting of old buildings typical of the lake's fishing ports, and some works by Sommarciga, a major Italian art nouveau architect.

Return to Iseo is now made through **Paratico**, where, it is said, Dante once stayed in the now ruined castle, and Clusane, a village noted for its roast lake tench – *tinca al farno con polenta* – and with the Castello del Carmagnola, a fifteenth-century castle.

VAL CAMONICA

Returning to Pisogne, an exploration of the Val Camonica can begin. In the valley, through which the Oglio river flows, the first place of consequence reached is **Boario Terme**, a town that has built up, like the spas of England, around its thermal springs.

The Healing Waters of Boario

There are four springs supplying warm, min-eralised water to the Thermal Establishment – a fine building set in magnificent, wooded parkland – for use in various ways to treat a variety of ailments. The spa is Italy's third biggest and specialises in liver and intestinal problems.

Also at Boario, or rather near to it, the famous rock engravings begin, the first being visible in **Parco di Luine**. The valley became famous when the first of the engravings (into the relatively soft Permian sandstone) was discovered, fame that grew rapidly to international status when the extent and age of the works was realised. Today almost 200,000 individual works have been catalogued, the engravings showing a range of subjects, but chiefly hunting scenes, scenes from ordinary life and religious themes.

The Naquane Rock in the **Parco della Incisioni Rupestiri** – the National Rock Engravings Park – has 900 figures carved on it. In age the carvings cover some 8,000 years from the Neolithic era through to Roman times, a truly amazing depiction of life as civilisation dawned. In 1979 UNESCO gave the site international protection as being of world importance.

The National Park is centred on **Capo di Ponte**, where the study centre for the carvings was set up in the 1960s. There is also a museum and exhibition of the carvings, while the Archeodromo reproduces village life from the time of the major carvings.

Between Boario Terme and Capo di Ponte there are several villages of interest. **Cividate Camuno** was the valley's chief town in Roman times and contains excellent remains of that period, some displayed in the town museum.

Breno is the valley's most important town today, set in the valley below a fourteenth-century castle which still has complete towers and, every school-child's dream – real underground dungeons. The key to their door can be borrowed from the town hall! In the church of Sant' Antonio and in the *Duomo* there are fine frescoes, while the town museum has much of interest from the local area, including some carvings.

VAL TROMPIA

The Val Trompia is immediately north of Brescia. Indeed, the Mella river which flows through the valley, also flows through the western part of the city, and the ridges which form the valley only fall onto the plain as the outskirts of Brescia are reached. Val Trompia runs parallel to Val Camonica, separated by the ridge of Monte Guglielmo, and crossed only once, to the south, by the road from Iseo which runs over the Tre Termini Pass to Concesio.

NORTH OF BRESCIA

The road to Val Trompia passes the Trebbi Botanical Garden, at **Mompiano** on the outskirts of Brescia, and has a fine collection of plants and can be visited on request. Further on, **Concesio** is the valley's first town, and is famous as the birthplace of Pope Paul VI. Beyond the town the valley is quite industrialised as far as **Sarezzo**, and to Lumezzane in a side valley (the Val Gobbia) from Sarezzo.

From Lumezzane a road links to the Val Sabbia. The industrial valley here is famous for its metal working, producing high-quality cutlery and kitchenware. This industry is a link with the history of Val Trompia, and specifically the next town, **Gardone Val Trompia**, which was once famous for the making of arms and armour.

Gardone Val Trompia

Today Gardone is world famous for the production of firearms, especially hunting guns. The arms industry here was first started by the Venetians, and another side to the Republic's influence can be seen in the **church of Santa Maria degli Angeli**, a fine, cloistered church, which has a number of paintings by artists of the Venetian school. The local Brescian school is also represented, the church's frescoes being by Paolo da Brescia.

North of Gardone

Val Trompia proper, from a tourist's point of view, starts at Brozzo. From there the valley (named from the Triumplini, a Celtic tribe that lived among the Ligurian Alps) is a landscape artist's dream: an array of greens, more than can be counted or appreciated; orchards of apples, plums and cherries; and a sprinkling of copses and larger woods, chiefly of chestnut trees.

Tavernole sul Mella is the ancient capital of the valley, and from it **Marmentino** can be reached, a lovely village set in lush meadows with chestnut and beech woods. In winter the skiing is good, though facilities are

lacking. The same comment can be made of **Pezzaze** and **Pezzoro** which are reached from the valley village of **Lavane**. In summer they make good starting points for walking on Monte Guglielmo, (6,400ft/1,950m).

Beyond Lavone a side valley can be followed to **Irma**, a clean, neat village in a magnificent position with expansive views to blue hills and walks over flower-studded meadows or through pine forests. **Bovegno**, at a height of 2,460ft (750m) as the valley begins to rise steeply, is equally well sited, and here some of the houses have more than a hint of the Tyrol to add a picturesque touch. Pineta Park has lovely pine woods to stroll in, and the church of San Giorgio has some interesting wood carvings.

At **Collio** the Mella river is a fast flowing stream of clear water running over a rock-strewn bed with mossy stones and wooded banks. The village itself is beautiful with white houses and red roofs, geraniums in the niches of old walls, blue pine woods in the background and meadows of startling green – their terraces sharply drawn by shadows. The village is a winter sports centre and has a cable car to a higher plateau, as well a a ski jump.

Beyond, **San Colombano** is the last valley village, another centre for winter sports. From there, torturous roads lead north to link with Val Camonica at Breno, and south to Val Sabbia at Anfo on Lake Idro.

VAL SABBIA AND LAKE IDRO

The Val Sabbia runs from Gavardo (a town on the main road from Brescia) to Saló on Lake Garda, and on to Ponte Caffaro at the northern end of Lake Idro. The Chiese river flows through the valley both feeding and draining Lake Idro. It is a valley of considerable scenic interest, with the added advantage of having a lake. As with Val Trompia, Val Sabbia is a place for the walker and the country enthusiast, although Lake Idro does add an extra dimension to a visit.

Gavardo, where the valley starts, is a pleasant town, split in half by the Chiese which appears to wash the foundations of the houses on both its banks. The town museum deals with the history of the Grotte mountains to the north of the town, mountains that form the western side of the valley and which separate Val Sabbia from Val Trompia. It has prehistoric and Roman items, and a skeleton of a cave bear.

From Gavardo the main road follows the valley, but a minor road on the opposite side of the river leads to Vallio Terme, a spa town whose mineral waters are used chiefly in the treatment of kidney and liver complaints. The spa's hydropathic centre is open from April to October. The water is also bottled locally and is available for sale.

At Tormini the main road divides, the right fork going to Salo and Lake Garda, the left continuing along the eastern bank of the Chiese. The route follows the left road to Vobarno, which has the remains of a medieval castle, and a bridge dating from the mid-sixteenth century of Venetian construction. The town is one of the valley's chief industrial centres.

NORTH OF SABBIO CHIESE

Beyond Sabbio Chiese the valley narrows: at Barghe the church has been built into the rocks of the mountain ridge, so close does it encroach; and roads from Barghe, on both sides of the valley, lead to beautifully set mountain villages which offer spectacular views and excellent walking.

Nozza is the old capital of the valley, while nearby Vestone still has

Sabbio Chiese's *Rocca*

Sabbio Chiese has a natural fortress, a *rocca*, that was once topped by a medieval castle, but is now transformed (in best swords into ploughshares fashion) into two churches. That might not seem so unusual, but here the churches are one on top of the other! There is a single campanile, still with the fish-tail crenellations so popular on the Lake Garda castles. The rocca also houses a museum of farming with a collection illustrating the development of techniques in the valley.

Mountain Villages

From Vestone, roads again lead off to the mountains on both sides of the valley, the road north going to a series of beautiful villages. One, Forno d'Ono, is probably the most picturesque of all the mountain villages, nestling below a gorge carved by a mountain stream and surrounded by meadows. In the Italian sunlight, which always seems so bright and 'clean', the shadows in the gorge and on the meadow terracing paint the most evocative pictures.

The spa buildings at Boario Terme

the valley's most important market on the first Monday in the month. Also here are the Ruscino Botanical Gardens, which include many plants local to the Val Sabbia.

Lavenone has a wonderful collection of very rich houses and considerable scenic attractiveness. Just beyond the village the jagged peaks of Corna Zeno and Corna Alta dominate the valleys of the Abbioccolo and Canale to the left (north), while soon Idro unfolds ahead.

Idro is the highest lake in Lombardy at 1,207ft (368m) above sea level and is 7 miles (11km) long, reaching 1.25 miles (2km) wide, and with a maximum depth of 1,200ft (368m). In places on its shore the surrounding mountains fall so steeply into it that from a distance they seem to rise straight out of the water. Despite that, there is a road, in one place tunnelled, along its western bank, the eastern bank being only sparsely populated.

The village of **Idro** is off the main road at the point where the Chiese river leaves the lake, and further along the western shore are the new villages of **Vantone** and **Vespa**. The first has several good camping sites, and from the second the visitor can walk to Prato della Fame, where the rocky backbone of Monte Calva dips into the lake and from where the lake views are the finest. From Vantone a road leads into the mountains to several good villages and the mountain-enfolded Lake Valvestino – all very fine walking country.

THE WESTERN SHORE OF LAKE IDRO

Travelling up the western shore from Idro, **Anfo** is found about half way along, built on a terrace sloping down to the lake. Nearby, the private castle on the Rocca d'Anfo was built by the Venetian Republic and was the headquarters of Garibaldi's forces in 1866. The church of Sant' Antonio has a twelfth-century campanile and contains some good paintings, including a set of Renaissance frescoes.

Beyond Anfo a road off left can be taken to **Bagolino**, a beautiful village of narrow streets and piled-up houses, thought by many to be the most picturesque village in the Val Sabbia, though, strictly, lying in a side valley. It also has, in the fifteenth-century church of San Rocco, one of the most important churches in the whole valley, the importance lying in the fine series of frescoes by da Cemmo.

Ponte Caffaro is the last village of Val Sabbia. Here are the ruins of the **castle of Santa Barbara** from which there are lovely views of the interesting 'quadri' squares on the Pian d'Oneda. The plain was reclaimed by Benedictine monks in the tenth century and is very fertile. In 1861 it was divided into lots, each separated from its neighbour by an irrigation ditch, which gives it its curious pattern. A better view is obtained by leaving the main road beyond Ponte Caffaro, crossing the Caffaro and Chiese rivers and going to Trentino's first village, Baitoni, and on to **Bondone**. From there both the Pian, the lake and the upper Chiese valley can be seen.

Border River

Today when visitors cross the Caffaro, one of the Lake Idro's inflowing rivers, they enter Trentino. Until 1918 the river marked the boundary not between two of Italy's regions, but between Italy and Austria.

BRESCIA

**Association of Art
and Spirituality**
9 Via A Monti
Open: all year, Saturday &
Sunday 4-7pm.
☎ 030 3753002

Castle Park
Colle Cidneo
Open: all year, daily 8am-8pm.

**City Museum
(Museo della Cittá)**
81b Via dei Musei
Open: June-September, Tuesday-
Sunday 10am-6pm; October-May,
Tuesday-Sunday 9.30am-5.30pm.
☎ 030 2977834

City Art Gallery
*Palazzo Martinengo da Barco,
1 Via Martinengo da Barco*
Open: June-September, Tuesday-
Sunday 10am-1pm, 2.30-6pm;
October-May, Tuesday-Sunday
9.30am-1pm, 2.30-5pm.
☎ 030 3774999

Diocesian Museum
13 Via Gasparo da Salò
Open: All year Tuesday-Sunday
10am-12noon, 3-6pm.
☎ 030 40233

**'Ken Damy' Museum of
Contemporary Photography**
22 Corsetto S Agata
Open: all year, Tuesday-
Sunday 3.30-7.30pm.
☎ 030 3750295

Luigi Marzoli Museum of Arms
Castle, Colle Cidneo
Open: June-September, Tuesday-
Sunday 10am-1pm, 2-6pm;
October-May, Tuesday-Sunday
9.30am-1pm, 2.30-5pm.
☎ 030 293292

Mille Miglia Museum
*Sant' Eutemia Monastery,
Via della Rimembranta, 3*

Open: all year, Tuesday-Sunday
9am-6pm. ☎ 030 3753418

Museum of Musical Instruments
34 Via Trieste
Open: all year, Monday-Friday
2.30-7.30pm.
☎ 030 3776040

**National Museum of
Photography**
16b Corso Matteotti
Open: All year Saturday 10am-
12noon, 3-6pm, Sunday 10am-
12noon, 4-7pm.
☎ 030 49137

Natural History Museum
4 Via Ozanam
Open: all year, daily 9am-5pm.
☎ 030 2978672

Risorgimento Museum
Castle, Colle Cidneo
Open: June-September, Tuesday-
Sunday 10am-5pm; October-
May, Tuesday-Sunday 9.30am-
1pm, 2.30-5pm.
☎ 030 44176

LAKE ISEO AND VAL CAMONICA

BOARIO TERME
Parco di Luine
Open: All year Tuesday-Sunday
9am-12noon,2-6pm (1-5pm from
October-March)
☎ 0348 7374467

CAPO DI PONTE
**Centre for the Study of the
Prehistory of Valcamonica**
7 Via G Marconi
Open: all year, Monday-
Friday 9am-4pm.
☎ 0364 42091

**Archeodromo (Museum of
Prehistoric Art and Life)**
4 Via Pieve San Siro
Open: all year, Monday-Friday
8am-4pm. ☎ 0364 42148

**National Park of
Rock Engravings**
Open: Tuesday-Sunday 8.30am-
7.30pm (4.30pm October-
February). Guided tours
available. ☎ 0364 42140 (Park)
or 42080 (Tourist Office)

CIVIDATE CAMUNO
Museum of Val Camonica
29 Via Roma
Open: all year, Tuesday-Sunday
8.30am-2pm. ☎ 0364 44301

ISEO
War Museum
Castello Oldofredi
Open: All year Saturday and
Sunday 9am-12noon, 3-6pm
☎ 030 980341

LOVERE
Tadini Gallery
Open: May-September, Monday-
Friday 3-6pm; Saturday &
Sunday 10am-12noon, 3-6pm.
☎ 035 960132

MARONE
Photographic Collection
c/o Public Library, 42 Via Roma
Open: All year Monday &
Wednesday 2-4.30pm, 6.15-7pm.
☎ 030 9877077

MONTE ISOLA
Museum of Fishing
Peschiera
Open: May-July, September,

Saturday & Sunday 10.30am-
5.30pm, August, daily 10am-
6pm. ☎ 030 9825226

VAL TROMPIA

MOMPIANO
Trebbi Botanical Gardens
119 Via Montini
Open: by request only.
☎ 030 2007704

VAL SABBIA

GAVARDO
Archaeological Museum
2 Piazza S Bernardino
Open: all year, Monday 8.30am-
12.30pm, 2-5pm, Tuesday,
Wednesday & Thursday 8.30am-
12.30pm, Friday 8.30am-
12.30pm, 8.30-11.30pm.
☎ 0365 371474

SABBIO CHIESE
Museum of Farming
Open: By request only, May-
September, Saturday and Sunday
2-6pm. ☎ 0365 85375 or 85127

Rocca
Open: By request only, Saturday
& Sunday 2-6pm.
☎ 0365 85168/85119

VESTONE
Ruscino Botanical Gardens
Open: by request only.
☎ 0365 81138 or 0365 81714

LAKE STEAMERS

On Lake Iseo, ferries leave the Sarnico terminus for Clusane, Predore,
Iseo, Sulzano, Tavernola Bergamasca, four ports on Monte Isola –
Sensole, Siviano, Carzano and Peschiera Maraglio – Sale Marasino,
Marone, Riva di Solto, Castro, Lovere and Pisogne. A full round trip,
including a visit to Monte Isola, takes about 4 hours, which gives some
idea of the size of one of the smallest northern lakes. ☎ 035 971483

At 145sq miles (370sq km), Lake Garda is the largest of the Italian lakes. The shallow shoreline in the south produces excellent beaches which, coupled with the area's very mild climate (in part due to the huge volume of water that acts like a storage radiator), its closeness to large population centres and its distance from the other large lakes means that the entire perimeter of the lake's southern shore seems to have been taken over by holidaymakers.

Do not let that observation deter you from visiting however. The near Mediterranean climate is of itself worth a trip, and it also encourages a luxuriant and very varied plant growth. The southern lake has much of interest and, in Sirmione, one of the most extraordinary towns on any of the lakes visited. The northern tip of the lake cut fjord-like into its enclosing hills is also worthwhile, the backdrop of hills to the blue lake waters never failing to stir the imagination.

SOUTHERN LAKE GARDA

DESENZANO DEL GARDA

The lake tour begins at Desenzano del Garda on the main railway from Milan to Venice, which has its own exit from the A4 *autostrada*. Desenzano also has a pleasant little harbour, being an important terminus for the lake steamers.

A stroll along the tree-lined lake front should take in the old quay. Desenzano has two quays, a large modern one that is the terminus for the lake steamers and an older one that nudges its way into the town. The latter is an absolute must, it is the most picturesque place in town and one of the best old ports on the lake.

If time permits, do also try to visit the **Duomo of Santa Maria Magdalene**, dating from the late sixteenth century and including a notable, and dramatic, painting of the Last Supper by the eighteenth-century Venetian artist G B Tiepolo. Try also to reach the archaeological museum to the east of the harbours which explores the local area's history from prehistoric times.

Away from the lake, some 2½ miles (4km) further on is **Lonato**, perched on a hill with a fine view of Desenzano. There is much of interest crammed into this typically airy but small town. It has a cathedral with a fine dome beside an excellent central *piazza*. The tenth century *rocca* is worth visiting for its remains and views. In addition to the remains are the **Casa del Podestà**, which has a library of 40,000 books, some of great rarity and the **Fondazione da Como** (named after an Italian senator who renovated the Casa), containing frescoes and antique furniture. Also of interest is an **ornithological museum** with over 700 specimens.

On the other side of Desenzano (to the east) and again inland, are two sites,

Roman Desenzano

The Roman link is strong here in Desenzano, the remains of a third-century AD **Roman villa** having been discovered not far from the harbour. Finest of the remains are the very large multi-coloured mosaics that have been compared favourably to those at Pompeii. Next to the villa a small museum contains some finds from the site, together with other items from a locally excavated prehistoric site. Of particular interest is the collection of very early Christian glassware.

The Roman link is maintained at **Capo la Terra**, the higher part of the town, where there are remains of a **castle**, constructed spasmodically from the thirteenth to the fifteenth centuries to guard against attacks by marauders from the north. The castle stands on the remains of a Roman fort, so the strategic merits of this spot must have been obvious 1,000 years ago. The Romans had a market here, chiefly for grain, and Desenzano held its position as an important market town right through to its time under Venetian rule.

Even today there is a market every Tuesday – a good day to come to absorb the atmosphere of the lively, small-town Italian market.

close to each other and historically inseparable, which is a must for all those interested in the Napoleonic campaigns.

At **San Martino della Battaglia**, on the 24 June (Midsummer's Day) 1859, a Piemontean army under Vittorio Emanuele II defeated the right wing of the Austrian army, while a short distance to the south at Solferino, Napoléon III crushed the main body of the Austrians, a victory commemorated in name by a bridge over the Seine in Paris. The day had few equals in the Wars of Italian Independence, but it also has a significance that was even more far-reaching as the Red Cross was set up as a direct result of the suffering of survivors of the battle at nearby **Solferino**.

SIRMIONE

Returning to the lakeside it seems impossible to escape from images of war, because the castle at Sirmione is another. However, one is soon to be distracted from grim thoughts by the beauties of the Sirmione peninsula. It starts straightforwardly enough, with a drive from the village of Colombare, but travelling about 2 miles (3km) to the end, it narrows remarkably down to a mere 400ft (120m) wide in places. Eventually drivers must leave their cars and walk to the town, because although the bridge connecting with the end of the peninsula is of car width, the town excludes all but essential vehicles.

Even though the bridge takes the visitor into the town, it feels as if you are actually entering the **Scaligeri Castle** which dominates the view rightwards.

Beside the castle is the town, which occupies about half of the 180 acres (70 or so hectares) that the peninsula's head comprises. Into that small area are packed an astonishing variety of things.

The Battle of Solferino and the Red Cross

On Midsummer's Day in 1859, while the battle of Solferino raged, J Henri Dunant, a Swiss traveller, was holidaying near the southern shores of Lake Garda. After the battle he visited the field and was appalled by the sufferings of the wounded of both sides. In the stiffling heat many were dying due to the lack of adequate medical care, and many that would survive were, he felt, being unnecessarily tortured by neglect.

Dunant wrote an account, *Souvenir of Solferino*, which was published in 1862. This account of the aftermath of the battle was instrumental in the setting up of the International Red Cross, and a memorial was erected at Solferino in 1959, the centenary of the battle. The memorial, of marble sent by nations from all over the world, stands beside the *rocca*, a huge tower built by the Scaligeri much earlier than the battle, in 1022, though restored in the early seventeenth century.

In contrast the round tower of San Martino does commemorate the battle. It is 210ft (64m) high and houses a museum with exhibits on the campaign that led to Solferino. From the top, the view over the Lombardian plain is excellent. Each of the sites has an ossuary – a sad reminder of suffering even if one of the world's finest charities was a direct result of it – and a museum.

For the sunlover there is a fine beach; the athletic can enjoy windsurfing or tennis, or wile away a more leisurely hour in one of the pedalo boats which characterise all the lakes; while the village explorer finds an abundance of narrow streets. There is also an international congress centre and a **thermal spa.**

The spa uses natural hot water from a spring on the bed of the lake (here only 65ft, 20m, down) at 158°F (70°C) to treat muscular ailments and sinus problems. Indeed there is a centre that is world famous for its treatment of a specific form (rhinogenous) of deafness.

Also worthy of note is the **church of San Pietro in Mavino**, built in the eighth century on the site of a pagan temple. It is beautifully positioned among the trees and has some fine thirteenth- and fourteenth-century frescoes. Outside is a bell monument to the dead and wounded of all wars.

Scaligeri Castle

The Scaligeri built both the castle and the town walls in the fifteenth century when they were lords of Verona, using Roman foundations for their fortress. Inside, the castle retains the machinery for a drawbridge, and the near perfect preservation of the upper battlements gives a good idea of the method of protection, by sentinel post and removable foot-bridges.

The castle, which also includes an embattled quay, must by sheer position have defended the entire southern end of the lake. It is an enchanting building, the fish-tail shaped battlements giving it a fairy tale quality, the archetypal child's castle.

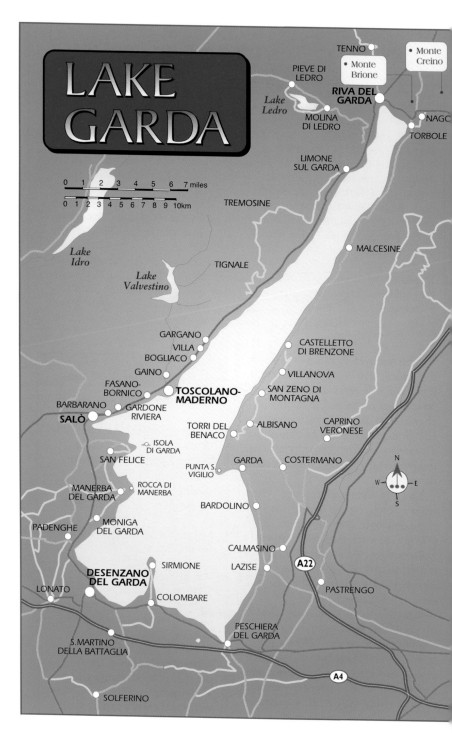

Catullus, the First Love Poet

Catullus, the greatest of Rome's lyrical poets, was born in Verona in about 84BC and is thought to have had a villa at Sirmione. Catullus is credited by some experts with the invention of the love poem, his works being dedicated to 'Lesbia', a married woman with whom he had an unsatisfactory love affair. He is said to have died of a broken heart at the age of 30 when Lesbia finally rejected him.

At the end of Sirmione's peninsula there are the romantic remains of either a large Roman villa or a public baths with water piped in from the natural hot spring. The remains are known as the Grotto of Catullus after the great poet who had a villa on the peninsula, and wrote glowingly of it several times, but there is no hard evidence to link him with this specific site. A small museum holds the best of the excavated finds.

PESCHIERA DEL GARDA

Continuing eastward along the lake from Sirmione, the visitor soon crosses the border from Lombardy to Veneto reaching, at Peschiera del Garda, the start of the 'Olive Tree Riviera', the name given to that part of the shoreline of Lake Garda which lies within Veneto.

Peschiera today is a pretty town with pleasant gardens to relax in, a fine multi-arched bridge across the Mincio and several good Renaissance buildings. The Austrian defences are interesting, and be sure to watch the hour chimed on the town hall clock in the main square, by the beaks of two bronze eagles. It is also a good place to explore

Scaligeri Castle, Sirmione

167

Peschiera has been fortified since earliest times. The Romans had a presence here, and in medieval times there was a castle and a walled harbour, proof of the importance of the site where the Mincio river leaves the lake. The castle was demolished and the wall made extra strong during the time of the Austrian occupation when the town formed part of the occupying army's primary defence, a quadrilateral with, at its corners, Peschiera, Verona, Legnago and Mantua. It is the ruins of those defences that now encompass the town.

In 1917, King Vittorio Emanuele III came here with allied commanders and decided to hold the Piave line (pivoted around Peschiera) to the last man.

the wine growing area of Lugana which lies to the south.

Also south, about 5 miles (8km), is the **Villa Sigurta** with a large, superbly laid out park that can be toured either by car, along specially prepared roads, or on foot. There are fine lawns, ponds and grottoes, the whole having been conceived by Count Sigurta over the last half century, as an example of peace and brotherhood through nature.

After crossing the river, turn northward to follow the eastern shore of Lake Garda, driving along the Gardesana Orientale.

THE EASTERN SHORE

LAZISE

On the shore line Lazise is the first town reached after going past several pleasant villages and an attractive line of camp sites – the whole eastern shoreline is, virtually, a beach to one side, a camp site to the other – each with good beaches, and sunsets, behind the hills that hem in Val Trompia, which are themselves worth a trip to Italy. Especially good is **Pacengo** which also has a church with some fine paintings.

Lazise is both impressive and charming, with parts of the old arched and embattled town wall on three sides, the lake on the fourth and the still strong

Children's Favourites

The first spots visited on the eastern side of the lake are not actually on the lakeside. Just outside Peschiera, on the road to Lazise, is **Gardaland**, with numerous rides which are free after paying the entrance fee. Further on towards Lazise is the **Caneva World** with a large variety of water chutes and pools. The nearby Caneva Movie Studios offer a glimpse of the world of cinema studios. Inland, at **Pastrengo**, is the **Parc Natura Viva**, with a conventional, driveable safari park area, a zoo and a model dinosaur park. South of Peschiera, near Valeggio Sul Mincio are the **Altomincio Acquapark** and the **Parco Acquatico Cavour**, each with a great collection of water chutes, pools and other water-based activities.

remains of a castle of the Scaligeri. The castle is private and cannot be visited. One interesting point here is the use of fish-tail battlements, and the delightful continuation of their use in one of the lakeside buildings.

From this castle a chain could be drawn across the harbour mouth, the town being known as 'The Key to the Lake' by the Venetian Republic who maintained warships here. The quayside itself is delightful, an array of small boats with a backdrop, from the church side, of fine tall buildings, each, in typical fashion, with a balcony.

Above Lazise, on the road through Vallesana, is **Calmasine**, a pretty village worth the detour for its view out over Lazise to the lake, with the peninsula of Sirmione in sharp relief and the hills north of Brescia on the skyline.

BARDOLINO

Alternatively, continue along the Gardesana Orientale to reach Bardolino, which also had a castle, the tower of which now forms part of a hotel. Bardolino is famous for its wine, and the vineyards from which it is produced spread up the hillside (too far south to be Monte Baldo as yet) that rises not too steeply here.

The whole of the town and its surrounding area lives up to the name of Olive Riviera: not only are there olives and vines, but also avenues of cypresses and other trees which crowd in on roads and houses alike.

The village contains five churches, each of considerable interest, but if time is limited then be sure to visit **San Zeno**, a tiny building dating from the eighth century, and **San Severo**, a magnificent eleventh-century building.

As would be expected on this holiday riviera, the holidaymaker is well catered for. The harbour area provides good sport and there is a good beach for swimming. In the town centre, the main street has a row of shops specialising in the necessities of beach life along one side, while the opposite side of the street is equipped with a line of typically Italian cafés and restaurants, some with road (rather than pavement) seating, to the confusion of the motorist.

GARDA TO TORRI DEI BENACO

North again are two huge lumps of rock, like the humps on a camel though flatter on the top, the larger of which has given its name to both the town and the lake at its foot, for this is the *rocca* of **Garda**. Not surprisingly the rock was used as a fortress from earliest

Garda's Rocca & Adelheid

In the tenth century the castle on Monte Garda was the most important and formidable on the lake. At that time much of Lombardy and Veneto was controlled by Berenger II, King of Piemonte. Berenger was a ruthless man who defeated another local king, Lothar, in battle and then, to reinforce his control of Lothar's lands, decided to marry Adelheid, his widow. When Adelheid declined his offer Berenger imprisoned her in the castle. Using a trusted servant, Adelheid had a message of help delivered to the German Emperor Otto. Otto brought an army south, defeated Berenger, married Adelheid and was crowned head of the Holy Roman Empire.

times. Today the visitor who walks up (allow about 45 minutes) is treated to a stunning view, can wander through a luxuriant natural garden, and gaze at all that remains of the final castle.

In the town at the base of the *rocca* there is a hotel named after Queen Adelheid, and the Palazzo del Capitani which was once occupied by the Captains of the Lake – an imposing building, arched at ground level. Look too for **Villa Albertini**, a romantic, castle-like villa where the treaty for the annexation of Lombardy to Piemonte was received by King Carlos Alberto in 1848, a prelude to the Risorgimento. Close to the town a series of important prehistoric rock engravings were discovered near Punta San Vigilio. Those tempted to look for the real thing at the Point should note that they are very, very difficult to find.

Outside **Costermano**, a village on the hill above Garda, is a German war cemetery, holding 22,000 German soldiers of World War II. It is a most moving place where lie, not enemies, but fellow humans.

ON TO MALCESINE

Next stop on the shoreline is **Torri del Benaco**, yet another Scaligeri castle and, again in keeping with its southern neighbours, the site has been fortified virtually continuously since Roman times. The castle still has attached to it part of the old town walls, which give a delightful period quality to the town and its picturesque harbour. Like the other towns on the eastern shore, however, this one has made significant concessions to tourism.

The lake's only car-ferry links Torri to Maderno, and there is a panoramic view of the town as you approach, of the castle, red-tiled houses, the backdrop of trees and the ridges of Monte Baldo.

Equally lovely is the view from **Albisano**, a village set on the hill above Torri, and reached by a winding road from the lakeside. An even better view, taking in almost the entire lake, (though not directly of Torri del Benaco) can be seen from **San Zeno di Montagna** about 4 miles (6km) further on along another winding road.

Continuing along the road from San Zeno, through a collection of little hamlets (from **Villanova** the energetic enthusiast can walk/scramble to the *orrido* (gorge) of Sandolino) the

Punta San Vigilio

The lake at Garda is a bay formed by the hooked nose of land poking out into the water to the north of the town. This is Punta San Vigilio, one of the highlights of any tour of Lake Garda. At the tip of the nose of land are a little church and the private sixteenth-century Villa Guarienti. The church is dedicated to San Vigilio of course – a simple, dignified building, a statue in a niche in the wall which is only visible from across the water.

The church and villa stand among tall, dark cypresses, the whole vision mirrored in the calm lake waters. Equally lovely is the view from the tip, either south across the bay to Garda, or westward, across the lake to Manerba and Gardone. Alternatively, on the northern side of the tip, the secluded Serene Bay offers marvellous views, with a beautiful mixture of greens and blues.

Above: Peschiera del Garda

Below: Garda and its rocca

visitor can reach **Castelletto di Brenzone** direct. The coast road is pleasant, but the views from the higher road make the detour worthwhile, though some will want to backtrack a few hundred metres to visit the twelfth-century church of San Zeno (not be be confused with the hill village of that name) – a romantically sited building.

Castelletto is the first of a collection of villages which are known collectively as Brenzone, though that name – said to derive from Bruncione, one of Charlemagne's paladins – is usually applied to Porta, the largest of the collection, about 2.5 miles (4km) north of Castelletto. However, Castelletto is probably the nicest, an ancient village retaining its character.

The **Piazza dell'Olivio** is almost too good to be true – tall trees, balconies covered in flowers and creepers, arched entrances, external staircases, shuttered windows – all the elements of the essential lake village.

MALCESINE

The last of the towns of the eastern shore that lie in Veneto, **Malcesine** is among the most famous, and offers the most interesting itinerary of any on the Olive Riviera. It also offers the most spectacular view, with its impressive Scaligeri castle, a huge, almost complete building perched right at the lake edge with a tall square central tower that dominates the town from any direction.

The approach to the town gives a very good view of the castle, and also of the Val di Sogno, a peaceful valley with flowers and fine villas. Offshore is Isola Val di Sogno, the Island of the Valley of Dreams.

Malcesine is a wonderful place, beloved over centuries by writers and artists. It is an apparently haphazard array of excellent buildings; unexpected eruptions of tall shady trees; a picturesque harbour almost totally enclosed and lined on two sides by arcaded, balconied buildings; and over everything the castle, tier upon tier of white stone, embattled walls and towers, competing for height with dark green cypresses and winning, finally, with the tower. From the tower the view to the town is worth every step of the climb.

The **castle**, built in the early fourteenth century, houses the **Museum of**

Johann Wolfgang Goethe and Malcesine

Be sure to find the stone dedicated to J W Goethe – there can be few towns anywhere which have raised a memorial to an arrest. The arrest occurred on 13 September 1786 when Johann Wolfgang Goethe visited Italy for the first time. At that time the border between Austria and Italy lay between Torbole and Malcesine, so on present day terms Goethe was already in Italy as he made his way from one town to the other.

In Malcesine he was impressed by the castle and paused to sketch it. He was seen, and promptly arrested as an Austrian spy, having no small difficulty in proving his innocence as a citizen of the Republic of Frankfurt. When he was released the great man saw the funny side of it all, writing a humorous account in his *Italian Tour*. The castle's **Pariani Museum** deals with Goethe's visit.

Monte Baldo

Monte Baldo, on Lake Garda's eastern shore, is occasionally known as the 'Botanical Garden of Italy' because of the variety and profusion of species which grow on its flanks. Two parks, the **Lastoni Selva Pezzi** and the **Gardesana Orientale**, have been set up to protect the plant life. The former is at the base of the ridge, the latter higher up, the plant species changing as altitude increases. In the lower park there are olive groves, then holm oak and Mediterranean pine, while higher up is a rich collection of alpine flower species.

Monte Baldo boasts three species which are unique to the high ridge: the anemone *Anemone baldensis*; the bedstraw *Galium baldensis;* and the speedwell *Veronica bonorata.*

Each park is crossed by way-marked paths – a map of these is available at the Information Centre – though the paths through the higher park do necessitate taking the cable car and some high-level walking.

building with its pillars and arcaded windows. Also do not miss the view across to the tiny Island of Olives.

In Via Novene Vecchia, which lies almost directly inland from the castle, the visitor can take a 30-minute ride in a cable car that rises 5,410ft (1,650m) to the flank of Monte Baldo. At the top of the *funivia* the visitor is only 1,475ft (450m) and 4 miles (6km) from the actual high point of the long, steeply sided ridge along a well used path. The last part of the ridge is rocky so great caution should be exercised, but the views are spectacular. Many however, settle for the more immediate panorama from the cable car terminus.

NORTH OF MALCESINE

Beyond Malcesine the Gardesana Orientale follows the lake edge, hugged on its eastern side by the steep wooded flank of Monte Baldo, so tightly in places that the road engineers had to resort to tunnelling. There are villages though, and a row of camping sites each with its own beach. Between Casello and Piano di Tempesta (where, until 1918 when some of the Tyrol was transferred to Italy, the route would have crossed into Austria) the visitor now crosses into Trentino, leaving Veneto and its Riviera of Olives.

Torbole

The first town in Trentino is Torbole, on the eastern bank of the Sarca river which is Garda's main feeder. The approach is a great sight, the Gardesana Orientale has reached its northern limit and the road turns westward towards the town, which lies on flat land broken by wedges of white rock as the pre-Alps to the north descend into the lake. The lake here is very deep, the enclosing ridges giving it a fjord-like appearance, and is, at this northern

the Lake, and among its exhibits are models and drawings of the transportation of Venetian war galleys across land for launching at Torbole.

Within the town any walk will pay dividends, but find time to see the fifteenth-century **Palazzo dei Capitani**, the palace of the Venetian Captains of the Lake near the quay, which is now the town hall, a most impressive extremity, excellent for sailing and wind-surfing. The sailors take advantage of the consistent winds – blowing from the north in the morning, from the south in the afternoon.

The town is grouped around its main port (there are several other quays and landing stages) and in its older parts is very picturesque.

It was from Torbole that Goethe sailed to Malcesine and arrest. A plaque below a medallion image of the writer notes the visit, a memorial to the fact that it was here, Goethe maintained, that he began to write *Iphigenia*. Be sure also to visit the public gardens, for a peaceful stroll in the shade of olive trees beside a quiet stream.

Equally peaceful is a walk in **Nago**, a quiet village behind Torbole in which to escape the bustle of the larger town. There you can visit the Marmitte dei Giganti, the **Giant's Pots**, a dozen smooth hollows scoured out by the action of whirling glacial meltwater.

Venetian War Galleys

In 1424 Milan and Venice went to war, Milan advancing east to besiege Brescia and Verona. To outflank the attackers Venice decided to launch a fleet of war-ships at Torbole, but there were no ships there. They therefore put ships on ox carts and towed them from Venice to the River Adige. From there the ships were rowed upstream to Roverto, towed to Lago di Loppio, sailed across and dismantled so they could be hauled over the San Giovanni Pass to Torbole. After a journey of three months the ships were finally floated on Lake Garda. The fleet, still barely serviceable, was sailed south and totally defeated by a fleet the Milanese had constructed at Maderno. But though the Venetians lost the battle they went on to win the war.

Malcesine & Monte Baldo from Eremo di'Montecastello, Tignale

The castle at Malcesine is the most distinctive on Lake Garda

passed, the road rounding and finally breaking through the rock mass.

Riva is the largest town at the northern end of the lake, though not as big as Desenzano where the tour started. Not only is it large – especially in comparison with the smaller, more manageable villages of the Olive Riviera – it is also very prosperous, a prosperity which it carries in sophisticated rather than gaudy style.

Riva is the most popular holiday centre with the largest number of tourists (the lake is sometimes an astonishing sight, such is the profusion and colourfulness of the windsurfers) and as a result, has the largest number of hotels, cafés etc, but it does retain much of its fishing/trading port atmosphere. Nowhere is this better seen than in the main square that fronts onto the lakeside – the water laps at your feet as

Also, stroll among the ruins of **Penede Castle**, almost returned now to nature, but offering good viewpoints for Torbole and the lake.

Another viewpoint should also not be missed, it is reached by taking the short but winding road to the top of Monte Brione, the wedge-shaped ridge on the opposite side of the Sarca. The panorama from there is very interesting as well as being expansive – the Sarca valley can be seen, as can the valley of Lake Loppio giving access to the *autostrada* for the Brenner Pass – and is the best of any on the northern end of the lake.

THE WESTERN SHORE

RIVA DEL GARDA

Only 2½ miles (4km) and the Sarca river separate Torbole from Riva del Garda, though Riva is not visible until the wedge of **Monte Brione** has been

Enjoying a lakeside promenade at Salò

you contemplate the port, its quays angled to provide a safe haven.

The square is the **Piazza Tre Novembre** and it is dominated by the huge but simple **Torre Apponale**, a clock tower from the thirteenth century. The **Palazzo Pretorio** is a century newer and the **Palazzo Communale** is a century later again. Between them are medieval arches and porticos. Elsewhere parts of the old town wall, as well as three wall towers, have been incorporated into newer buildings.

Riva's *Rocca*

Only a step away from the main square is the **moated castle**, the *rocca*, built by the Scaligeri in the twelfth century, though altered on several occasions, to defend the town against lake-borne pirates rather than land-borne adventurers. The castle is open to visitors and includes a museum in which are many of the artefacts from the Lake Ledro lake dwellings as well as interesting exhibits on the history of the town. There is also a permanent exhibition of paintings. The *rocca's* approach, over a double-arched bridge and old drawbridge, is utterly irresistible.

Also in connection with Lake Ledro, it is worth noticing the Ponale Hydroelectric Power Station in Riva, powered by water from that lake, which is brought along a pipe 4 miles (6km) long. A more exciting fall of water is to be seen about 2.5 miles (4km) north of Riva beside the road to **Tenno**. Here the

Cascata del Varonne falls nearly 300ft (almost 90m) in two leaps, each in a tightly enclosed, dark gorge that amplifies the noise and concentrates the spray.

There are the ruins of a medieval castle at Tenno and a museum of old agricultural machinery. Close by, **Canale** is one of the best preserved medieval villages in the area.

Northwards, but still within the town, on Via Roma (the road to Arco) is the **church of the Inviolate** with an octagonal interior in baroque style and containing stucco and gilded work of considerable interest. The ceiling of the octagonal cupola is especially good.

A little way south of Riva, on the road along the lake's western shore, the **Bastione** is topped by an early sixteenth-century round tower built by the Venetians, and from which there are excellent panoramic views. This outcrop, and others around Riva, were fortified by the Austrians during World War I, and though the artillery was ordered not to shell the town when the Italian army advanced in 1915, it was badly damaged by the fighting. Fortunately, much that is interesting has survived.

SOUTH OF RIVA

The road south from Riva is the **Gardesana Occidentale**, a fine road that bores its way innumerable times through the steep cliffs that fall into the lake and delivers the traveller speedily to his chosen spot on the lakeside. The first chosen spot on this route is soon after the *funivia*, where an older road that also tunnels its way southwards is followed.

After the second tunnel the road heads up the valley of the Ponale river passing, almost immediately, the noted, but frankly disappointing Cascata del Ponale. The gorge of the river itself is

Bronze-age Lake Dwellings

At the pleasant village of **Molina di Ledro** there is, near the lake shore, a small **museum** that deals with the lake dwellings found near the village during construction work, in 1929, for the pipeline to the hydro-electric station at Riva. If the power station demands more water than the lake inflow it supplies, the fall in the lake level reveals some of the nearly 15,000 wooden stakes that the lake dwellings comprised. The site, and another found more recently, are now confidently ascribed to the Bronze Age. Altogether this is a most interesting site.

much less disappointing, the road being on a shelf cut out from the rock.

Lake Ledro itself, though small, is about 2 miles long and, on average, $\frac{1}{2}$ a mile wide (3km by 1km). It is a beautiful lake, well sited among high hills, but with a wide enough valley to give flat land at the shoreline so there is ample space for several good camping sites and beaches. **Pieve de Ledro**, at the opposite end of the lake from Molina, is the valley's holiday resort, a pleasant village with good sports facilities.

Back on the Gardesana Occidentale (which can only be regained by returning along the same road, though it is, of course, straightforward to continue from Lake Ledro into the upper Val Sabbia and down to Lake Idro) the drive south is through a succession of tunnels. The entrance to one marks the boundary between Trentino and the Brescian province of Lombardy, and is where the route crosses into the Riviera del Garda.

LIMONE SUL GARDA

Limone has a beautiful old quarter associated with the old fishing port, with picturesque houses, arches, window boxes, balconies and shutters all piled on top of each other. And above it all are the white cliffs of Cima di Mughera, speckled with plant life in many shades of green.

Today Limone has expanded outwards from the old fishing port, reaching across two rivers, the Pura and San Giovanni torrents, between which, up on the hill, is the **church of San Pietro**. This formerly stood in a village, where now there is only an olive grove. It is an ancient church and on one outside wall notable events in the history of the village are inscribed, remembering the pestilence of 1630, the poor olive harvest of 1822, the cold winter of 1857, but not the death of the community it served.

The First Lemons

Limone sul Garda is probably named after the lemon trees which, it is believed, were grown here for the first time in Europe. The name could, however, derive from the town's position on the border between Austria and Italy, or from the name of a son of the lake god Benacus.

Lemons still grow here, in terraces overlooking the lake and in numerous greenhouses which they share with oranges and mandarins. Elsewhere there are olive groves and other trees typical of Mediterranean areas, indicative of a very good climate.

COPPA VERSIGLIANA

Pavement café, Riva del Garda

TREMOSINE & TIGNALE

From Limone a road above the Gardesana Occidentale leads to Tremosine and Tignale, collections of small villages on plateaux apparently hewn out of the high rocks of the pre-Alps.

The Church of Madonna di Montecastello in Tignale

The Scaligeri, masters of Verona, built a castle on a rock above the village of Gárdola on Tignale. When this was destroyed a church was raised on the site after a series of miracles occurred at the nearby chapel. Today, the sanctuary of Madonna di Montecastello is famed for the view and its art treasures. Four paintings on copper are attributed to Palma the Younger while the fresco of *The Coronation of the Virgin* is by the school of Giotto but, some experts believe it is actually by the master himself.

This is one of the most beautiful areas anywhere on Garda. There are meadows full of flowers, with dairy farms, some making and selling butter and cheese, gentle wooded slopes, huge rock faces (the village of **Pieve** is perched right on the edge of a precipice and from the lake it seems to hang in space) and waterfalls. It is an ancient landscape – evidence of Etruscans and Gauls have been discovered – and full

advantage of its timeless qualities can be taken by following any of a series of waymarked trails that crisscross the ridges and valleys.

Details of these are on a pamphlet issued by the Tourist Offices at Gargnano and Limone, as well as in Tignale and Tremosine themselves. It is advisable to obtain the leaflet because some of the routes, though well marked, are for experienced walkers only, and also because it has a good panoramic map of the area. Since the plateaux also have good restaurants and excellent sports facilities, they can be recommended as excellent holiday centres.

GARGNANO

From either the high plateaux or the Gardesana Occidentale, the visitor will arrive at Gargnano, a well known and well loved sailing town – the **Centomiglia sailing competition** brings boats from all over Europe to the lake here in September. The winds on Lake Garda are dependable, but the lake does also suffer from spasmodic winds that bring cool air down from the pre-Alps and Dolomites.

These winds, and the more continuous morning and afternoon winds, seem more persistent than on the other lakes and Garda appears more rarely to be flat calm. For the sailors this is a bonus, though not for some residents. One patch of green, set among high cliffs and, before the road, provisioned by boat alone, was known as 'Hungry Meadow' because the lake's fierce winter winds prevented boats from landing.

One of most interesting aspects of Gargnano is the array of terraced citrus orchards beside the town, eager farmers having pressed every last square centimetre of soil into service. Equally good is the **Franciscan monastery**, dating from the thirteenth and fourteenth centuries, with a fine cloister.

From the village a road leads to Val Toscolano and Lake Valvestino, named after the valley beyond it. From the lake's northern end a road winds down to Lake Idro, another which winds even more, can be used to explore the lonely, isolated villages of Valvestino itself. The valleys are excellent and the lake (dammed and used as a source of hydro-electric power) well set, but the area does not have the beauty of the high plateaux that have already been visited.

Back in Gargnano, walk along the lake shore, admiring the lines of the **Villa Feltrinelli**, home to the Italian government during the time of the Salò Republic. Mussolini himself stayed in another villa of the Feltrinelli family also in the town, which is now home to foreign students from the University of Milan when they attend summer courses in the Italian language.

The Marks of Battle

The sixteenth-century town hall in Gargnano still bears the marks of an Austrian bombardment of 1886. Cannon balls and a stone memorial bear witness to this event.

On the lakeside are locals who grow fruit on the hillside terraces and bring it here to sell. No fruit tastes better than the sun-warmed, fresh and ripe fruit from these stalls.

Away from the lakeside the town has older, picturesque areas. In one alley the houses are bridged at first floor level, the visitor walking under a

succession of stone arches, each with its own light, and everywhere the window boxes are alive with colour.

Within the commune of Gargnano are several outlying villages. In one of these, **Bogliaco,** is the **Villa Bettoni,** an eighteenth-century building of immense size and majestic lines that contains an art gallery with a collection of art from the same period. The villa is open to visitors on request and is worth visiting for the array of statuary in the gardens. Another lakeside village, **Villa,** was visited by D H Lawrence who, it is claimed, was inspired by his stay to write *Lady Chatterley's Lover.*

TOSCOLANO-MADERNO TO GARDONE

The next town is, in fact, two – Toscolano, of Etruscan origin, now linked to Maderno, of Roman origin, across the diameter of a circular blob of land thrust into the lake about 3 miles (5km) south of Bogliaco's Villa Bettoni.

From Toscolano, which is reached first (a village famous for its paper mills: there is now an interesting museum to the industry), a road leading up the valley of the Toscolano river reaches **Gaino,** an excellent viewpoint. The river has partly helped create the button of land that supports the two villages, but its aid has created fertile, rather than picturesque land. The villages have turned this to advantage, every spare piece of soil having been utilised in the growing of trees or shrubs, adding a real garden feel to any walk.

Maderno is the terminal port for the lake's car ferry (from Torri Benaco), but has much more than that to offer any visitor. The **basilica of Sant' Andrea** is a fine twelfth-century Romanesque building, with some Byzantine additions, and contains the painting, *The Vir-*

gin and the Angel, by Paolo Veneziano.

Across from the church is an Ionic column topped by the winged lion of St Mark, Maderno being the only village of Lake Garda that retains such a memory of the rule of the Venetians. Also nearby is a statue of Sant' Ercolano, on an extremely tall pedestal, now only the local patron saint, but once the protector of the lake and its voyagers.

Beyond Maderno is a small bay created by the Toscolano-Maderno semi-circle, and a similar but smaller combination of towns which is **Fasano-Bornico**. This is a pleasant town and the only one that historians agree definitely existed as such in Roman times.

Next comes **Gardone Riviera** marking one end of a much more defined bay, the Gulf of Salò. It must have become apparent that the Riviera del Garda on the western shore is more sheltered and hence has a better climate for plant life than Veneto's Riviera of Olives. The climate was noted in the late nineteenth century by Dr Ludovic Rohden, a German expert in climate, who did much to popularise the area. So famous did it become that the Austrian Emperor had the Villa Alba built here in 1904, though he never actually stayed in, or visited, it.

GARDONE RIVIERA

Any lingering doubts on the climate will be cast aside with a walk through the parks of Gardone or, indeed, on any walk at all through the town. But most of all it is obvious at the **Hruska Botanical Gardens**, named after Dr Arthur Hruska who lived here until his death in 1971, where 2,000 varieties of plants and flowers thrive, and where there are the finest rock-gardens in Italy, if not in Europe.

The gardens have now been taken over by the artist André Heller who has added works which combine art and ecology. No visit to Gardone, or for that matter to Lake Garda itself, should fail to include a visit to the gardens, which are in **Via Roma** that leads off northwards from Corso Zanardelli near Piazza Marconi, close to the steamer landing stage.

Those who follow Via Roma will eventually reach the Vittoriale degli Italiani, though it is easier to go directly along Via Panoramica which leaves the lake road just north of the Torre San Marco – a fine tower.

Il Vittoriale was bought and extended by Gabriele d'Annunzio and is open to the public. It contains many mild surprises, together with the odd major one. At one point, between the

D'Annunzio and *Il Vittoriale*

Gabriele d'Annunzio was one of Italy's larger-than-life historical figures. He was a poet with a verse style that has been described by words from sensuous to decadent. He was also leader of the disastrous campaign to occupy Fiume (Rijeka) when Italy lost part of Istria in 1919. In his will d'Annunzio left *Il Vittoriale* to the state. It is a collection of buildings, many in Art Nouveau style, and an open air theatre.

D'Annunzio's old house is much as he left it – he disliked daylight and painted most of the windows black – and visitors can also see his mausoleum, built in as flamboyant a style as the man who now occupies it.

(cont'd on page 184)

Limone sul Garda

cypresses, there is a ship, the *Puglia* – no ordinary ship, being in part original and in part stone. The ship recalls the expedition to Fiume. The ships captain, though sadly wounded, succeeded in rescuing some of D'Annunzio's men. In hospital the captain ignored medical advice and removed bandages to inspect his wounds – and promptly died. D'Annunzio approved of such gallantry.

Elsewhere there is a magnificent open-air theatre. This, together with the concert hall, is administered by the Fondazione del Vittoriale, and regular festivals are held in the summer months.

Throughout the grounds there are memorials to d'Annunzio, including his tomb at the top of a hugely elaborate, three concentric-ringed mausoleum that also holds the tombs of several of his war comrades. In addition, the villa is a museum to the man, poet and soldier.

A walk along the Gardone lakeside is one of the great pleasures of a trip to Lake Garda, but the town has much more than such good, but conventional, pleasures. The Barbarano stream which runs into the western edge of the town can be followed back to the hills, through little gorges and over little falls, past old iron forges and the occasional water-wheel.

At **San Michele** a detour can be made to the tiny church, set among hills crowned with chestnut trees. And even when the Barbarano is finally crossed, the town of **Salò**, lying at the back edge of the square lake gulf that bears its name, is equally elegant.

First however, between the San Michelle and Salò, is the **Palazzo Martinengo**, a sixteenth-century villa that played a part, in the latter part of that century, in the tale of murder and intrigue that is recalled in John Webster's play *The White Devil*. The *palazzo*, named after a Brescian family whose name is synonymous with the history of that city, is open to visitors who request permission in writing.

SALÒ AND THE SOUTH

Salò, beyond the *palazzo*, has a fine **cathedral**, built in Gothic style in the fifteenth century, with a now familiar dome. Inside, it is a towering combination of dark stone and colourful paintings, with a floor of an unusual, but very effective, geometric design. Some of the artwork is both excellent and of historical interest.

As if to maintain its reputation for diversity, Salò has two other claims to fame. The brothers Bertolotti lived here, both musicians, and one of whose sons was Gasparo da Salò who is credited with having invented the violin. An excellent statue of the great man at work on a violin can be seen on the first floor of the sixteenth-century **Palazzo Municipale**, the town hall.

Centuries later Salò was created capital of its own republic (the Republic of Salò) which was formed by Mussolini towards the end of World War II when the Italian Fascist state had collapsed and Il Duce's world was crumbling.

Aside from these tales, Salò is an excellent place to wander around, another town that makes the most of its considerable assets of climate and position. The **Palazzo Fantoni**, near the cathedral, houses the **Biblioteca Atenco**, a library with a great number of rare books.

The Salò Republic

Italy's involvement in the 1939-45 War was largely the work of Mussolini, popular feeling never genuinely supporting the campaigns in Albania and Greece. When half the 100,000 soldiers sent to fight on the Russian front died the anti-Fascist movement grew and when, in 1943, Sicily was invaded Mussolini was forced from power. With the new Italian government poised to change sides, Germany poured troops into Italy and established Mussolini as head of a puppet 'republic' centred on Salò. However, the Salò Republic was short-lived and the escaping Mussolini was caught and executed by partisans on the shores of Lake Como.

Closer to the lake, in the fourteenth-century **Palazzo del Capitano Rettore** attached to the town hall, the Town Museum houses exhibits of Salò's history.

Quite a different museum is the **Museo Storico 'Nastro Azzuro'**, the museum of the history of the blue ribbon – all Italian gallantry awards are gold with a blue ribbon. The museum follows the history of the Italian army from Napoleonic times to World War II.

From Salò the main road leaves the lake, making directly for Desenzano, but there is merit in taking the minor road that stays close to the shore. Between Porto Portese and San Felice del Benaco the view is dominated by Isola di Garda, the lake's largest island, on which is a magnificent villa set in equally good gardens – shades of Isola Bella. The villa is private property though, which can only be viewed from afar, either from the lakeside or from a round-the-island boat trip.

In **San Felice**, at the head of the Valtens (a valley running parallel to the lake shore) the sanctuary of Madonna di Carmine has fine fifteenth and sixteenth-century frescoes, recently and lovingly restored. At **Manerba del Garda** there is a rocky headland offering fine views over the lake, the *rocca* being known (not a compliment) as Dante's profile! Manerba also has a museum of local archaeology.

Moniga del Garda has a wonderful little port (take advantage, it is the last) and a medieval castle, while at nearby **Padenghe** there is a castle within the walls of which houses have been built, so that it now appears as a hill-top walled hamlet.

Opposite page: Statue of Gasparo da Salò

SOUTHERN SHORE

DESENZANO DEL GARDA
Archaeological Museum
Chiostro Santa Maria de Senioribus, 22 Via Anelli
Open: all year, Tuesday and Friday-Sunday 3-7pm.
☎ 030 030 9144529/9994215

Roman Villa & Museum
22 Via Crocifisso
Open: All year Tuesday-Sunday 8.30am-7.30pm (5pm October - February)
☎ 030 9143547

LONATO
Foundation Como/Museum
Casa del Podestà
Open: all year, daily 10am-12noon, 2.30-6.30pm.
☎ 030 9130060

***Rocca*/Ornithological Museum**
Open: all year, daily 10am-12noon, 2.30-6.30pm.
☎ 030 9130060

SAN MARTINO DELLA BATTAGLIA
Tower & Museum
Open: all year, Monday-Saturday 9am-12.30pm, 2-7pm.
☎ 030 9910370

SIRMIONE
Castle
Open: All year Tuesday-Sunday 8.30am-7pm (4.30pm October-March).
☎ 030 916468

Grotte di Catullo
Open: March-September Tuesday-Sunday 8.30am-7pm; October-February Tuesday-Sunday 8.30am-5pm.
☎ 030 916157/9906002

SOLFERINO
Ossuary Chapel/Tower/Museum
Open: All year except for two weeks in early December. Tuesday-Sunday 9am-12.30pm, 2-6.30pm
☎ 0376 854019

(cont'd overleaf)

The castle moat at Riva del Garda

An ideal place to relax at Malcesine on Lake Garda

(cont'd from previous page)

EASTERN SHORE

MALCESINE
Castle/Museums
Open: daily May-September,
9am-8pm; October-March,
Saturday and Sunday
9am-1pm, 3-6pm.
☎ 045 7400837

Palazzo dei Capitani
Open: May-September,
daily 9am-8pm.
☎ 045 7400024 or 7400346

MALCESINE TO MONTE BALDO
Funivia (cablecar)
Open: all year, daily from 8am.
Cars run every 30 mins and the
journey yakes 10mins. Time of
last car varies, 7pm from mid-
May-mid-September, 6pm in
spring and autumn and usually
4.30pm or 5pm in winter.
System usually closed late Nov,
early Dec for maintenance.
☎ 045 7400206 or 7400044

PASTRENGO
**Parco Natura Viva
(Garda Safari Park & Zoo)**
Zoo & Dinosaur Park open:
March-October, daily 9am-6pm;
November to mid-March,
Thursday-Tuesday 9am-5pm.
Auto Safari open: mid-March
to October, daily 9.30am-6pm;
November to mid-March,
holidays and holiday
evenings only 9.30am-4pm.
☎ 045 7170113

PESCHIERA DEL GARDA
Acquapark Altominicio
Valeggio Sul Minicio
Open: late May-early-
September, daily 10am-7pm.
☎ 045 7945131

Caneva World
Open: May-September,
daily 9.30am-7pm.
☎ 045 6969700

Caneva Movie Studios
Same times as Caneva World.
☎ 045 6969800

Gardaland
Open: Late March-September
daily 9.30am-6pm (open until
midnight in late June, all of July
& August, and early September).
Also open on Saturdays and
Sundays in October & December
9.30am-7pm. ☎ 045 6449777

Parco Acquatico Cavour
*Borghetto, near Valeggio Sul
Mincio.* Open: May-September,
daily 9.30am-7pm.
☎ 045 7950904

Villa Sigurta
Open: March-November,
daily 9am-6pm. ☎ 045 6371033

TORRI DEL BENACO
Castle/Museum
Open: all year, Tuesday-Sunday
9.30am-12noon, 3-5pm.
For information ☎ 045 6296111.

NORTHERN & WESTERN SHORE

BOGLIACO
Villa Bettoni
Open: by request during the
working day. For information
☎ 0365 71222.

GARDONE RIVIERA
**Hruska (or Heller)
Botanical Gardens**
Via Roma
Open: mid-March-mid-October
daily 9am-7pm
☎ 0336 410877

VITTORIALE DEGLI ITALIANI
Gardone Sopra
Open; *Gardens*: Daliy 8.30am-8pm (9am-5pm October-March). *House*: April-September, Tuesday-Sunday 9.30am-7pm, Oct-March Tuesday-Sunday 9am-1pm, 2-5pm. *War Museum*: April-September, daliy, except Wed, 9.30am-7pm, Oct-Mar, daily, except Wed 9am-1pm, 2-5pm. ☎ 0365 296511

GARGNANO
Villa Feltrinelli
Permission to view may be granted. Ask at Tourist Office (☎ 0365 71222).

MANERBA DEL GARDA
Museum
Piazza S Bernardo
Open: September-June, Saturday 2-4pm, Sunday 10am-12noon; July & August, Friday 9.30am-12.30pm, Tuesday 8.30-10.30pm. ☎ 0365 552548/552533

MOLINA DI LEDRO
Museum
Open: Tuesday-Sunday 9am-12noon, 1-6pm.
For information ☎ 0464 514444

RIVA DEL GARDA
Castle
Open: mid-March-Sep, Tues-Sun 10am-6pm. ☎ 0464 573869

Apponale Tower
Open: mid-March-October, Tuesday-Sunday 10am-6pm.
☎ 0464 573869.

Museum of Agricultural Machinery
Tenno. Open: mid June-Sep daily, 10am-12noon, 2-6pm.
For information ☎ 0464 502171.

SALÒ
Blue Ribbon Museum (Museo 'Nastro Azzuro')
49 Via Fantoni
Open: Under review at time of writing. ☎ 0365 20804/21603

Museum
Lungolago Zanardelli
Closed at time of writing, for information ☎ 0365 21423.

TIGNALE
Church of Montecastello
Open: mid-March-October daily 10am-5pm
☎ 0365 73019

TOSCOLANO - MADERNO
Museum of Paper
Casa di Luseti, Valle della Cartiere. Open: by request.
☎ 0365 643192

LAKE STEAMERS

On the largest lake there is a full range of diesel and hydrofoil services with restaurants and bars. There are also additional steamers offering day and night-time cruises.

Desenzano is the terminus for Garda steamers. From it the ferries visit Sirmione, Peschiera del Garda, Lazise, Bardolino, Garda, Salò, Gardone Riviera, Fasano, Maderno, Torri del Benaco, Gargnano, Brenzone, Assenza, Malcesine, Limone sul Garda, Torbole and Riva del Garda, with occasional boats calling at Manerba and Moniga south of Salò, from Sirmione.

A round trip from Desenzano to Riva takes around 6 hours. In addition, there is a single car ferry service from Maderno to Torri del Benaco, which takes about 30 minutes (☎ 030 9149511).

10. Verona

HISTORY

Verona is a very old city, so old that its true origins are uncertain. By the first century BC it was already an important Roman city, built on an S-bend of the Adige river and on important roads going north through the Alps and east to west across the Lombardy plain. In terms of its Roman past, Verona is second only to Rome itself in the quality of its surviving structures. Its amphitheatre, smaller only than Rome's Colosseum and the one at Capua, is arguably the most magnificent of all such structures.

Verona maintained its importance into the Middle Ages. Berengar died here in 924, and Otto I stayed during his mission to free Adelheid on Lake Garda. As a free state the city was ahead of its time, forming the Veronese League before the formation of the Lombard League, and defeating Barbarossa in 1164 before joining with Milan to defeat him decisively in 1176 at Legnano. Following this there were severe feuds between rival rich families within the

city, one of which formed the basis for the story of Romeo and Juliet.

The feuding stopped when the city was taken by Ezzelino da Romano, a savage tyrant who ruled, or dictated, until his death around 1260. Next came Mastino della Scala, first of a family which was to give Milan's opera house its name and whose name, Scaligeri, is associated with so many of the fishtail embattled castles seen on Garda's shore. Mastino in Italian means mastiff, and many subsequent members of the Scaligeri had their names prefixed by *can* (dog), as a mark of respect.

The most famous ruler was Francesco della Scala, who was known as 'Cangrande', Great Dog, under whose rule Verona had its greatest sphere of influence. Following banishment from Florence, Dante came here and received Cangrande's protection, dedicating the third section (*Paradise*) of the *Divine Comedy* to him. In keeping with the dog allusions, one later member of the family, not noted for his thoughtful dignity, was Canrabbiaso, Mad Dog.

A later Scaligeri, the second Great Dog, Cangrande II, built the city's castle, but by the end of the fourteenth century the family's rule was at an end, Verona falling firstly to the Viscontis and then becoming part of the Venetian Empire. During the four centuries of Venetian rule, the city grew in stature, its artistic development being greatly assisted by the presence

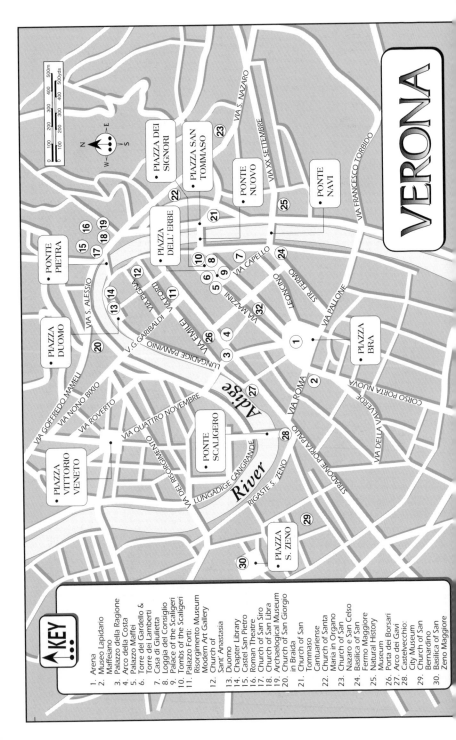

of the brilliant Renaissance architect Michele Sanmicheli and the artist Andrea Mantegna.

Ultimately the Venetian Empire collapsed, and the city was occupied in 1796 by the French. The following year saw the 'Pasque Veronesi', the Veronese Easter, when the city rose and killed the new ruler's men who were quartered there, an uprising that was swiftly avenged with considerable damage to the city's fabric. Thereafter the city was held by French or Austrians until the Risorgimento when it became part of the unified Italy.

TOUR OF THE CITY

PIAZZA BRA

The swift tour of the city will start in Piazza Bra – the name deriving from the Latin *pratum*, a meadow – where the **Arena**, the Roman amphitheatre, immediately takes the eye.

The Roman Arena

The arena is elliptical, the struc-ture originally covering a site measuring 499ft by 403ft (152m by 123m). The arena floor measures 243ft by 144ft (74m by 44m). The whole was built of local stone in the last years of the first century AD. When the arena was first built the structure had a three-tier perimeter wall, only a small section of which (known locally as the *ala* (the wing)) remains, following a destructive earthquake in 1183.

Inside, the amphitheatre is wonderfully imposing, and it takes a moment to remember that amid this splendour gladiators died on the sand-strewn floor. Thankfully, the only spectacles to be seen here today are operas performed during a season that runs from mid-July to the end of August.

Piazza Bra is a spacious square, one of the largest in Italy, with elegant buildings on all sides and a formal fountain garden at its centre. The wide pavements, the *Listone*, of the north-west side are ideal for strolling, and while doing so, be sure to notice Sanmicheli's **Palazzo Guastavera**. On the corner of Via Roma is the **Museo Lapidario Maffeiano** with the oldest collection of ancient inscriptions in Europe.

PIAZZA DELL'ERBE

North-east from Piazza Bra is Piazza dell'Erbe occupying, almost exactly, the position of the Roman forum. It is a delightful place, one of the most picturesque spots in the whole of Italy with its array of umbrellas protecting its fruit and vegetable market, stallholders and shoppers. In the square there is much of interest: just relax and stroll, but do not fail to see the **Palazzo della Ragione**, founded in the twelfth century, but much altered except for the tower, the Torre delle Carceri; or the **Arco della Costa** beside it, the Arch of the Rib, so called because of the whale's rib that hangs by it.

On the north-western side is the baroque **Palazzo Maffei** from the seventeenth century with, beside it, the **Torre del Gardello** from the fourteenth century. In front of the *palazzo* is the **Colonna di San Marco**, the lion symbol of the Venetian empire, destroyed after the Pasque Veronesi, but now restored. Note too, the fourteenth-century fountain with a statue. The statue is Roman, but the bizarre head is not original, making the whole thing a bit odd, but it

(cont'd on page 196)

The market in Piazza dell' Erbe seen from the LamBerti Tower

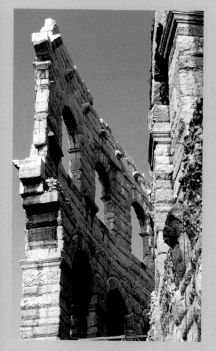

The 'wing' of the Arena

Ponte Scaligero

Piazza dei Signori

195

is revered as the Madonna Verona. The 276ft (84m) **Torre dei Lamberti** beside the Palazzo della Ragione can be climbed to improve the view.

A little way from the *piazza* is Via Cappello, and the **Casa di Giulietta,** Juliet's House. For lovers of the story there is also **Romeo's House**, on the corner of Via delle Arche Scaligeri, near Piazza dei Signori.

PIAZZA DEI SIGNORI

Piazza dei Signori is reached through the Rib Arch. By contrast to Erbe it is small, quiet and dignified. To the right on entering, another archway leads to the Old Market, a beautiful courtyard formed within the Palazzo della Ragione. Here is a first glimpse of the red and white horizontal zebra stripes that will become so familiar on the tour of the city. In the old courtyard they act as a perfect backdrop to an elegant stairway.

In the centre of Piazza dei Signori is a statue of Dante, his back to the **Loggia del Consiglio,** an elegantly arcaded and painted fifteenth-century Renaissance building, crowned by statues of famous men of Verona, including Catullus and Pliny the Elder. To Dante's left is the **Palace of the Scaligeri,** a much altered twelfth-century building with fishtail battlements. Beside the palace an archway leads to the small Romanesque **church of Santa Maria Antica**.

Beside the church are the **Tombs of the Scaligeri,** an extraordinary assembly of monuments damaged by an earthquake in 1976, but now almost restored. The tombs can be seen as marvels of Veronese art of the thirteenth and fourteenth centuries, or

---

Romeo and Juliet

The late twelfth/early thirteenth century feuding between the noble families of Verona that followed the defeat of Barbarossa at Legnano in 1176 was the basis of a story by the sixteenth-century Italian writer Luigi da Porto. His story involved the Cappelletti and Montechi families whose names, anglicised to Capulet and Montague, were taken by Shakespeare when he adopted the story for Romeo and Juliet, still perhaps the most famous association that the city offers tourists.

Though the story has a basis in truth, all the sites in Verona now associated with the play are of doubtful (to say the least) veracity. **Juliet's House**, with its façade of golden brown brick and a balcony of cream marble, is exquisite, and being thirteenth century does have the merit of being from the right period (well, almost, it is actually a little too new). However, the climb to the balcony is too difficult and the strength of the house's claim lies in the name of the street, itself taken from an old inn – Il Cappello – which is claimed to once have stood in it.

Close by is **Romeo's House**, which has a history which is even more dubious. It also lacks the romantic appeal of Juliet's House. At least, with the former, the 'feel' is correct even if the history is unsupportive. Standing in the delightful courtyard while a young visitor plays Juliet for her camera-clicking family, it is easy to form the impression that, if this was not actually Juliet's House, then it should have been.

an over-elaborate self-indulgence. Their nicest part is the exquisite wrought iron grille surrounding them, which incorporates the five-ringed ladder used by the family as a symbol. The equestrian statue of Cangrande that surmounts the topmost pyramid of his tomb is a masterpiece by an unknown artist, and is a copy, the original being in the city's Castle Museum.

Going north from the tombs, the visitor passes, on the corner of Via Emilei and Via Forti, **Palazzo Forti** where Napoleon stayed, and which now houses the city's **Modern Art Gallery**. Nearby is the **church of Sant' Anastasia**, the largest in the city, and in a beautiful position beside the river. The main doorway is superb, though the façade in which it is set is unfinished, 700 years after work began. Inside, do not miss the *gobbi* (hunchbacks), who support the Holy Water stoups at the first column bases, the terracotta scenes from the life of Christ, and some good frescoes.

Near the *Duomo*, the **Chapter Library** can be visited. Founded in the

eighth century, it contains many interesting and valuable texts.

ACROSS THE RIVER VIA PONTE PIETRA

From the *Duomo* cross Ponte Pietra, one of the two original Roman bridges though little is of that age now. The bridge was almost completely destroyed in 1945, but the stones were dredged from the river and faithfully restored to position. Ahead now is the **Castel San Pietro**, an Austrian fortress which dominates the **Roman Theatre**.

The theatre, which was not rediscovered until the early nineteenth century is thought to be older than the Arena. The view from the top of the seating tiers, both of the theatre and the city, is excellent. Also on the site are small fourteenth-century churches to **San Siro** and **San Libera**, and an **Archaeological Museum** – reached by lift from the back of the theatre – with items from both the theatre and Verona's Roman past.

Nearby, is one of the city's newest museums, the **Museum of African Art and Civilisation**.

If, after crossing Ponte Pietra, a left turn instead of a right is taken, the **church of San Giorgio in Braida**, will be reached. This contains many fine paintings, and the cupola is by Sanmicheli.

BACK AROSS THE RIVER VIA PONTE NUOVO

Going east from the Scaligeri tombs, the river is crossed by way of Ponte Nuovo, and, in Piazza San Tommaso is a church dedicated to **San Tommaso Cantuariense** – Thomas of Canterbury – in which the architect Sanmicheli is buried. A little north is the **church of**

The *Duomo*

In contrast to the church, the city cathedral (*Duomo*), further north, seems disproportionate – too many changes of idea, too much over-emphasis. It was once described as 'architecture in colour' which seems a back-handed compliment. Inside, however, it is light and spacious and has a superb Titian altarpiece – *The Assumption* – his only work in the town and worth the journey to see.

(cont'd on page 200)

Archaeological Museum and Roman Theatre
Rigaste Redentore, 2
Open: All year Monday 1.30-7.30pm, Tuesday-Sunday 9am-7.30pm (closes at 3pm October-April). ☎ 045 8000360

Arena
Piazza Bra
Open: All year, Monday 1.30-7.15pm, Tuesday-Sunday 8.30am-7.15pm (9am-3.30pm during the opera season).
☎ 045 8003204

Basilica of San Zeno Maggiore
Piazza San Zeno
Open: All year, Monday-Saturday 8.30am-6pm, Sunday 1-6pm.

Chapter Library
Piazza del Duomo, 13
Open: all year (except July) daily 9.30am-12.30pm; Thursday & Friday 3.30-6.30pm.
☎ 045 596516

Church of Santa Anastasia
Corso Santa Anastasia
Open: daily 9am-6pm (1-6pm on Sunday).

City Museum
Castelvecchio
Open: All year, Monday 1.30-7.30pm, Tuesday-Sunday 8.30am-7.30pm. ☎ 045 8062611

Guisti Gardens
Via Giardino Giusti, 2
Open: May-September daily 9am-8pm; October-April daily 9am-sunset. ☎ 045 8034029

Juliet's House (Casa di Giulietta)
23 Via Cappello
Open: All year, Monday 1.30-7.30pm, Tuesday-Sunday 8.30am-7.30pm.
☎ 045 8034303

Juliet's Tomb/Museum of Frescoes
Via del Pontiere, 35
Open: All year, Monday 1.30-7.30pm, Tuesday-Sunday 8.30am-7.30pm.
☎ 045 8000361

Maffeiano Lapidary Museum
Piazza Bra, 28
Open: All year, Monday 1.30-7.30pm, Tuesday-Sunday 8.30am-2pm.
☎ 045 590087

Museum of African Art and Civilisation
Vicolo Pozzo,1
San Giovanni in Valle
Closed for restoration at time of writing.
☎ 045 8092100

Natural History Museum
Palazzo Pompei,
Lungadige Porta Vittoria, 9
Open: all year, Monday-Thursday & Saturday 9am-7pm, Sunday 2-7pm.
☎ 045 8079400

Gallery of Modern Art
Palazzo Forti (entrance in Corso Sant' Anastasia)
Open: all year, times vary with exhibitions.
☎ 045 8001903

Tombs of the Scaligeri
Piazza dei Signori
No entrance, but visible from the street.

Torre dei Lamberti
Piazza dei Signori
Open: All year, Monday 1.30-7.30pm, Tuesday-Sunday 9.30am-7.30pm.
☎ 045 8032726

The balcony of Casa di Guiletta, reputedly the one immortalised by Shakespeare

Santa Maria in Organo, the interior of which is covered in frescoes and has some exceptionally good woodcarving. Note especially the Palm Sunday carving of Christ on a donkey.

Eastward are the **Giusti Gardens**, the Italian-style gardens of the sixteenth-century Palazzo Guisti. Here, as one would expect with the formal Italian style, are statues, fountains and well defined flower beds. But there is also a maze and some beautiful, very old, cypresses. South-east from the gardens, the **church of San Nazaro e San Celso** has some fine paintings.

Next is the city's **Natural History Museum**, housed in Sanmicheli's Palazzo Pompei. The museum is considered to be one of the finest of its type in Italy and has an especially good collection of local fossils.

RE-CROSS PONTE NAVI

South from the Scaligeri tombs, at the western end of the Ponte Navi, is the **basilica of San Fermo Maggiore**, colourful in stripes of red brick and yellow stone. The basilica is actually two churches, a lower, Romanesque one from the twelfth century and an upper, Gothic one from the fourteenth century. Beside the basilica is a fine campanile, most unusually topped by a stub spire. The campanile is also in marble and brick, but here the builder was not successful in his layering! Inside, the basilica has a magnificent wooden ceiling and superb frescoes.

Continue to the south to reach the grounds of a former Capuchin convent, of which only the cloisters and a small chapel remain. Here is **Juliet's Tomb**, a fourteenth-century stone sarcophagus that traditionally is ascribed to Shakespeare's heroine. There is also a modern bust of Shakespeare, and a small museum of detached frescoes.

West from the Scaligeri tombs is the **Porta dei Borsari**, a Roman gateway derived from the word *bursarii*, Latin for tax collectors, this being a tollgate into the old city. The gateway is an imposing double archway of marble, and is inscribed 'Colonia *Verona Augusta*'.

Further along the riverside road is another Roman archway, the **Arco dei Gavi**. This formerly stood elsewhere in the city and was demolished by the French, being rebuilt here from its original fragments supplemented with new material, in 1932. The arch is older, more delicate, and more beautiful then the Borsari Gate.

CASTELVECCHIO

Next comes the Scaligeri castle, the Castelvecchio, one of the undoubted highlights of a tour of Verona. The castle was built by Cangrande II in the years around 1350 and was subsequently used by the Venetians as a college, by the French, and Austrians as a barracks and it was here that Count Ciano, Mussolini's son-in-law, was tried in 1944.

The castle is quite magnificent, embodying all of the features seen in the Garda castles and setting them in a superb riverside position. The river itself is crossed by the **Ponte Scaligero**, a bridge incorporated into the original design as part of the defences. During World War II the bridge was almost totally destroyed, but has been lovingly restored to its former massive glory.

Today the castle holds the **City Museum**, which houses some excellent items including the original equestrian statue from the tomb of Cangrande I, works by Mantegna and Paolo Veronese, some fine early and Renaissance sculpture, jewellery and gold, medieval glass, a collection of ancient firearms, detached early frescoes and many works from the Veronese and Venetian schools.

West from the castle, the **church of San Bernardino** has some good frescoes and a fine chapel – Cappella Pellegrini – by Sanmicheli.

Basilica of San Zeno Maggiore

North from here is San Zeno Maggiore thought by many to be the most beautiful Romanesque church in northern Italy. The basilica, dating from the early twelfth century, dominates a large, paved square, its own façade being dominated equally by a huge rose window.

To one side of the church is an elegant, slender twelfth-century campanile in similar golden stone, while on the other side stands the embattled tower of a former monastery, looking out of character in its red brick and heavy design. Behind the church, its cloisters are breathtakingly beautiful, arcaded with a tiled roof, above which are two tiers of red and yellow striped walls each with its own tiled roof.

The **basilica doors** consist of forty-eight panels of bronze depicting biblical scenes, dating chiefly from the twelfth century with a few added in the thirteenth century when the doors were enlarged. The bronze reliefs are in one sense very primitive in layout and characterisation, but are very dynamic, foreshadowing the change to come in the nature of art.

Inside, the basilica is very simple, elegantly so, with a minimum of artwork. There is a porphyry bowl in the north-west corner that some say was given by San Zeno, an African, to the Roman Emperor Gallienus in the fourth century, but legend says it was placed here by the devil, though quite why he should want to is not clear. There is also a triptych by Andrea Mantegna – partly a copy, as some of the original is in the Louvre having been removed by Napoleon. The church's crypt holds an urn containing the remains of San Zeno.

ACCOMMODATION

Hotels

Reservations cannot be made through ENIT offices. They do, however, hold lists of organisations who can book hotels, (normally 4 or 5-star), in all major tourist areas. The tourist (APT) offices in the regional centres, the local tourist offices (Aziende Autonome di Cura e Soggiorno – AACST) in larger towns/villages, and the Pro Loco offices in small villages also hold lists of hotels.

See under **Hotels and Restaurants** for a list of recommended hotels for each chapter.

Camping

Camping is popular all over Italy. The tourist offices will provide details of sites and their standard. Alternatively, two lists can be obtained. The first contains details of all of Italy's sites, some 1,600, and must be purchased. The second is an abbreviated list and is free. Each can be obtained from:

> **Confederaziane Italiana Campeggiatori**
> Via Vittorio Emanuele, 11,
> 50041 Calenzano,
> Firenze
> ☎ 055 882391

Mountain Huts

The Italian Alpine Club owns most of the mountain huts in upland Italy. The huts offer cheap overnight accommodation with basic facilities. Details from:

> **Club Alpino Italiano**
> Via Petrella 19,
> 20124 Milan
> ☎ 02 802554 or 8057519

Youth Hostels & Student Hostels

The Italian Youth Hostel Association has over fifty youth hostels in Italy, including Bergamo, Como, Domaso, Milan, Riva del Garda and Verona. Information from:

> **Associazione Italiana Alberghi per la Gioventu**
> Via Carour 44,
> 00184 Roma,
> ☎ 06 4871152

In addition several of the larger towns have student hostels available to visiting students. Ask about Casa della Studente at the Milan Tourist Office. Milan is the only town in the area with such a hostel.

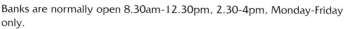

BANKS, CREDIT CARDS & CURRENCY

Banks are normally open 8.30am-12.30pm, 2.30-4pm, Monday-Friday only.

Most major credit cards (MasterCard, Visa, American Express etc) are taken at most large restaurants, hotels and shops. Eurocheques and traveller's cheques (checks) are also accepted. The notable exceptions are gas stations which, as a rule, do not accept anything but money or fuel coupons.

The Italian monetary unit is the lira (plural = lire). No traveller may import or export more than 20 million lire or its equivalent in other currencies, or may re-export currency to the same value unless they have completed customs form V2 on entry.

CLIMATE

The lakes themselves are so large that they act as temperature regulators, warming the area like giant storage radiators in winter and acting as heat sinks to take the edge off the summer's heat. As a result the summers are dry and hot, but usually without the sticky humidity of more southerly resort areas. The winters are cool and wet, with snow usually confined to the high ridges.

The graphs show that there is a pronounced difference between the temperature and rainfall of the western lakes of Maggiore, Lugano and Como, and the eastern lakes of Iseo and Garda. In reality due to the proximity of the Piedmontian Alps Lake Maggiore is about 1°C cooler than Lake Como.

Much of the rain in summer is associated with thunderstorms, particularly near Lake Garda, hence the high figures for summer and autumn. There the summer is dry and hot, but punctuated by very occasional – though heavy – rainfall, the accompanying thunderstorms giving superb displays of lightning.

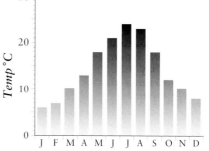

Average Daily Temperatures

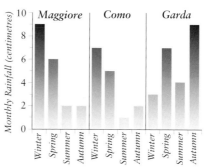

Average Monthly Rainfall

CONSULATES

Great Britain
7 Via San Paolo,
Milan
Open: 9am-12noon, 2.30-4.30pm
daily except Saturday.
☎ 02 723001

Canada
19 Via V Pisani,
Milan
Open: 8.45am-12.30pm, 1.30-
5.15pm daily except Saturday.
☎ 02 657581

United States of America
Via Amedeo 2/10,
Milan
Open: 9am-12noon, 2-4pm
daily except Saturday.
☎ 02 290351

CUSTOMS & ENTRY REGULATIONS

Normal EU customs regulations apply. The Italian age limit for the import of duty-free alcohol and tobacco is 17. Normal personal equipment – cameras, jewellery etc – can be taken into the country, but professional photographers need an AFA Carnet for the importation of their equipment.

No visa is required for stays of less than 3 months for holders of passports from the European Union, Canada or the United States. A valid passport is required.

All tourists must register with the police within 3 days of entering the country. If you stay at a hotel, campsite etc this registration will be carried out for you.

ELECTRICITY

The electricity is 220 volts AC, 50 Hertz (cycles/sec). Four different types of plug are commonly in use – two with two pins and two with three pins in a line. While a two-pin continental adapter is recommended, purchasing plugs on arrival is easy and inexpensive.

EMERGENCIES

Emergency Assistance/Police	113
Fire	115
Health Emergency	118
Motoring Aid	116

For immediate attention at airports, railway stations or hospitals look for the sign PRONTO SOCCORSO.

HEALTH CARE

Visitors from the European Union have a right to claim health services in Italy by virtue of EEC regulations. Form E111 – available in Britain from Post Offices and the Department of Health and Social Security – should be obtained to avoid complications.

Canadian and American tourists should check their personal health insurance to ensure they are adequately covered.

If drugs are prescribed by a doctor and these are dispensed at a pharmacy (*farmacia*), a minimal local tax is payable which will not be reimbursed.

HOLIDAYS & FESTIVALS

Italy has the following national holidays:

New Year's Day	Assumption Day (15 August)
Epiphany (6 January)	All Saint's Day (1 November)
Easter Monday	Immaculate Conception
Liberation Day (25 April)	(8 December)
Labour Day (1 May)	Christmas (25 and 26 December)

In addition, some towns celebrate the patron saint's day with a holiday. Museums, etc also occasionally close on other saint's days.

Most of the major festivals in the area are mentioned in the text, but are gathered here for completeness:

Festivals on the Lakes

3-5 January

- **Canto della Stella**, Tignale, Lake Garda. Translating as Starlight Singing, this event re-enacts the journey of the Magi with night-time procession accompanied by the singing of choirs.

31 January

- **Boat Festival**, Orta San Giulio, Lake Orta

February

- **Carnival season**. The most famous of all carnivals is that at Venice. Staying within the Lakes' area, the best is at Verona (the Gnoccho Bacchanalia).

March

- **Autumn fashion collections**, Milan

Lent

- **'Hag's Trials'**, Gargagno and Gardone, Lake Garda. The effigy of an old woman is burnt on a bonfire, a memorial of a less savoury aspect of medieval life, though the event is now a much jollier affair.

Fact File

Easter

- **Traditional processions** in the Swiss villages of Lake Lugano. Processions are often held on both Maundy Thursday and Good Friday

9-10 April

- **Pageant** to commemorate the creation of the Lombard League, Bergamo

24 June

- On the Sunday following St John the Baptist's day a **procession** of boats takes people to Isola Comacina, Lake Como for an outdoor mass in the ruined church. There are also boat races between local crews in traditional lake boats.
- At San Martino della Battaglia groups dress in authentic costumes and re-enact the famous battle.

June to July

- **Shakespeare season**, Verona

July

- **Folklore Festival**, Val Cannobina, Lake Maggiore
- **Festival of traditional music and dance**, Quarna Sopra, Lake Orta
- **Jazz Festival**, Lugano (first week in the month)
- **Music Festival**, Lugano (last week in the month)
- **International Sailing Regatta**, Gargagno, Lake Garda
- **Il Redentore** (The Redeemer) – the procession of gondolas and other craft at Venice held over a weekend in mid-month

July to August

- **Opera season**, Verona. The operas are staged open-air in the Roman Arena.
- **Season of open-air plays** at Il Vittoriale, Gardone Riviera, Lake Garda

August

- **Compagna di Ballori**, Ponte Caffaro, Lake Ledro. Traditional music and dance festival with musicians in ancient dress playing old instruments. The event is accompanied by a day-long carnival. (Dates change, please consult local Tourist Office)
- **International Film Festival**, Locarno, Lake Maggiore

Mid-august to mid-September

- **International Music Festival** (Settimane Musicali), Stresa, Lake Maggiore. World famous event with top musicians and conductors.

September to mid-October

- **Music Festival**, Ascona, Lake Maggiore. Timed so that some of the players from Stresa can appear again.

Carnival time at Laveno, Lake Maggiore

Mid-September to October

- Lake Maggiore villages celebrate a **festival of local foods** with special menus in the restaurants.

September

- **Grape Festival**, Bardolino, Lake Garda (last weekend of month)
- **Firework Spectacular,** Sirmione, Lake Garda
- **Palio del Baradello**, Como. This largely comprises boat and horse races between the districts of the city, but concludes with a spectacular procession through the city of men dressed in medieval costume. The procession is always on a Sunday, and usually coincides with the Italian Grand Prix at Monza.
- **Italian Grand Prix**, Monza.

October

- **Spring fashion collections**, Milan.

7 December

- First night of the **opera season** in La Scala, Milan.
- There are operas throughout the year in the Donizetti Theatre, Bergamo.

Christmas

- At Laveno, Lake Maggiore, divers create an underwater crib in the bay on 20 December. This is floodlit and on 24 December the baby Jesus is lowered into position with great ceremony. The ceremony pre-dates floodlighting and, though clear, the lake waters are too murky for the crib to have been seen in earliest times making the origins of the event a mystery.

HOTELS AND RESTAURANTS

Most Italian hotels at the lower end of the price spectrum (*** and below) do not have restaurants, offering only breakfast. Most quoted prices will not include breakfast (colazione non incluso). In the following sections, a few hotels in each star category are given as indications of the type of position and facilities available. It must be stressed that for these, and for the restaurants which follow them, the information is correct at the time of writing and is based on personal observation. Should readers find the information to be at fault, they should contact Landmark Publishing. Key: $ average, $$ good, $$$ excellent, L luxury.

Chapter 1 — Milan

HOTELS

Grand Hotel et de Milan *****
Via Manzoni, 29
20121 Milano
Almost off the price scale.

All possible facilities. Situated within a short walk of the *duomo*. Two excellent restaurants. $$$
☎ 02 723141, Fax 02 86460861

Michelangelo****
Via Scarlatti, 33
20124 Milano
Close to the Central Station. A 'No
smoking' hotel. Good sized rooms
and excellent restaurant. $$$
☎ 02 67551, Fax 02 6694232

Bolzano***
Via Boscovitch, 21
20124 Milano
Close to Central Station. Small,
quiet rooms, redecorated a few
years ago in modern, but tasteful
style. No restaurant. $$
☎ 02 6691451, Fax 02 6691455

Lancaster***
Via Abbondio San Giorgio, 16
20145 Milano
A small and neat hotel, unusual
for Milan in being on the western
side of Sempione Park. No
restaurant and usually closed
throughout August. $$
☎ 02 344705, Fax 02 344649

London**
Via Rovello, 3
20121 Milano
A small hotel very close to the
main attractions. No restaurant,
but the Opera Prima restaurant
(which is excellent) is in the
same building. $
☎ 02 72020166, Fax 02 8057037

Star**
Via dei Bossi, 5
20121 Milano
Another small hotel very close
to the main attractions. No
restaurant. $
☎ 02 801501, Fax 02 861787

RESTAURANTS

Savini*****
Galleria Vittorio Emanuele II
21012 Milano
The most famous restaurant in
the city, filling with opera goers
as soon as the curtain comes
down at La Scala. $$$$
☎ 02 72003433

Alfredo-Gran San Bernardo ****
Via Borgese, 14
20154 Milano
Probably the best place in the
city for true Milanese cooking.
Try the risottos and the cotoletta
Milanese and be amazed. Not
cheap, out by the Fiera (Milan's
international fair centre) but worth
the journey and the bill. $$$
☎ 02 3319000

Al Mercante***
Piazza Mercanti, 17
20123 Milano
The most romantic setting in
town – dine outdoors in a
small, enclosed *piazza*. $$
☎ 02 8052198

Don Lisander **
Via Manzoni, 12
20121 Milano
A great place to eat in summer
when the tables are set in the
beautiful garden. Good interna-
tional menu which changes
regularly. Closed on Sundays. $$
☎ 02 76020130

La Tavernetta-da-Elio*
Via Fatebenefratelli, 30
20121 Milano
Quiet and out of the way,
but excellent pasta. $
☎ 02 653441

Trattoria all'Antica *
Via Montevideo, 4
20144 Milano
In the Naviglia district of the
city, but well known for serving
excellent food at reasonable
prices and so justifiably popular.
Closed during the winter and
on Sundays. $
☎ 02 58104860

Bellagio, Lake Como

Fact File

Chapter 2 – Orta

HOTELS

L'Approdo**
Corso Roma, 80
28028 Pettenasco
A sumptuous new hotel with swimming pool and lake frontage. Good restaurant. $$$
☎ 0323 89346, Fax 0323 89338

Orta***
Piazza Motta, 1
28016 Orta San Giulio
Set right on the lake front in the most picturesque of Orta's villages. Fine old building with well furnished rooms and a pleasant restaurant. $$
☎ 0322 90253, Fax 0322 905646

Belvedere**
Via Belvedere, 8
28020 Quarna Sopra
Aptly named for its magnificent views of the lake – arguably the best from any Orta hotel. Good restaurant. $
☎ 0323 826198

RESTAURANTS

Trattoria Toscana**
Via G. Mazzini, 153
28026 Omegna
One of the best places on the lake: try the speciality 'mountain recipe' gnocchi or the lake fish. Closed on Wednesdays. $$
☎ 0323 62460.

Sacro Monte**
Via Scare Monte, 5
28016 Orta San Giulio
Worth trying for the house speciality desserts alone, but try the 'Pollo alla Sacre Monte' too. $$
☎ 0323 90220

Venus*
Piazza Motta, 50
28016 Orta San Giulio
Almost too romantic.
Set right on the lake side.

Straightforward menu, but well prepared. $
☎ 0323 90362

Chapter 3 – Maggiore

The Piemonte shore of Lake Maggiore offers the better accommodation with numerous hotels in all categories. On the Lombardian shore the hotels tend to be smaller and have fewer stars.

HOTELS

Grand Hotel des Îles Borromées***L**
Corso Umberto I, 67
28838 Stresa
The ultimate in luxury, matched only by Lake Como's Villa d'Este. Everything you could want and a lake view. $$$$
☎ 0323 938938, Fax 0323 32405

Camin***
Viale Dante, 35
21016 Luino
Very small and exclusive. Elegantly positioned and very comfortable. Good restaurant. $$$
☎ 0332 530118, Fax 0332 537226

Hotel Villa Carlotta***
Via Mazzini, 121
28832 Belgirate
A fabulous palazzo set on the lakeside. Swimming pool and sun terrace. Excellent restaurant. $$$
☎ 0322 76461, Fax 0322 76705

La Palma***
Corso Umberto, 33
28838 Stresa
A modern hotel on the lakeside road, with a swimming pool beside the lake. Most rooms have a lake view. Very pleasant restaurant. $$$
☎ 0323 32401, Fax 0323 933930

Beau Rivage***
Via della Vittoria, 16
28831 Baveno
Elegant old-style pink hotel set

Fact File

on the lake shore. Good
restaurant. $$
☎ 0323 924534, Fax 0323 925253

La Fontana***
Via Sempione Nord, 1
28049 Stresa
A little way out of the town
and with no restaurant, but
more than compensating with
beautiful grounds and elegant,
high-ceilinged rooms. $$
☎ 0323 32707, Fax 0323 32708

Hotel Cannero*****
Lungo Lago, 2
28821 Cannero
Small, old-style hotel set
very conveniently right on
the lakeside. $$
☎ 0323 788046, Fax 0323 788048

Conca Azzurra ***
Via Alberto, 53
21020 Ranco
Situated in a village just north
of Angera. Tidy little hotel with
reasonable facilities and a
good restaurant. $$
☎ 0331 976526, Fax 0331 976721

Mignon*
21021 Angera
Small and quiet, nicely set in
the village at the southern end
of the lake. No restaurant. $
☎ 0331 930141, Fax 0331 930141

Moderno*
21014 Laveno
Simple, but well maintained.
Useful for the lake car ferry. $
☎ 0332 668373

RESTAURANTS

The most romantic way of eating
on Lake Maggiore is on a night-
time lake steamer as it cruises the
lake. For those who prefer the
shore there are:

L'Emiliano***
Corso Italia, 50
28838 Stresa
Very fine food and surroundings.

Specialities include ravioli
and mountain lamb. $$$
☎ 0323 70595

Charleston ***
*Hotel Regina Palace, Corso
Umberti I, 13328922 Pallanza*
Wonderfully set at the lakeside
and with a very good menu. $$$
☎ 0323 31160

Saleggi**
Via Angelo Nessi, 38
Locarno, Switzerland
Good Ticinese cuisine in
elegant surroundings. $$
☎ 093 314171

Il Porticciolo-Bellevue**
*On the lakeside road, about 2km
(1 mile) south of Laveno*
Good lake fish dishes and a
terrace with a beautiful view of
the lake. $$
☎ 0332 667257

Cà Blanca*
28821 Cannero Riviera
Good food and a fine view of the
Cannero (Malpaga) castles. $
☎ 0323 788038

Ristorante Al Camino*
On the road from Lesa to Comnago
Small restaurant (booking advised)
which offers a very good local
menu and lovely views of the
lake and hills. $
☎ 0322 7471

Chapter 4 – Varese

HOTELS

City ***
Via Medaglie d'Oro, 35
21100 Varese
For those looking for a city hotel
within reach of the western lakes.
Positioned near the centre of
Varese and with good facilities.
No restaurant, but good places
just a short walk away. $$
☎ 0332 281304, Fax 0332 232882

La Vecchia Rotaia***
21013 Gallarate
Conveniently positioned for
Malpensa airport and the
autostrada. Very good
restaurant. $$
☎ 0331 792140

Hotel Lido*
21026 Gavirate
Small and basic, but very clean
and hospitable and with a
surprisingly good restaurant. $
☎ 0332 743443

RESTAURANTS

Ristorante Lago Maggiore***
Via Carrobbio, 19
21100 Varese
The best place in town. The
pistacchio tortellini and lamb
with herb sauce are worth
travelling miles to try. $$
☎ 0332 231183

Casa Radice**
Via Roma, 8
21052 Busto Arsizio
Excellent choice and very
pleasant surroundings. $$
☎ 0331 620454

Hotel del Pittore*
21030 Casalzuigno-Arcummegia
Excellent food to satisfy an
appetite from the outdoor art
exhibition that is Arcummegia. $
☎ 0332 650116

Chapter 5 – Lugano

HOTELS

*Hotel Bellevue au Lac****
Riva Caccia, 10
Lugano, Switzerland*
Large, but well sited.
Swimming pool and sun terrace.
Excellent restaurant. $$$
☎ 091 9943333

Hotel del Pesce**
Ponte Tresa, Switzerland

Medium-sized hotel on the
lakeside, with good opportunities
for water sports. $$
☎ 091 711146

Hotel Du Lac*
21037 Ponte Tresa, Italy
As elegantly sited as the name
implies. Small and well kept and
with an excellent restaurant. $
☎ 0332 550308 or 550463

RESTAURANTS

Locanda del Boschetta***
Via Boschetto, 8
Lugano, Switzerland
Open until midnight for those
wanting to eat late. The menu is
mostly Ticinese specialities, well
cooked and beautifully served. $$$
☎ 091 9942493

Da Candida **
Via Marco, 4
22060 Campione d'Italia
Terrific place in every sense.
Lovely old building, excellent
menu, fine service, good food.
Try the lamb or one of the more
exotic choices. $$
☎ 091 6497541

L'Ancora *
Via Mazzini, 3
Porto Ceresio
Lovely little place at the heart
of an equally attractive village.
Typical Italian albergo, with a
small number of rooms, restaurant
and pizzeria. Very good food. $
☎ 0332 917240

Chapter 6 – Lake Como

The southern end of that arm of
the lake, which extends to Como
itself, has long been renowned as
a holiday paradise. The hotels tend
to be on the western shore as that
receives the early morning sun and
more sun in winter. At the

Fact File

northern end of the lake, and on the Lecco arm, the hotels tend to be smaller and of a lower star category. The notable exception is Bellagio which has hotels of exceptional quality.

HOTELS

Grand Hotel Villa d'Este *****L
22010 Cernobbio
The ultimate in luxury, a truly magnificent building, richly decorated and set in equally splendid grounds. The rooms would grace a museum of style. Lakeside position, and offering everything you could want, including a floating swimming pool. $$$$
☎ 031-53481, Fax 031-348844

Grand Hotel Villa Serbelloni*****L
22021 Bellagio
A magnificent old palazzo standing in its own grounds. Again with every conceivable luxury. $$$$
☎ 031 950216, Fax 031 951259

Barchetta Excelsior****
Piazza Cavour, 1
22100 Como
Beautifully positioned on the main square in Como, overlooking the lake. Comfortable modern decoration. Good restaurant. $$$
☎ 031 3221, Fax 031 302622

Grand Hotel Tremezzo****
22019 Tremezzo
Superb hotel, one of the oldest on the lake. Built in grand style, with gardens to match. Some rooms have balconies overlooking the lake. Walking distance to Villa Colotta and ferry to Bellagio. $$$
☎ 034 442491, Fax 034 40201

Grand Hotel Victoria ****
Lungolago Castelli, 7
22017 Menaggio
Beautiful old building in delightful grounds. Very pleasant restaurant with outdoor dining. $$$
☎ 0344 32003, Fax 0344 32992

Firenze***
Piazza Volta
22100 Como
Small hotel in central Como. Well appointed. No restaurant. $$
☎ 031 300333, Fax 031 300101

Royal Victoria***
Piazza San Giorgio, 5
23829 Varenna
Well positioned for exploring the top end of the lake, and close to the ferry. Very well decorated. $$
☎ 0341 815111, Fax 0341 830722

Centrale**
Via Regina, 39
22012 Cernobbio
Fine old building in the centre of town, just a few steps away from the lake steamer quay. Excellent restaurant, with an al fresco option in the garden in summer. $$
☎ 031 511411, Fax 031 341900

Moderno**
Piazza Diaz, 5
22053 Lecco
Deserves to be more popular, as does this arm of the lake. Well positioned for exploring the high hills on the lake's eastern shore. Well appointed, but no restaurant. $
☎ 0341 286519

Regina**
Lungolago Matteotti, 11
22018 Porlezza
Very pleasant hotel with good decor. $$
☎ 0344 61228, Fax 0344 72031

Villa Marie**
Via Regina, 30
2019 Tremezzo
Simple, but well maintained. Close to Villa Carlotta and very useful for the lake car ferry. $
☎ 0344 40427, Fax, same as Tel no.

Above: The village of Iseo on Lake Iseo

Below: The Apponale Tower, Riva del Garda

Fact File

RESTAURANTS

Imbarcadero***
Piazza Cavour, 20
22100 Como
Part of the Hotel Metropole
Suisse. Superb menu with dining
on the square if you wish. Try the
lake perch and rice. $$$
☎ 031 270166

Imperialino***
Via Antica Regina, 26
22010 Moltrasio
Very high quality restaurant in
village now bypassed by main
lake road. As a result, peace and
quiet is also on the menu. $$$
☎ 031 346600

Al Porticciolo 84**
Via Valsecchi, 5/7
23900 Lecco
Small restaurant (booking advisable, particularly in high season)
specialising in lake fish dishes. $$
☎ 0341 498103

Antico Ristorante
Grotto del Misto**
22020 Pognana Lario
Situated at the Cavaclub, a water
sports centre on the eastern
shore of the Como arm of the
lake. Specialises in lake fish
served overlooking the water.
☎ 031 309857

Bilacus*
22021 Bellagio
One of the best places to eat
in the town, good food at
reasonable prices and served
in a pleasant garden. $
☎ 031 950480

Del Duca*
Piazza Mazzini
22100 Como
Recently converted from a
restaurant to a small hotel, but
retaining its reputation as one of
the best little eateries in the city. In
a small square close to the main
square. $ ☎ 031 266166

Chapter 7 –
Bergamo

HOTELS

Excelsior San Marco****
Piazza della Repubblica, 6
24100 Bergamo
Very comfortable hotel with
all modern facilities set close to
both the upper city and the
new city centre. $$$
☎ 035 366111, Fax 035 223201

Cappello d'Oro ***
Viale Papa Giovanni XXIII, 12
24121 Bergamo (lower city)
In the lower city, but just a short
walk from the lower station of
the *funivia* to the upper town.
Very well appointed and with a
good restaurant. $$$
☎ 035 232503, Fax 035 242946

Hotel Europa*
Lungo Mallero Cadorna
23100 Sondrio
Neat and comfortable, and well
sited to explore the Valtellina.
☎ 0342 515010, Fax 0342 512895

RESTAURANTS

Colleoni & dell'Angelo***
Piazza Vecchia, 7
24100 Bergamo Upper City
Situated at the very heart of the
upper city. Absolutely superb,
with a terrific menu of Bergamo
dishes, good cooking and
excellent service in a magnificent
palazzo. $$$
☎ 035 232596

Taverna Valtellinese**
Via Tiraboschi, 57
24100 Bergamo
Just as the name implies,
specialising in cooking from the
Valtellina. Almost everything
worth a try! Closed Mondays. $$
☎ 035 243331

Ristorante Dei Castelli**
23020 Montagna in Valtellina
Just a short distance from Sondrio
and specialising in local cuisine. $$
☎ 0342 380445

Chapter 8 — Brescia

HOTELS
Master****
Via Apollonio, 72
225100 Brescia
Elegant old palazzo beside the
Castello. Very comfortable and
an excellent restaurant. $$$
☎ 030 399037, Fax 030 3701331

Hotel i Due Roccoli****
Via San Bonomelli
25049 Iseo
Very comfortable, with gardens,
swimming pool, tennis courts
and a very good restaurant. $$$
☎ 030 9822977, Fax 030 9822980

Hotel Alpino***
Via Lungolago
Località Crone
25074 Idro
Small hotel with limited facilities,
but very pleasant and in a
delightful position. Good
restaurant. $$
☎ 0365 83146, Fax 0365 823143

Ambra**
Porto Bagriele Rosa, 2
25049 Iseo
Small and simple, but very
comfortable and very well
positioned. $
☎ 030 980130 Fax 030 9821361

Bellavista**
Via Roma, 65
25050 Monte Isola
Elegance coupled with an exotic
location on the island in Lake
Iseo. Good restaurant and
pleasant grounds. $
☎ 030 9886106

Hotel Val Palot*
Via Val Palot, 34
Pisogne
Small and basic, but very clean
and hospitable. Limited number
of rooms with their own bath
or shower. $
☎ 0364 880553

RESTAURANTS
La Sosta***
Via San Martino della Battaglia, 20
25100 Brescia
Housed in a beautiful 17th century
building, with elegant decoration
and excellent menu. $$$
☎ 030 295603

IL Paiolo***
Piazza Mazzini, 9
Iseo
Best restaurant in the area with a
wide menu and superb desserts.
$$
☎ 030 9821074

Alpino***
Via Lungolago, Località Crone
25074 Idro
The hotel's restaurant is one of the
best places to eat in the area. $$
☎ 0365 83146

Turistico del Sebino*
24067 Sarnico
Very pleasant atmosphere and
garden dining in a good position
at the southern tip of Lake Iseo. $
☎ 035 910043

Chapter 9 — Lake Garda

Lake Garda is an important tourist
area with a huge number of hotels
at all grades.

Fact File

HOTELS

Continental****
Via Punta Staffalo, 7/9
25019 Sirmione
Beautiful hotel close to one of
the most romantic sites on the
lake. Excellent facilities and
restaurant. $$$
☎ 030 9905711, Fax 030 916278

Hotel du Lac et du Parc*****
Viale Rovereto, 44
38066 Riva del Garda
A fabulous hotel with all possible
facilities including swimming
pool, tennis courts etc. $$$$
☎ 0464 551500, Fax 0464 555200

Hotel Leonardo da Vinci****
Via 4 Novembre, 3
25010 Limone sul Garda
As elegant as the name. Swim-
ming pool, sun terrace and
excellent restaurant. $$$
☎ 0365 954351, Fax 0365 954432

Regina Adelaide****
Via San Franceso d'Assisi 23
37016 Garda
Large hotel set close to the lake
and with superb facilities. $$$
☎ 045 7255977, Fax 045 7256263

Villa Paradiso****
Corso Zanardelli, 192
25083 Gardone Riviera
Worth the name. Very
comfortable rooms and grounds
overlooking the lake. $$$
☎ 0365 21883, Fax 0365 20269

Benaco***
Lungolago Zanardelli, 44
25087 Salò
Small, but well sited and
decorated hotel. Very good
restaurant. $$
☎ 0365 20308, Fax 0365 21049

Benacus**
Via Monte Brisne, 18
38066 Riva del Garda
Secluded position, but balconies
make most of the view. Very
comfortable. Only open April-
October. $$
☎ 0464 552737, Fax 0464 551030

Vittorio***
Via Porto Vecchio, 4
25015 Desenzano del Garda
Best hotel in town for position,
right at the edge of the old
harbour. Very pleasant. No
restaurant, but easy access to
some of the best in town. $$
☎030 9912245/58, Fax 030
9912270

Erika*
37018 Malcesine
Simple, but well maintained
hotel in one of the lake's most
romantic villages. Own garden
and car park. $
☎ 045 7400451, Fax 045 7400451

Garden**
Via Stazione, 18
37019 Peshiera del Garda
Nicely positioned for exploring
the lake. Well appointed, but
no restaurant. $
☎ 045 7553644, Fax 045 7553644

La Pescatrice**
Via Porto, 10
25080 Moniga del Garda
Off-the-beaten-track, but neat
and tidy. Surprisingly good
restaurant. $
☎ 0365 502043

RESTAURANTS

Vecchia Riva***
Via Bastione, 3
38066 Riva del Garda
Limited seating, so booking
advised, but worth the effort
for the magnificent cuisine. $$$
☎ 0464 555061

Villa Fiordaliso***
Corso Zanardelli, 132
25083 Gardone Riviera
Beautiful old palazzo that also has
a small number of rooms to let.
Excellent menu and service. $$$
☎ 0365 20158

Botticelli**
37017 Lazise
Pleasant dining in the garden,
with a good menu. $
☎ 045 7581194

Grifone da Luciano**
Via delle Bisse, 5
25019 Sirmione
Marvellous position, with dining in
a garden overlooking the lake. $$
☎ 031 309857

Il Giardino delle Esperidi **
Via Mameli, 1
37011 Bardolino
Beautiful garden restaurant
with menu and food to match.
☎ 045 6210477

Pizzeria al Marconi*
Via Marconi, 111
25080 Padenghe sul Garda
Off-the-beaten-track pizza house
with a good menu and very
pleasant terrace beside the lake. $
☎ 030 9912563

Chapter 10 – Verona

HOTELS
Due Torri Baglioni*****
Piazza Sant' Anastasia, 4
37100 Verona
Luxurious hotel set between
the river and the old centre.
The L'Aquila restaurant is one
of the best in town. $$$$
☎ 045 595044, Fax 045 8004130

Victoria****
Via Adua, 6
37100 Verona
Excellent hotel in a quiet location,
but no restaurant. $$$
☎ 045 590566, Fax 045 590155

San Luca***
Vicolo Volta San Luca, 8
37122Verona
Well appointed and neat hotel
close to the Roman Arena. No
restaurant. $$
☎ 045 591333, Fax 045 8002143

Cavour**
Vicolo Chiodo, 4
37100 Verona
Small, but very comfortable
hotel close to the Scaligeri castle.
No restaurant. $
☎ 045 590166, Fax 045 590508

RESTAURANTS
Nuove Marconi ***
Via dalle Fogge, 4
37100 Verona
Famous for its cuisine. Close to
the best of Verona's squares for
that after dinner stroll. $$$
☎ 045 591910

Accademia **
Via Scala, 10
37100 Verona
Excellent menu and friendly
service. $$
☎ 045 8006072

Bottega del Vino*
Via Scudo di Francia, 3
Splendidly named little restaurant
with no frills but excellent food. $
☎ 045 8004535

Fact File

LANGUAGE

Italian is a straightforward language, with each letter being pronounced, and always being pronounced in the same way. There are differences in pronunciation from English however: *c* before *e* and *i* is pronounced ch, eg *dolce* – dole chay, *cinque* – chin kway

elsewhere *c* is pronounced *k*
ch is pronounced *k*
g before *e* and *i* is pronounced *j*
elsewhere *g* is hard
gh is pronounced as a hard *g*
gl is pronounced *ly*

gn is pronounced *ne*
h is silent
sc before *e* and *i* is pronounced *sh*
elsewhere *sc* is pronounced *sk*
z and *zz* are pronounced *ts*,
though occasionally as *ds*

Some Useful Words & Phrases

Si	Yes	*Parla inglese?*	Do you speak English?
No	No		
Per piacere or *per favore*	Please	*Non capisco*	I do not understand
		Possa avere?	Can I have?
Grazie	Thank you	*Puo dirmi?*	Can you tell me?
Prego	You're welcome, OK	*Vorrei*	I would like
Va bene	That's alright	*aperto*	open
Buongiorno	Good morning/ afternoon	*chiuso*	closed
		caldo	hot
Buona Sera	Good evening	*freddo*	cold
Buona Notte	Good night	*grande*	big
Dov'e...?	Where is...?	*piccolo*	small
Quando?	When?	*buono*	good
Che cosa?	What?	*cattivo*	bad
Quanta costa?	How much?	*cambio*	currency exchange

Numbers

zero	0	*dieci*	10
uno	1	*cento*	100
due	2	*mille*	1,000
tre	3	but	
quattro	4	*duemila*	2,000
cinque	5	*cinquemila*	5,000
sei	6	etc	
sette	7	*primo*	1st
otto	8	*secondo*	2nd
nove	9	*terzo*	3rd

Days of the week

Domenica	Sunday	*Giovedi*	Thursday
Lunedi	Monday	*Venerdi*	Friday
Martedi	Tuesday	*Sabato*	Saturday
Mercoledi	Wednesday		

Countries

Gran Bretagna	Great Britain
Canada	Canada
Stati Unita	United States
Inglese	British
Canadese	Canadian
Americano	American

In the Hotel

una camera	a room
con bagno	with bathroom
con doccia	with shower
con gabinetto	with toilet
giorni	days
una settimana	one week
la colazione	breakfast

MUSEUMS

Most museums charge for admission. Current opening times are given in the Places to Visit at the end of each chapter, but check locally as they are subject to slight alteration from year to year.

POST & TELEPHONE SERVICES

Stamps *(francoboli)* are sold at both Post Offices and tobacconists. Post Offices are normally open from 8.30am-1pm, some in large towns remain open until 7 or 8pm. Tobacconists open from 8.30 or 9am-1pm and from 3.30 or 4-7.30 or 8pm.

Phones in phone-booths occasionally take coins – usually 200 lire coins – but these, and all older phones, take *gettone*, a 200 lire token available at post offices, tobacconists, bars and some news stands.

Some bars will allow you to phone, taking a note of the time of the call and charging you when you have finished. This is more convenient, but there may be a bar 'surcharge' and the phone will not have a meter advising you of time or cost.

In larger towns look for the SIP 'shop' where you can phone from a sound-proof booth and a meter will advise you of cost. Again you pay after your call.

The dial codes from Italy are:

Great Britain	00 44	**USA**	00 1
Canada	00 1	**Australia**	00 61

Remember to leave out the first zero of your home country number – eg. to dial the Italian Tourist Office in London (020 7408 1254) from Italy, dial 00 44 20 7408 1254.

RESTAURANTS

See under ***Hotels and Restaurants*** above for list of recommended restaurants for each chapter.

SPORTS

Water Sports

Apart from Lakes Varese and Comabbio which are closed to swimmers because of pollution, swimming is allowed in all the lakes and each

Above: Varenna, Lake Como

Below: Leisurely boat hire at Riva del Garda, Lake Garda

town (indeed virtually all camp or holiday sites) is provided with its own beach. Swimming is, in general, very safe, with gently sloping – though frequently stony – lake bottoms. There are places where the lakes are shelved, but these are easy to spot, the general lie of the fore-shore land giving the clue. If there are steep cliffs, take care. The lack of tides and currents adds to the safety, the chief hazard the swimmer faces is the wash from a ferry or the occasional trainee windsurfer.

The lakes are the place to learn or practise board sailing. The dependable winds, normally blowing from the north in the mornings, and from the south in the afternoons and evenings, and the combination of warm sun and warm water, do much to encourage the beginner, and to give the expert the opportunity to display his skills. On all the lakes the winds are stronger and more dependable the further north the sailor travels.

All the above comments on windsurfing apply equally well to dinghy or yacht sailors. All major villages and many hotel and camp sites have public launch points and berthing arrangements. If in doubt, contact the local Tourist Office.

Walking

The lake foreshores are more for strolling than walking, but the ridges that confine the lakes and the high valleys that link them, offer enormous potential for the serious walkers. Though some of the peaks rise to 8,000ft or more (above about 2,500m) there are many cableways offering easy access to high ridges, and the mountains themselves are, in the main, pre-Alpine, that is, rounded and grassed, rather than rocky and angular.

The Lombardy Tourist Authority produce an excellent leaflet *Trekking in Lombardy* giving details of superb 7-day treks in the region's uplands. In the area covered by this book they include Valsassina to the east of Lake Como; Valmasino and Valmalenco, near Sondrio; the upper reaches of Val Seriana, north of Bergamo; and the upper part of Val Camonica, north of Brescia and Lake Iseo. Each of the itineraries uses mountain huts or small hotels for sleeping, and offers a daily walk of around 5 hours.

Even those who feel that to devote a full week to such a tour is to give too much time, should consider including a one-day walk in their holiday; some of the upland scenery is magnificent, the views to the lakes quite superb and there is always the chance of seeing some of the unusual alpine animals.

As walking increases in popularity, more towns are recognising the enormous potential that the ridges which form their back gardens offer to complement the lakeside front gardens. Many places now have waymarked paths and local guide books – the Tremosine/Tignale area above the western shore of Lake Garda being the best example – that offer short, half-day, walks.

Those wanting a greater freedom, but not wanting to take to the mountains, should consider the longer trail which is waymarked from Cernobbio to Sorico, staying above Lake Como's western shore at all times and visiting Val d'Intelvi. The walk usually takes 4 days, but any section, Cernobbio to San Fedele, San Fedele to Grandola ed Uniti, Grandola to Garzeno, and Garzeno to Sorico, is worthwhile.

As a complete change, there is a waymarked geological trail that traverses the interesting section of the High Brianza near Canzo, to the south of Lake Como.

Adventure Sports

The Grigna peaks and the mountains to the north of Riva del Garda, around Arco especially, are famous for their rock-climbing. There are clubs in the area, but limited facilities for those wanting to learn to climb. The local tourist offices will have details.

An alternative for those with a head for heights, but not wanting to commit to climbing is a Via Ferrata. Vie Ferrate (*vie* is the plural of *via*) are, literally, iron roads, sections of cliff which have been rigged with ladders and pegs to allow mere mortals (those most definitely with a head for heights) to explore places they would otherwise have no hope of reaching. Vie Ferrata are fully protected by wires running beside the ladders, or across sections of cliff where climbers can more easily ascend.

However, to make full use of any Via Ferrata it is necessary to have a kit which allows the climber to be continuously clipped into the safety line and to absorb the impact in the event of a fall. This kit requires a full climbing harness to be worn. Although the heartland of Vie Ferrata is the Dolomites there are excellent routes on the Resegone and Monte Grona, both above Lake Como, and in the Brenta Dolomites to the north of Lake Garda.

The gorges to the north of Lake Garda are ideal for the exacting sport of canyoning. This potentially dangerous sport should not be attempted alone by beginners: Groups may be seen advertising locally, but the visitor should always be cautious when selecting a leader: please ask for advice at the local tourist office.

Winter Sports

Obviously these are limited to the upland area, and in the main have limited facilities when compared to the internationally famous resorts such as Bormio. They do offer a very different holiday, being quieter and less bustling, and many summer tourists book hotels for a winter return. The major resort within the area covered by the book is Aprica, near Sondrio, which has excellent facilities and snow.

Hunting & Fishing

Italy is one of the few European countries which still has a strong hunting tradition, a tradition frequently at odds with Europe's new ecological movement. Details on seasons, licences etc can be obtained at the local tourist offices.

Both the lakes and the rivers that feed them offer considerable scope for fishermen. Again details on times, licences, etc are obtainable at the tourist offices.

Golf

Golf is increasing in popularity in Italy, and with the climate and the magnificent views from some of the local courses the visitor with an enthusiasm for the game is now well catered for. Local tourist offices will have details of clubs in the area which accept visiting golfers.

Horse Riding

Horses are available for hire or trek at: Oleggio, Castello, Lossone (Switzerland), Mesenzana, Marchirolo, Ghirla, Caravate, Brenno Useria, Cantello, Varese, Bodio, Cargenno and Angera near Lakes Orta, Maggiore and Lugano.

At Grandate ed Uniti, Magriglio, Canzo, Poncia and Alzate, Brianze, near Lake Como.

At Boario Terme, near Lake Iseo, and at Lonato, Desenzano, Manerba and Padenghe near Lake Garda.

Swimming Pools

Public pools are available at: Meina, Lesa, Baveno, Verbania Pallanza, Luino, Marchirolo, Besozzo, Comerio, Induno Olona, Castiglione Olona, Varese, Azzate, and Ispra near Lakes Orta, Maggiore and Lugano.

At Como, Cernobbio and Lecco near Lake Como, at Iseo, Crone (near Idro) and Collio near Brescia and at Cisano, Salo, Manerba and Padenghe near Lake Garda.

TIPPING

A service charge of 15 per cent and IVA (VAT) of 19 per cent are included on most restaurant and hotel bills. However it is usual to give an extra 5 per cent of the bill for satisfactory service. The same is also true of cafés and bars, particularly in the more upmarket places. In Italy there is also a table charge for sitting in a café. Cinema and theatre usherettes expect small tips, as do washroom attendants and service station attendants who clean the windscreen. Taxi drivers expect a tip of 10 per cent.

TOURIST INFORMATION OFFICES

ENIT (Italian Tourist) Offices

Great Britain
1 Princes Street
London W1B 2AY
☎ 020 7408 1254,
Fax 020 7493 6695

USA
Suite 1565, Rockefeller Centre
630 Fifth Avenue
New York
NY 10111
☎ (212) 245 5095,
Fax (212) 586 9249

Suite 1046
500 North Michigan Avenue
Chicago
IL 60611
☎ (312) 644 0996,
Fax (312) 644 3019

Suite 550
12400 Wiltshire Boulevard
Los Angeles, CA90025
☎ (310) 820 1898,
Fax (310) 820 6357

Canada
Store 56, Plaza
3 Place Ville Marie
Montreal, Quebec H3B 2E3
☎ (514) 866 7667/7668/7669

c/o Alitalia
120 Adelaide Street West
Toronto
☎ (416) 3631348

Tourist Offices in Italy

Most of the lakeside towns and the majority of the larger mountain villages have tourist/accommodation offices.

The main provincial (APT) offices are always found in the provincial capitals, and these are listed below.

The tourist offices can assist with all queries regarding accommodation, local festivals, etc as well as some more interesting items. For example, Varese has a list of farms where the visitor can live and work for a few days, a fascinating chance to see Italian life at first hand.

Piemonte

The main provincial office close to Lakes Orta and Maggiore is at:

Novara, 2 Corso Cavour (☎ 0321 27238). Though for information on the sections of Lakes Orta and Maggiore that lie in Piemonte it is better to contact offices at:

Orta San Guilio
Via Panoramica
28016 Orta San Giulio
☎ 0322 905614, Fax 0322 905800

Stresa
Piazza Marconi, 16
☎ 0323 30150, Fax 0323 32561

Lombardy

The regional office for Lombardian tourism is at:

Milan
Via Marconi, 1 (Beside cathedral / *Duomo*)
☎ 02 72524301, Fax 02 72524350

The Lombardian provincial offices are at:

Bergamo
Viale Vittorio Emanule, 20
☎ 035 210204, Fax 035 230184

Brescia
Corso Zanardelli, 34
☎ 030 43418, Fax 030 293284

Como
Piazza Cavour, 17
☎ 031 269712, Fax 031 261152

Sondrio
Via Trieste
☎ 0342 512500, Fax 0342 212590

Varese
Viale Ippodromo. 9
☎ 0332 284624, Fax 0332 222107

Veneto

The main provincial Veneto office close to Lake Garda is at:

Verona
Via degli Alpini, 9
☎ 045 8068680,
Fax 045 8003638

Though for Lake Garda itself it is advisable to contact the local village offices, the main ones being at:

Malcesine
Palazzo dei Capitanai
☎ 045 7400044, Fax 045 7401633

Cernobbio, Lake Como

Fact File

Trentino/Alto Adige

The main provincial Trentino office close to Lake Garda is at:

Trento
Via Manci, 2,
☎ 0461 983880,
Fax 0461 984508.

Though for Lake Garda itself it is advisable to contact the local village offices, chief of which is at:

Riva del Garda
Giardini di P Orientale 8
☎ 0464 554444, Fax 0464 520308

Swiss lake Shores
Locarno
Largo Zorzi, 1,
☎ 091 7510333,
Fax 091 7519070.

Lugano
Riva Albertolli, 5,
☎ 091 33232,
Fax 092 27653.

TRAVEL & TRANSPORT

Air

At the time of writing the Italians are attempting to change the local international airport from Linate, to the east of Milan, to Malpensa, near the southern tip of Lake Maggiore. In future Linate will serve domestic flights only. This move is being resisted by international carriers as the destination of business passengers is, invariably, Milan. At present, therefore, most international carriers fly to both Linate and Malpensa, with fewer (but more crowded) flights to the former.

Malpensa has a train station, but Linate is not served by train. Each airport has bus connections to Milan from where the lakes can be reached by train.

Linate airport is 7 miles (5km) from Milan city centre. The airport lies just 2km from Milan's *autostrada* ring. If you are approaching Linate from the south (i.e. you are heading north) the exit slip road is to your right, as usual, but please note that if you are approaching from the north (i.e. you are heading south) the slip road is on the left, that is you exit from the outside (fast) lane. This catches many visitors unawares as the signing for the exit is a little late.

There is a combined telephone number for information for the two airports, ☎ 02 74852200.

There are also airports at Bergamo (Orio sul Serio) and Verona (Villafranca), both situated beside the A4 *autostrada*. Although these are mainly used for Italian national flights, some charter flight companies use them more regularly.

Full time students up to the age of 26 receive a 25 per cent discount on flight fares. A certificate from school, college or university must be presented to the flight operator. All major Italian airports have duty-free facilities.

Rail

The cities of the Lombardy plain, Milan, Varese, Como, Bergamo and Brescia, together with Verona, are linked by a very efficient railway system. From the cities, branch lines penetrate some of the valleys that hold the lakes. The eastern shore of Lake Orta, and the western shore of Lake Maggiore as far as the Toce river, are served by lines that meet at

Cuzzago in the Val d'Ossola before crossing into Switzerland via the Simplon tunnel.

The remainder of Lake Maggiore's western shore has no railway, though a line runs continuously along the eastern shore from Sesto Calende into Switzerland.

Lake Lugano is not well served by rail, though a line from Varese terminates at Porto Ceresio, and one from Como goes from Capolago along the lake to Lugano, after crossing the lake bridge.

On Lake Como the only railway line runs from Lecco up the eastern shore before serving the length of the Valtellina. A line runs up Lake Iseo's eastern shore and on up Val Camonica, but none of the Lake Garda towns, apart from Desenzano and Peschiera, are served by rail.

A French motorail service takes cars to Milan's Porta Garibaldi station. The journey's French terminus is either Paris or Boulogne, the latter being ideal for English travellers. The service is not cheap, but to leave Boulogne at around lunchtime one day and to wake (all passenger accommodation is in sleeper coaches) fresh, in time for a free breakfast at Milan, saving at least a day's holiday, is to many people worth the expense.

A second motorail service runs through the Simplon tunnel, cars loading and off-loading at each end, Brig and Varzo. This service is of more debatable merit, as the traveller saves little time and very few miles, those saved being through some of Europe's finest rock-gorge scenery.

A 'travel-at-will' ticket – *Biglietto touristico libera circolazione* – is available to tourists whose place of residence is outside of Italy. The ticket allows unlimited travel on the Italian railway system, and does not require a supplement for travel on the *Rapido* (see below). State tourist offices in your home country will have details of where the tickets can be purchased. In Italy they can only be obtained from a limited number of stations. In the area covered by this book, there are only two: Milan Central (Centrale) and Milan Porta Garibaldi. The tickets can be first or second class, and there is a 50 per cent reduction for children under 12. Other reductions, for circular journeys, 3-day returns, party and family tickets, are also available.

On all rail journeys children under 4 not occupying a seat travel free, children under 12 receive a 50 per cent reduction. Full-time students can obtain reduced rates on most tickets.

Italian trains have the following specifications:

Super-Rapido
Luxury first class only running between **TEE** major cities. Special supplements charged, seat bookings obligatory.

Rapido
Fast trains between major cities. Some trains are first class only. Supplement charged (about 30 per cent of standard fare and children pay full supplement). On some trains seat booking is obligatory.

Espresso
Long-distance express trains, stopping at major stations only.

LANDMARK
Publishing Ltd ● ● ● ●

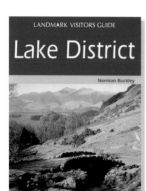

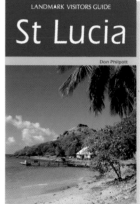

UK	EUROPE	WORLD
Lake District	**Cote D'Azur**	**St Lucia**
ISBN 1 84306 113 9 Pages 224 £10.95	ISBN 1 84306 217 8 Pages 112 £7.50	ISBN 1 84306 178 3 Pages 144 £6.99
All of the well-known sites are included to give an in-depth under-standing of the area	Covers Nice, Cannes, St Tropez, Monaco, Menton & the Mercantour	Includes tours of the island; extensive eating-out giudes
Devon	**Italian Lakes**	**Bermuda**
Dorset	**France from the Channel Ports**	**Cayman Islands**
North Devon & Exmoor		**The Gambia**
Jersey		**Florida: The Keys**
Peak District		
Cornwall & The Isles of Scilly		

Available from all good bookshops

LANDMARK
Publishing Ltd ● ● ●

LANDMARK VISITORS GUIDE

Bruges
Christopher Turner

LANDMARK VISITORS GUIDE

Northern
Cyprus
Kristina Gürsoy & Lavinia Neville Smith

LANDMARK VISITORS GUIDE

France:
Dordogne
Mike Smith

CITIES	ISLANDS	REGIONS
Bruges	**Northern Cyprus**	**Dordogne**
ISBN 1 84306 119 8 Pages 112 £7.50	ISBN 1 84306 056 6 Pages 176 £10.99	ISBN 1 84306 166 X Pages 176 £11.99
Includes four routes around the city	The authors live and work in Cyprus and they drew on their extensive local knowledge to produce this comprehensive guide	Includes 6 car tours, plus walking trails around Sarlat and Périgueux
Oxford	**Kefalonia**	**Cornwall & The Isles of Scilly**
Cracow	**Isle of Wight**	
Riga and its beaches	**Mull, Iona & Staffa**	
	Tenerife	
	Zakinthos	

See pages 238-239 for a full list of our titles

Diretto

Trains stopping at most stations.

Locale

Local trains, stopping at all stations.

Road

Coaches & Buses

Italy has an extensive long-distance coach system, and good local bus services. Most major cities offer specific bus tours.

Milan has an underground (*Metropolitano*) train service with a single-priced ticket, and a good tram service.

Cars

Travelling from within Italy the area of the northern lakes is easily reached by the excellent *autostrada* system that uses Milan as a hub. From outside Italy the alpine chain must be breached, the most popular routes being through the Great St Bernard Pass to the Aosta valley which, though involving a drive of some distance to Milan (around 125 miles/200km), does pass through some interesting countryside; the Simplon Pass from Brig in Switzerland to Domodossola and Lake Maggiore; the St Gotthard and San Bernardino Passes to Bellinzona and Lakes Maggiore, Lugano and Como; the Spluga Pass from Chur, the Maloja and Bernina Passes from St Moritz; the Ponte del Gallo and Stelvio Passes into the Valtellina; and the Brenner Pass from Austria into Trentino and the north tip of Lake Garda.

At any frontier crossing point that has an Italian Automobile Club (ACI) office (all the above crossings do) the visitor may buy a booklet of fuel coupons, either for northern or for southern Italy. The booklet for northern Italy contains vouchers for the lire equivalent of about 150 litres of fuel and offers a discount of about 10 per cent on pump prices. The coupons can be exchanged at most garages. The figures are approximate because the vouchers are for 'lire's worth' of fuel, not for 'litre's-worth', and so depend upon the current price.

In addition to the above benefits each booklet contains five 2,000 lire motorway toll vouchers. All Italian *autostradas* are tollways, the traveller taking a ticket from an automatic machine on entry to the system and paying on exit. Purchase of the booklet also entitles the buyer to call on the free breakdown assistance of the ACI. For assistance dial 116 on any phone, or ask for ACI at the *autostrada* SOS columns, situated every 1¼ miles (2km) along the roadside.

Possession of a booklet entitles the driver whose car is off the road for at least 12 hours for repair after a breakdown or accident, to a free hire car for up to 10 days. This concession does not apply to coaches or motorcycles. To buy a coupon booklet the driver must be driving a foreign car (not a rented Italian car) and be able to produce the vehicle registration document.

Speed limits (in km/h) on Italian roads are:

	Engine capacity	Autostradas	Other roads
Cars	up to 1099cc	110 (68mph)	90 (56mph)
	over 1100cc	130 (80mph)	90 (56mph)
Motor cycles	150-349cc	110 (68mph)	90 (56mph)
	over 350cc	130 (80mph)	90 (56mph)

In built up areas the speed limit is 31mph (50kmph). These limits should be adhered to as there is an on-the-spot fine system for motoring, including parking, offences. Both the fines and their immediate payment are non-negotiable. Besides the fines, which can be as high as £500 ($800), an offender faces the risk of imprisonment.

The wearing of seatbelts by both front and rear seat passengers is compulsory. Children under 12 years of age must travel in rear seats. The carrying of the vehicle registration and the owner's written permission for the driving of the vehicle if the driver is not the owner are also compulsory. Left side wing mirrors are compulsory on all vehicles, including those with right-hand drive, and drivers should carry a valid insurance certificate ('Green Cards' are not compulsory, but it is advisable to carry one).

Italy has random breath-testing to detect alcohol. The legal limit is 80 micrograms of alcohol in 100ml of breath.

Car Rental

Car rental is available at airports, major stations and in most big towns. The major international companies – Hertz, Avis etc – serve Italy, supplemented by larger domestic companies, eg. Maggiore. A large range of (mainly Italian) cars is offered.

Parking

Can be difficult in many Italian towns, and it is usually advisable to use one of the large car parks, occasionally administered by ACI, as their fee is much less than the fine incurred for illegal parking.

Italian Automobile Club (ACI)
Head Office
8 Via Marsala, 00185 Rome
☎ 06 4998

There are regional offices in Bergamo, Brescia, Como, Domodossola, Milan, Novara, Sondrio, Trento and Varese.

Road Signs

Accendere i fari in Galleria	Use headlights in tunnel
Accostore a destra (sinistra)	Keep right (left)
Avanti	Walk (seen at pedestrian lights)
Divieto di Sosta or Sosta Vietata	No parking
Entrata	Entrance
Lavori in Corso	Road works ahead
	(literally workmen in the road)

Pericolo	Danger
Polizia Stradale	Highway police
Rallentare	Reduce speed
Senso Unico	One way
Senso Vietato	No entry
Sosta Autorizzata	Parking allowed (followed by times)
Uscita	Exit
Vicolo Cicco	No through road
Zona Pedonale	Pedestrian zone

Lake Steamers

Although there are now very few steamers on the lakes, the word is still used to describe the variety of passenger boats that daily criss-cross the waters of the larger lakes – Orta, Maggiore, Lugano, Como, Iseo and Garda. The services are mainly modern diesel ferry boats, with a number of the more exciting hydrofoils (*aliscafo*) which reduce crossing times for a price supplement that is generally about 50 per cent. To take advantage of their speed the hydrofoils do not call at all ports, taking more direct lines between the lake ends.

Price reductions are also available for those who buy 'season' tickets, which are available for 1 day, several days, 1 or 2 weeks. The diesel and hydrofoil ferry services, together with the car-ferries that offer limited crossings on the three major lakes, are scheduled services operating every day.

In addition the steamer companies run special services in the summer months, offering sight-seeing tours, together with excellent night-time trips on light-bedecked boats with dancing to live music. Some of these trips are by 'old-fashioned' paddle steamer, offering an unforgettable outing, particularly when the trip passes close to some of the floodlit highlights of the lakes, the Rocca d'Angera on Lake Maggiore and Malcesine's castle on Lake Garda for example. The boats for these trips have restaurants and bars, full air-conditioning, and the best of sound systems.

Further details of the boat services on the various lakes are given at the end of each chapter.